# MAKING A CASE IN CHILD PROTECTION

**Other titles from Longman**

NSPCC: *Child Sexual Abuse: Listening, Hearing and Validating the Experiences of Children* by Corinne Wattam, John Hughes and Harry Blagg

NSPCC: *Listening to Children: The Professional Response to Hearing the Abused Child* edited by Anne Bannister, Kevin Barrett, and Eileen Shearer

NSPCC: *From Hearing to Healing: Working with the Aftermath of Child Sexual Abuse* edited by Anne Bannister

*Making Sense of the Children Act* (2nd edition) by Nick Allen

NSPCC: *Key Issues in Child Protection for Health Visitors and Nurses* edited by Jane Naish and Christopher Cloke

# MAKING A CASE IN CHILD PROTECTION

Corinne Wattam
NSPCC Research Fellow, Lancaster University

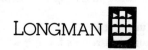

LONGMAN

*Published by* Longman Industry and Public Service Management,
Longman Group UK Ltd, 6th Floor, Westgate House,
The High, Harlow, Essex CM20 1YR, England and
Associated Companies throughout the world

A catalogue record for this book is available from
The British Library

ISBN 0-582-09281-7

**Dedication**
To Doreen, Graham, Ann and John.
Thank you for caring.

Phototypeset by The Midlands Book Typesetting Company,
Loughborough LE11 1HH
Printed and bound in Great Britain by
Biddles Ltd, Guildford and King's Lynn

# Contents

This book reflects the practice, experience and views of the author
and does not necessarily reflect or express NSPCC policy

# Foreword

The publication of *Making a Case in Child Protection* is timely. With the Children Act 1989 beginning to have an influence on service provision and the Home Office Memorandum of Good Practice on Child Evidence being introduced, child protection practice is in a state of change. *Making a Case in Child Protection* explores a number of themes which are central to the interface between the Children Act and the Criminal Justice Act 1991; between civil and criminal proceedings; between meeting the needs of children and securing successful prosecutions.

The resounding message which comes across clearly from this book is that establishing what has happened to children who may have been abused is not a straightforward process and that investigating cases requires immense skills, experience and patience. It is not simply a matter of carrying out the law or government guidelines. Interpretation, negotiation and mediation are also necessary in this process and the interests of children may be lost or relegated. Children's circumstances differ and they have varying needs. There is no single right way of responding to abused children. It is important to give serious attention to the differences between children and their experiences and to use the legal processes if it is appropriate.

Drawing on a wealth of research, derived from painstaking interviews with children and the professionals working with them, and from observation and file studies, Corinne Wattam demonstrates the complex dynamics which interact when it comes to establishing that a child has been abused. The simple premise that children should be listened to, taken seriously and not dismissed because they are not understood is all too often ignored or overruled in the investigation and interviewing process. Children are not listened to. Wattam answers the frequent question of how it can happen that children are abused yet the people believed to be responsible are not prosecuted. As a consequence they receive no therapeutic help and are able to reoffend. This is not in children's interest and safety, and both child protection practitioners and policy makers must consider how this significant shortcoming can be rectified.

Corinne Wattam's book will be of great value in helping us think through a series of dilemmas in child protection work. She analyses the investigation and prosecution processes paying particular attention to the difficult task of how children are interviewed. Practical advice is given on how effective, child centred decision-making can be achieved. *Making a Case in Child Protection* will help practitioners in all disciplines really hear what children are saying and act appropriately.

Importantly, the book also points to the need for legal reforms. Undoubtedly great strides have been made with recent legislation – the Children Act 1989 and Criminal Justice Acts of 1988 and 1990 – but these reforms do not go far enough. As Wattam demonstrates, the government procedures and guidelines of *Working Together Under the Children Act* and the *Memorandum of Good Practice on Child Evidence* do not sufficiently meet the complex requirements of good practice. The NSPCC has long campaigned for law and social policy reforms to meet the needs of children. In 1889 the Society was instrumental in bringing on to the statute book the Cruelty Act – at its time hailed as a 'Children's Charter'. Over a hundred years later we are campaigning for reforms which will eliminate the trauma caused to children by the investigation, prosecution and court processes. *Making a Case in Child Protection* gives further weight to the argument that the Pigot Committee recommendations should be implemented in full, particularly the proposal that video recorded interviews with children at a pre-trial hearing should be admissible as evidence so that a child need never face the distressing experience of giving live evidence at a trial. Such humane reforms should be introduced as a matter of priority.

Legislative reform, while crucially important, is not of itself sufficient for achieving improved practice. Changes in professional thinking and attitudes towards children and the development of appropriate skills are also essential. These can be developed through training. It is also necessary to provide professionals with time to move at the child's own pace and put into practice the principles of interdisciplinary working. Training and time are prerequisites to child centred practice and they both cost money. They are not luxuries and we cannot afford to ignore these needs. Child protection services must be adequately resourced.

*Making a Case in Child Protection* brings together the research, practice and policy experience of the NSPCC. Corinne Wattam is an NSPCC Research Fellow at the University of Lancaster and has played a significant part in synthesising these disciplines. Child protection is the richer for that and we are indebted to Corinne for her pioneering work in this area. The NSPCC is committed to both developing such an approach to working with children and to taking forward the issues identified in this book through further research, practice innovation, and policy development.

**Christopher Brown**
**Director, NSPCC**

# Acknowledgements

Detection is not so much a process of discovery as it is an act of invention, a making and unmaking of the world. Professor Theresa Coletti

If I'd have known what I was letting myself in for, I'd never have done it. Girl, aged 16, during research interview for the child protection study.

This book is an acknowledgement to the achievement of our practices, actions and work in child protection. It is not possible within the research approach I use here, and continue to develop, to suggest that practitioners are 'only doing their job'. The products of the job are the cases of children whom practitioners encounter in their day-to-day work. I do research, and write, in the hope that our response to them can improve.

There are so many people who have assisted in the research, in the discussion of ideas, and with practical help, all of which enabled me to complete this project. Overall, the research could not have been conducted without the co-operation of its subjects; the social work and legal practitioners and the children whom I observed and interviewed. In particular, I thank Jean Horn, John Bates, Brian Wilson and all the social workers and CPS personnel who participated from the area I worked in. They know who they are, even if others cannot. I am deeply indebted to the NSPCC who have supported my work throughout. Special thanks are due to Karen Nevard and Cathy Tite at the Hedley Library (a unique resource for anyone undertaking research in this subject area), Chris Cloke for his persistence, Philip Noyes for his unstinting dedication to purpose, Helen Westcott and Sue Creighton. For comment and constructive thought, I am grateful to Michael King, Ray Bull, David Thorpe, Mel Cabaniuk and, as always, John Hughes. On a practical level, my thanks are owed to family and friends who have helped out in so many ways, and to Thea and Jos who have spurred me on, albeit for the sake of their Nintendo.

It has been necessary throughout the book to use case examples to illustrate the points made. Where such material is drawn upon all details which might identify the subjects of the extracts have been altered. This has been done carefully, in a way which does not detract from the reason for using the case as an example.

A note on transcription
Records, notes, interviews and conversations have all been transcribed using the following notations:

. . .        — part of the text has been omitted
(     )      — text is unclear
/            — next speaker comes in
(pause) —  pause over 30 seconds.

# Introduction

This book is a consequence of research that throws some light on to what has become a very complex and skilled task. That task is to do with the requirement for practitioners not only to protect children but to do it in accountable terms. Children who are victims of avoidable, adult-inflicted, harm and injury, now more than ever before, must make their case and have their case made for them by social workers, police officers, lawyers, judges and other legal practitioners who have the job of juxtaposing the competing needs and rights of children, with those of parents and those of the state. Over recent years, including the public 'shock' (DOH, 1991a) about events in Cleveland, protecting children from sexual harm or injury has been much highlighted and subject to wide public scrutiny. There has been previous acknowledgement of the problematic nature of the work and the 'no win' situation that social workers have found themselves in (Dingwall et al., 1983) but, up until Cleveland, most exposure has centred on physical harm or injury. Recent attention has shifted towards sexual and ritual abuse. It is ironic that, as awareness of the incidence, prevalence and nature of child harm has developed with greater sophistication than ever, the task of protecting children has become so complex that it leaves many practitioners bewildered and confused as to how to act in the child's best interests.

Although child abuse, whatever its form, is almost universally acknowledged as a social problem, what is less obvious, perhaps, is that, as a social problem, it has much to do with the culture of our society. The very terms 'child' and 'abuse' involve and invoke culturally acquired, understood and institutionalised categories and standards which underpin actions to, for example, protect children, identify and name behaviour, prosecute members, provide news, assault fellow prisoners, telephone a helpline, and so forth. In other words, such conceptions shape our everyday actions in a myriad of ways, both ordinary and exceptional. They define for us our social relationships, their character, our obligations and our attitudes toward our fellow members of society. However, even though there is agreement between some people about what does, or does not, constitute child abuse, this does not constitute complete agreement.

Bringing culture to the fore like this raises the issue of relativism and, particularly, the relativism of child abuse and its relation to child protection. In terms of making a case, the definition of the phenomenon for which a case is made becomes acutely relevant, and the fact that definition is problematic is central to the making of it. The notion of relativism is not new to the topic. Historical accounts of childhood can depict behaviours which, at the time, were considered to be quite acceptable (Aries, 1973), but which would not be so today. Cross-cultural studies similarly point to the acceptance of certain practices, such as female circumcision, which would be abhorrent to many people of different cultures (Korbin, 1981). Intra-cultural differences, such as those between social groups, have long been identified in social work training and practice. The issue is not simply that people from different cultures entertain different conceptions of, among other things, children, their rights and obligations, their status and their treatment, but that such conceptions, even within a single culture, can penetrate deeply into the practice of child protection itself. For example, there has been attention paid to the use of 'value judgements' in relation to child harm and injury, mainly in terms of the way in which certain professionals may use their own 'values' to make judgements about 'clients', who may hold different 'values' (see for example, Higginson, 1990) .

Perhaps the most well-known use of relativism is that of Dingwall, Eekelaar and Murray (1983) who, on the basis of their own research, identified 'cultural relativism' as a tool of the child protection trade. They maintain that practitioners operate under a 'rule of optimism' accepting that parents love and care for their children unless there is substantial evidence to the contrary. In attempting to explain why some cases are acted upon and others are not, they give examples of how practitioners use an understanding of the relativity of cultures to justify their judgement and response. So that, for example, in an accident and emergency department where a child is presented by a black father with what might be a dislocated elbow, it is remarked upon that the father does not show much 'love' for the child (Dingwall et al., 1983). Whereas, for a white family this might be perceived as indicative of potential risk because of its significance in relation to bonding and attachment, for this father it is almost dismissed as a 'cultural' phenomenon. Thus, it can be said that a child is cared for in a characteristic way for a particular neighbourhood, and if, for example, his parents occasionally leave him alone, send him out in inappropriate clothing when there are no other clothes to be had, feed him constantly on 'butties' and so forth, this is treated as the 'norm' for this particular family, against which its subsequent behaviours are interpreted and judged. There can be some acknowledgement of concern that the situation is not good, but an acceptance that things are probably as good as they can be under the circumstances, and, particularly if there is a display of 'natural love', action is unlikely to be taken.

It is widely recognised that there are differences in upbringing styles, attitudes toward children, and so on, which are explicable, although not always consistently, in terms of belonging to some larger collectivity, be it that of social class, of ethnicity, of neighbourhood, region, or whatever. This notion of cultural relativism is not simply to do with the fact that there are differences in outlook and behaviour between people and groups, but that such differences can very often have a great deal to do with the determination of facts and their significance. That one family might perceive smacking a child as a disciplinary action, whereas another might see it as an assault. The act of identifying an event which, in one culture or historical time, is not considered abusive, represents a gauge of the moral discourse on acceptable behaviour towards children. A second feature of the rule of optimism, that of natural love was identified by Dingwall et al. (1983). In order to use cultural relativism as a justification for inaction, there needs to be a further standard by which to judge behaviour — otherwise anything would be acceptable, which clearly is not the case in our culture. If one family sees smacking as discipline they still display the culturally same interpretation, that parents love their children, since discipline can be seen as an expression of care. However, there are limits in that not any so-called disciplinary behaviour is justifiable as care and affection, and these limits need to be arbitrated. Within our society this is, in part at least, the responsibility of the legal and social welfare system. For the practitioners in these institutions, finding and arbitrating limits and justifying them is a day-to-day issue in their work. Thus:

> . . . the core dispute is over the point at which intervention may be justified. What this means is that the very definition of maltreatment becomes a relative matter. Where do we draw the line between firm discipline and physical abuse? How is neglect to be distinguished from low standards of parental competence? What marks off sexual abuse from intimate displays of affection between family members? It is on the answers to these questions that advocates of state intervention and family rights ultimately establish their positions. (Dingwall et al., 1983)

Child protection work involves negotiating through, and by means of, the categories provided by our culture and, as legal gatekeepers of our behaviour towards children, justify whatever actions they take, including 'no action'. Child protection agencies receive many referrals which turn out to be unsubstantiated and lead to no further action. What is clear is that the majority of child protection cases referred to social work agencies drop out of the system at an early stage (Giller et al., 1992; Thorpe, 1991; Besharov, 1986). On the assumption that social workers are operating under the 'rule of optimism', it could be anticipated that the grounds to proceed in the cases acted on, would be those which satisfy a pessimistic prognosis for the child. However, on the basis of the research reported in this book, it would appear that matters are not so clear cut and that there are further factors to consider.

When I first embarked on the research on which much of this book draws, my aim was to examine decision-making in child protection intervention. Hitherto, this topic had been treated in at least three ways. First, by examining the organisation of communication between practitioners and agencies, characteristic of Inquiries in the 1970s and 1980s (DHSS, 1982; DOH, 1991a). Secondly, by examining the types of cases on which emergency child protection orders are imposed (Packman, 1989), initial intervention is warranted (Dingwall et al., 1983), and registration takes place (Giller et al., 1992; Creighton & Noyes, 1989). Thirdly, by examining the effectiveness of risk factors in predicting avoidable harms and injuries (Parton, 1989; Underwager & Wakefield, 1990). I have taken a somewhat different approach to an analysis of decision-making, founded on a theoretical framework which examines the social organisation and structure, that is, the formal properties of the practical action of decision-taking. This approach develops from the work of Garfinkel (1967) and Sacks (1966), particularly that in relation to documentary evidence and recording practices, the social organisation of conversational interaction and categorisation work. Chapter 3 is given over wholly to the findings of my analysis and the structures that I identified in examining the investigative and prosecution process. These were the structures of motive, corroboration, specificity and categorisation. Wherever one looks, these structures are pervasive, and, more importantly, they can predict how cases will proceed. From the first phone call to a long-awaited court appearance, these structures can help account for the response, whether it be a home visit or a guilty plea. It is these structured assemblages of cultural categories and their 'rules' of use which create the relevancies of the facts for the decisions that social workers, police officers and lawyers and judges have to make. While it is important to know about the quality of parental relationship, the frequency with which a child is hit, the stressful circumstances of a particular client, and so on, it is also important to know how these matters are formatted as information. To know that if, for example, a child is able to give a great deal of detail (the structure of specificity), s/he is more likely to be thought to be telling the truth and thus the information will be acted on. Or, that if a child is referred by a parent who is seen to have interests other than those immediately concerning the allegation, such as an access problem (the structure of motive) the information is likely to be queried and less likely to be substantiated. Very often risk assessment is the product of such structures, yet I have rarely seen them openly acknowledged as operational factors, and never have I known them to be analyzed in terms of their appropriateness. In other words, I have never known it to be asked whether these are the right structures by which to assess information from and about children who have been the victims of adult inflicted harm or injury. It may well be that, whilst they are unavoidable in terms of practical reasoning, their use should, at the very least, be recognised, and their impact compensated for, within any assessment of risk.

These structures effectively make or break cases, both in social work settings and in the courts. They underlie the construction of evidence, both social and legal, and it is legal evidence which is increasingly the criteria by which cases are judged. Confirming that a child has been the victim of assault is a serious and accountable matter, and one which might eventually be open to critical legal scrutiny. It is in this potential legal context that practitioners operate and the construction and interpretation of evidence starts to take place.

For some, particularly those who have no encounter either with child protection or its professional workers, it might be hard to understand why the legal context presents such a problem. Why is it the case that, for a child who is abused and presents, or has presented on her/his behalf, information which reveals that abuse has occurred, that in some cases legal action is not taken? The very posing of the question raises some important issues that are the concern of this book. Bluntly put, if harm or injury cannot be proved in a legal setting, can it be said that it has occurred? Many social workers would say it could, many lawyers would say it couldn't. Much of the discussion in this book is intended to show how this disjuncture can occur. At the root of it is the notion of evidence; what can be said to stand for what in the ordinary every-day world of the law, of the social world, and of the lives of ordinary children.

The public find it hard to accept that, if children are abused, those responsible will not be dealt with accordingly, and the child will be protected. If the information is not sufficient to prosecute, or seek a protection order, it cannot be a 'serious' case of child abuse, and those originally believed responsible should be vindicated. This was a clear message in the media coverage of Cleveland, and, from it, the parental rights lobby gained great strength. There is a tendency in such cases to cry 'where's the evidence?' and to retort, 'if there is no evidence, there is no case'. In the final chapters of the book I show how evidence in a legal sense is constructed and used in the legal process. This builds on a growing body of literature in socio-legal studies which views the legal process in terms of its social construction. In these chapters I identify how it can come about that a criminal act can be perpetrated on a child, and for that not to be substantiated in a legal context. It is already recognised that the legal system is not child 'friendly'. Many measures have been introduced and proposed to improve the process. Preparation of witnesses (Bray, 1989; Dent & Flin, 1992; Plotnikoff, 1992), the introduction of 'live' link (Davies & Noon, 1991), recommendations for de-robing and making courts less intimidating have all been advocated. What has received less attention has been the character of legal discourse itself and the place of evidence concerning children within it. Single issues to do with the formal rules of the discourse, such as hearsay and the 'warning' on uncorroborated evidence are noted with concern (Home Office, 1989; Spencer, 1990). However, the informal 'rules' that guide decision-making in cases of offences against children have received less attention. These have more to do with methods of assessing the credibility of witnesses, including the sense made of expert information, and methods employed to protect children from court by keeping them out of the process altogether, including the 'meaningful discussion' that surrounds the acceptance of pleas. Amongst the consequences of what can be called informal decision-making about children's cases are that people are convicted of lesser offences, receive lower sentences, are freed and found not guilty, and children are occasionally returned to high-risk situations. I hope to show, by examining the topic in this way, how practitioners might start to make reasoned decisions about whether it is in the child's interests to enter the legal process at all.

The accountability of practitioners is linked, as the quotation from Dingwall et al. (1983) suggests, to the issue of 'rights', in particular, to the right of the state to intervene in family life. This is an enduring philosophical and political problem, and one which underpinned the considerations of a number of inquiries during the 1980s (DOH, 1991a). Too often, rights language offers a 'win or lose' formula which is ill suited to the complexities of the child protection task (Midgely, 1991). With the introduction of the Children Act, 1989, practitioners must now consider such notions as the 'rights of the child' versus the 'rights of the parents' with some practical intent. This is, I would argue, a new development in child protection. Hitherto, child protection has been dominated by norms and values of the professional relationship. Social workers, for example, will consider the effects of their action on their relationship with the client. Doctors are reluctant to disclose information to other practitioners in order to protect their relationship with their patient (Williams et al., 1985), teachers will not pass on confidential information before their relationship with a pupil licenses the transmission of such knowledge (Wattam, 1989).

Arguably, one catalyst for this change was the way in which parents were not acknowledged to retain their rights as parents once the state began to intervene, both in an informal and formal way. This can be seen in the press coverage of the Cleveland crisis. It was also alleged that children were not accorded certain rights, particularly the right to be listened to. The phrase from the Cleveland report which refers to the child as a person and not an object of concern has been so often quoted that its impact has been lessened. However, in Chapter 1 it is argued that, in making this statement in the context of Cleveland, the reverse has occurred. The Cleveland Inquiry sustained the momentum of the Beckford Inquiry (London Borough of Brent, 1985) which reinforced the situation of child protection practice within the legal framework (Parton, 1991). Events in Brent were interpreted in terms of an exercise of legal powers, found to be lacking. Cleveland was about the evidence on which these powers rest, which actually had the effect of beginning the transformation of children from 'people' into evidential objects. Judgements in Rochdale and Manchester strengthened the transformation further, which has been sealed by the Children Act, 1989. Now, orders can only be made on the basis of evidence to show that it is better than making no order at all. This, in conjunction with the need for strong evidence in prosecution cases, has located child protection in the realms of the forensic, and what children say has become the basis for this evidence. Whilst this has been a practical consideration in child sexual assault cases for some time, the duty to ascertain the feelings and wishes of the child (Children Act, 1989) and the wide range of offences pertaining to the admissibility of pre-recorded video evidence (Criminal Justice Act, 1991) mean that, increasingly, this is going to be the case for all types of harm and injury.

The Advisory Group on Video Evidence recommended that a 'Code of Practice' be drawn up to assist practitioners in the interviewing process. This document, now known as the *Memorandum of Good Practice* (Home Office, 1992) provides a framework for interviewing child witnesses in a legally acceptable way. The admissibility of pre-recorded video evidence allows the child's account to be 'bottled' at the early stages of the investigation, with a recipe provided by the *Memorandum of Good Practice* (*MOGP*). It contains advice on when, and how, to do a 'substantive interview', what technical knowledge and equipment is required, and the legal rules of evidence by which any interview will be judged. The overall requirements of a child protection investigation are referred to in *Working Together* under the Children Act, 1989, (DOH, 1991*b*). This document itself refers to the advice contained in the MOGP for interviewing purposes. Ideally, the two should complement each other, and, taken together, provide all the guidance needed for investigative assessment. However, the practical consequence of having two documents is that the two processes, interviewing and investigation, remain distinct. Nothing has been stated in either document about the implications of a focus on evidence, particularly that obtained by criminal justice criteria, for the child. Nor is there any direction about principles which should underpin a child centred investigative assessment, in terms of deciding on which approach to take in the child's interests. If a practitioner decides that a legal route is probable, the guidance on interviewing is there. If, however, an alternative route is to be considered which is an increasing possibility under the Children Act, 1989, there is no guidance, and crucially, no advice on how to reach this decision. These matters are consequential for making a case in child protection and are discussed throughout this book.

In Chapter 5, the topic of interviewing children as it was observed in practice, is presented to show how the child, and the evidence, have been treated as objects of organisational concern in the past. It is difficult to pay attention to the right of the child, and the parents, to be 'listened to' (if such a right exists) without deconstructing the ways in which the process of investigation, prosecution and adults, in general, orient to children. My materials point to how it comes about that children appear to have minimal rights in the process of investigating, substantiating and prosecuting harmful actions perpetrated on them, because cultural and organisational constraints operate to make it very difficult to do otherwise. One upshot of this is the conclusion that, if the child is seriously to be treated as a person with rights, organisations are going to have to work very differently — not least in the way in which they make use of, and structure their work through, the legal system.

The claim to a right is to enunciate a 'rule' which pertains to the status or treatment of a person. The claim could be that such a rule would apply to all persons in general, for example, the 18th century debates on natural rights, or to particular sub-groups. The rule like character of 'rights' holds, however, irrespective of their authorisation in statute or more informally as a presumption underpinning case law, as in the UK. What rights in effect do is to propose a rule by, and through which, persons are treated. However, no rule dictates its own application, but needs to be applied in particular cases: a feature which applies to rules as diverse as those of games, to those of inalienable human rights. The right to 'life, liberty and the pursuit of happiness' is, in practice, hedged around with qualifications, caveats, restrictions and so on, which make it less than universal. This does not mean that the right is of no relevance, for it is the qualifications which make it applicable as a moral principle relevant to the practical world. However, it is in the application of rules such as this, and legal rules need to be included here, that conflicts are likely to arise, not only between varying interpretations of the same rule, but between the competing claims of different rules. For example, in drawing up the guidelines contained in the MOGP for interviewing children on video, the committee had to consider the issue of the disclosure of evidential videos to the defence. Under the law, the defendant has the right to access to the case to be made against her/him. This brought into sharp relief the rights of the complainant versus the rights of the defendant. The question was: should the defendant have access, which might be abused because of the value of such videos to those who might exploit them? Alternatively, did the child have rights to be protected from such potential misuse, further abuse and exploitation? In the event, the rights of the defendant prevailed but with restrictions which become the responsibility of the defendant's legal representative.[1]

This clash of 'rights' in a practical context presents a number of problems. For example, if children have rights (as persons) and they identify an action made towards them as abusive, and if parents have rights and they do not identify that same action as abusive, who acts as the arbiter? A practical every-day concern for social workers, police officers, doctors, teachers, lawyers, health visitors and the like is the injunction to decide, on a case-by-case basis, what is, or is not, a case of child 'abuse', and thereafter to decide what should be done about it. This concern, as it relates to the rights of children and parents, will become of increasing importance as the implementation of the Children Act, 1989 proceeds. Ultimately, in a climate of 'no order' and resource constraints, it may be that the law becomes the final arbiter. Thus cases which have a legal consequence will be the cases attended to; 'the rear end', serious cases which constitute from between 10% and 20%, will continue to act as the filter (Thorpe, 1991).

With the legal discourse as the dominant discourse in child protection, this represents a very narrow definition of avoidable child harm and injury. In times of resource constraint and a 'purchaser provider' climate, it presents a worrying picture for children who may be disadvantaged, deprived and not achieving their full potential. This situation typifies chronic neglect and emotional harm, which are the cases least representative of legal intervention. In Chapter 2, I show that whether a child receives attention at all depends on how the referral is oriented to, as much as whether anything has happened. The whole system of referral, investigation, conference and registration, prosecution and treatment is designed to filter out the 'least serious' cases. Yet, 'serious' harm or injury is a moral judgement as well as a physical condition, and 'serious' risk even more so. Whilst this book comments largely on the legal criteria for making a case, it also suggests strongly that other forms of intervention are just as important. Thus making a case has as much to do with providing the right environment to be able to respond to a child in need, as it does with acceptability to the legal process. Cases can be made for resources as well as for orders and convictions.

One difficulty with the notions of 'value' or 'relativism' is that they can be taken to indicate a less than factual status of a phenomenon. Problems identified by other people's values are subject to debate, and child 'abuse' is no exception. A recourse to this is to suggest that there is something like a 'bottom line' in the argument, for example, wilful murder of a child, serious physical and/or sexual assault, total social and/or physical deprivation, and so on. Of course, it could also be argued that 'assaults' or 'deprivation', 'wilful' or 'serious' are themselves subject to debate. The 'bottom line' is (generally) taken to be something the majority of 'reasonable' persons would agree upon. But the construction of child harm or injury, under this 'bottom line' category of seriousness, has tended to result in 'tunnel vision'. This is not a criticism, but a recognition of how 'serious' avoidable harm and injury to children has become the yardstick by which child health is measured in an investigative context. We cannot know what happens to the children who are filtered out, nor about those who are never referred. A completely different strategy and approach would need to be adopted if child health and protection was measured in positive terms.

In some senses, what is surprising is that social workers manage to carry out the child protection task at all. How do they daily sift through information offered to them about children thought to be at risk and decide what constitutes a case warranting their intervention. Parents are assumed respectable, and 'loving' unless proved otherwise.

> We can characterize this as an injunction to front line workers to interpret the available 'facts' as evidence that parents are honest, competent and caring, unless an exhaustive inquiry into their motivation renders this impossible. If parental failure is established these same facts can be read in a quite different fashion. Dingwall et al., 1983, p.78

Thus, the key to making a case here is evidence of parental failure. This citation also points to the fact that evidence is not a static, given phenomenon. It is (a) produced and (b) interpreted, (c) over time, (d) in various settings and (e) through different media. These facets of evidence do not happen in sequence, they are mutually interdependent features, which turn out to have several applied consequences for the investigation of, and response to, child abuse. Essentially, that is the theme of this book, the aim of which is to explicate the process of constructing a child protection case in the hope that this will give practitioners a base on which to make informed decisions; to reflect upon what kind of a case they have been making, and make reasoned assessments about routes to protect children which are in the child's best interests, rather than those of agency, organisation and law.

Before proceeding further, there are two points that require clarification. First, there is an organisational distinction made between different types of harm or injury. Many of the materials in this book pertain to child sexual assault, rather than to emotional, physical or neglectful harms. Whilst there is a great deal of common ground to be found between the different categories of harm in terms of the 'rules' operating in relation to evidence, there are also some clear differences. One crucial difference, which has relevance to much of what follows, is that evidence in cases of sexual assault quite often consists wholly, or in large part, of the child's account. Whereas cases of physical harm are unlikely to proceed to prosecution, or even care proceedings, without clear medical and/or forensic evidence, cases of child sexual assault might do. I do not wish to accentuate this difference too much, since it is quite possible that much of what follows will turn out in future to be of relevance to all categories of harm or injury for which evidence is required. This is because, with the admissibility of pre-recorded video interviews as evidence, and the opportunity afforded to the

child to express their feelings and wishes, the accounts of children
are set to become more available to legal and public scrutiny.

The second point is that there is also an organisational distinction
between civil and criminal proceedings and the standard of proof
applied to evidence in each. Thus there is a legal tradition, which
has been oriented to in child protection practice, to see the two
forms of evidence as distinct. This is exemplified in the almost
complete emphasis given to civil proceedings in the overview by
Dingwall et al. When they were writing in 1983, child sexual
abuse had not been a major public concern, and it did not
become an official criteria for registration until 1988. Whilst
the importance of multi-agency working was stressed prior to
this, the advocacy of 'joint working', that is police and social
service co-operation in investigation, did not gather momentum
and official sanction until the Cleveland inquiry where it was thrown
into sharp relief. The Bexley experiment (Metropolitan Police &
Bexley Social Services, 1987) and *Working Together* (DOH, 1988;
DOH, 1991*b*) have all promoted joint police and social services
working policy. This shift towards combining evidential and child
protection roles has been accentuated by the perceived requirements
of child sexual abuse cases, although there is no reason why, in
theory, such methods of working should not have been applied to
all types of child harm or injury. The introduction of the MOGP
has, however, had important implications for child protection
investigation, with the consequence that standards of proof whilst
legally remaining distinct, in practice, turn out to rest on similar
evidential considerations.

The Children Act, 1989, clearly gives practitioners a licence to
act in the 'best interests' of children. This means weighing up the
requirements of evidence in a legal sense, particularly in relation
to the MOGP on interviewing children, the organisational demands
imposed by multi-agency agency working and particularly by joint
working between the police and social services, and the needs of
particular children and their families. Social workers and child
advocates are in, what is likely to be, an extremely uncomfortable
cleft stick if they take into account all the directives enshrined in
the Children Act, the *Memorandum of Good Practice* and *Working
Together*.

The research on which this book is based was conducted between
1988 and 1991 in the North West of England. It comprises two
studies, one based in a child protection team (referred to throughout
as the child protection study), the other in the Crown Prosecution
Service (referred to as the CPS study). I undertook an ethnographic
analysis in both, but the first study had a stronger participant
observation component. The initial study was on the disclosure

of child sexual abuse. In addition to participant observation, I also coded information about cases into a quantitative format for computer analysis.[2] In both studies I conducted a document analysis of the files, video-recorded or taped interviews, and conducted interviews; with teachers (Wattam, 1989), social workers, police officers (Wattam, 1991), CPS personnel, and children.

## A note on methodology

There are at least two ways in which an ethnographic approach can assist in developing the overall corpus of knowledge about child abuse. First, in order to decide in a practical way what is and is not child abuse, practitioners, legal professionals and jurors must draw on cultural knowledge about children, normal families, adults, and particularly child abuse. Thus (and this is no reflection on their competence) like all of us, in order to make the judgements they did, they had to make recourse to their own common-sense knowledge of social life as well as their more specialised 'professional' knowledge. In other words, defining whether or not a child had been the victim of 'abuse' is involved in so much else that we, as competent members of our society and culture, know and understand about the social world. Thus, an ethnography of decision-making in cases of offences against children explicates something of the social organisation of children and families within our culture.

The second point is more of a methodological kind, and has to do with the validity and generalisable qualities of research studies in this area. Finkelhor (1986) bemoaned the deficiencies in research relating to lack of accepted criteria for definition, inadequate control and sampling techniques, and the tendency towards clinical case study techniques which are restricted as to their wider application. More rigorous quantitative research was advocated. A common misconception of ethnographic approaches is that they necessarily provide only particular information about individual instances and cases which may not be generalisable to a wider population; the very criticism Finkelhor has levelled at clinical studies. This is not the place for a debate on the merits and demerits of quantitative and qualitative research in this respect. However, it is necessary to understand that the current study does portray more than the local practice on which it reports. This claim is linked to the first point, that practitioners must draw on the culture in order to make sense of presenting information, and make sense of it to others. They do not begin from a standpoint of knowing that only a few (local) people will understand what it is they are saying and will see it in the same way. Rather, they utilise 'rules' that are shared in common, in much the same way as the rules of language are. That the 'rules' or methods are generalisable, is their rationale for use. As Sacks (Atkinson & Heritage, 1984) points out

> The methods persons employ to produce their activities permit formal description of singular occurrences that are generalizable in intuitively nonapparent ways and are highly reproducibly usable.

It is this 'reproducible' feature of practical reasoning that defence lawyers, for example, call on in presenting their case to juries. They base their talk on what any 'reasonable' person can expect; the devices, criteria and methods that people-in-general can be anticipated to use to draw conclusions about character, and culpability.

The key which distinguishes this study, and others like it, from a clinical case study approach is that the focus is not on any particular case, but on the 'methods' practitioners employed to produce their activities, to do their work. One does not need to look at vast numbers of cases in order to explicate such methods. For example, the simple fact that, as a rule, participants take turns in conversation, can be gleaned from looking at a very small number of conversations. This is not because the conversations studied are representative in a statistical sense of all conversations — how could such a sample be drawn? — but because each conversation is the product of conversationalists using the methods for producing conversational exchanges within our culture.

The primary data sources were field observations and files. In the child protection study, I was a 'team member' from commencement of the project in January, 1988. Field notes were largely written during the earlier part of the three-year study, and updated subsequently, when I shared a room with two other team members and thus gained access to talk about the work. There were certain factors which prevented me from watching a case in its entirety. Cases are visible in many ways: telephone conversations, 'write-ups', dictation, 'chatting', talking about cases in meetings, visiting at home, doing office interviews, videos of office interviews, supervision sessions, talk in other places such as hospitals, case conferences, to other practitioners, letters and memorandums, forms, audio-tapes and so on. In order to get access to the whole picture, I would have had to shadow a worker and the child simultaneously, 24 hours a day. This was, quite obviously, not possible. What I did have was access to all those sites of 'articulation' in an organisational setting at some point or another, for some case or another, in addition to having the 'gaps' filled in by the workers concerned. Thus, my field notes generally reflect the points of 'articulation' encountered in offices during the course of a working day.

Files were an important source of information. In the child protection study, 237 files were examined representing a total sample of child sexual abuse referrals in the area for a two-year period. In the CPS study, 62 files were identified as cases of offences against children over a six-month period. In each study, the whole file was read. Records on file present accountable information. When Garfinkel (1967b) attempted to use clinical records as a means of identifying by what criteria applicants were selected for treatment, he found that the records were notable for the 'unavailable information' they contained. This was a feature commonly found in records. He went on to note that the troubles of 'bad records' are 'normal, natural' troubles, so described because the recorders were acting in compliance with the rules of organisational practice and procedure. These need not be the officially stated rules, but rather the rules which members of organisations attend to as a practical concern in order to conduct their work. In his study, people were not recording badly, they were recording in a context of organisational requirements, and producing records which, unless notable in organisational terms for their badness (an entirely different matter) were adequate for organisational purposes.

Whilst absence of file information is a useful analytic device, files also contain the information any practitioner selects to record as relevant to the task at hand. Social workers do not record what they had for breakfast, they act as recorders in an organisational capacity. Thus

> Reporting procedures, their results, and the uses of these results are integral features of the same social orders they describe.
> Garfinkel, 1967, p.114

That is, if they stand as acceptable records in organisational practice, they might tell us something about organisational practice requirements. A reading of the files shows that, amongst other things, matters that justify (for whatever reason) actions taken and decisions made, are generally recordable. In relation to truth and belief in the process of investigation, for example, social workers rarely recorded such statements as 'I believed X' or 'X was telling me the truth'. However, the files are replete with accounts of interactions with children and their carers which are accounted in such a way as to substantiate, or not to substantiate, the validity of their claims. The following is an illustration concerning an 11 year-old girl allegedly assaulted by her uncle

> . . . She had witnessed white, sticky stuff and that it had hurt her. She also advised that there had been threats made upon her to keep silent. It appears that most of the incidents took place in his bedroom. The policewoman interviewing the child then began to discuss the subject of lie telling and whether or not [child], whose mental age is only 8, understood what telling lies involved. I considered that this process of the interview was unduly lengthy, and it appeared to me that [child] had been subjected to considerable questioning about the validity of her story, however, she did maintain the story throughout. Times and events did alter, and at one time she did retract but then reiterated her original story . . .

This is not a straightforward she said/he said account, nor a transcript of the interview, but a particular way of recording what has happened. It is a record of what was considered to be relevant at this stage of the investigation. Having established that what is recorded is what is relevant, we can now ask how it becomes relevant to record these features. Sense can only be made of this account if it is accepted as a commentary on a story, offered by a child, which is available for scrutiny as an accurate narrative of what has happened. If its validity was not in question, or going to be open to question in some prospective sense, these criteria would not have been used. It would be possible to comment on the child's story as a 'sad story', or an 'alarming indictment on adult's actions towards children'. By taking this methodological approach, by describing what criteria practitioners opt to use to obtain an account from a child — in this case what the child had seen and heard, where the event occurred, whether the child understood lies and lie telling, and consistency — a picture can be developed of the 'rules' or methods in use. The information is treated in a very particular way, and begins to exhibit, in data form, the construction of children as evidential objects.

Three sets of interviews were conducted in the child protection study: the first with teachers, the second with social workers and the third with children. The interviews with teachers are reported elsewhere (Wattam, 1989). Fifteen children and 16 social workers in three social service teams were presented with a brief explanation of the project, and a request that the child or social worker said anything they wanted to say on the topic. They lasted from 30 minutes to one hour. All the interviews were taped and transcribed where permission for taping was given. They were entirely unstructured, since their analysis depended on what the subjects offered, that is, what they saw as relevant information. Access to children was restricted by going through social workers, with the criteria that the child would have been in some kind of therapeutic relationship. This was the only way to ensure that the trauma of such an interview would be minimised. It also ensured that it was safe to approach the child, whatever the domestic circumstances. This limited the sample considerably, but necessarily. Very few children had received any treatment or therapy after their allegation had been investigated. Forty-one children (18%) continued to receive individual social work support, but this did not necessarily constitute a therapeutic relationship. Intervention varied from routine visiting to check on the child to individual counselling and group therapy.

In the CPS study, informal interviews were conducted with all Crown Court clerks responsible for the cases selected. These interviews were structured by a questionnaire and centred on any comment the clerk had to make about the child, the child's appearance in court as a witness, and the outcome of the case. These interviews were conducted to supplement the file information because, apart from witness assessments, there was very little descriptive recording on file. In addition, observations were made of the clerks at work, which included accompanying them to court. However, the main sources of material for this study were the file documents.

## Summary

Within a social constructionist framework, child harm and injury is subject to the operational definitions of the parties involved in it; those believed responsible, the victims, social workers and police officers, patents, relatives, lawyers, judges, jurors, doctors and so forth. Each of these parties acts at different points in the process of responding to any child victim, to arbitrate on whether they are dealing with a case of child 'abuse'. For practitioners in an organisational context, the definition and response appears to be dominated by the legal discourse and the pursuit of evidence. The introduction of the Memorandum of Good Practice represents the most recent attempt to refine this process further. Whilst such prescriptive guidance can give direction on the formal rules about what constitutes good evidence, there appears to be a set of other, less formal, 'rules' which are important in determining whether a case becomes a case or not, and how it is proceeded on.

The book is based on recently completed research along with the relevant literature and aims to illustrate the practical task of making a case in child protection work. Procedures and guidelines, particularly *Working Together* (DOH, 1991*b*) and the *Memorandum of Good Practice* (Home Office, 1992) are referred to throughout. The book thus represents an attempt to guide practitioners in the context of current practice requirements; explicit, formal, practical, informal, and professional. It is not a 'how to do' book, rather it is a book about the 'rules' as they were observed in practice, and as they are defined by procedural guidance and law. My hope is that practitioners will be able to make more reasoned decisions in the light of their depiction, particularly in relation to decision-making with, and on behalf of, the child.

## Notes

1   Law Society's recommendation.
2   I used the INTERACT programme devised by Dr D. Thorpe for monitoring and evaluating child protection in Western Australia. This programme is custom-made for the child protection process, and derives from a systems analysis of career types.

# 1 Foundations

The steering group for the *Memorandum of Good Practice* (*MOGP*) deliberated over its contents for several months and discussed in four very long meetings the issues that surrounded it. The topics that were raised repeatedly were those at the very heart of child protection practice and reflected a much wider and longer-term trend in the political response to child abuse, largely as a consequence of child abuse tragedies. Government working parties, inquiries, research and a major overhaul of child care law (for review see Parton, 1991) had identified, and in some cases tried to come to terms with the following issues: legal versus therapeutic responses to child abuse, the rights of the child versus the rights of the accused, and the need for legally formulated evidence versus what can be known from professional knowledge and experience. These are the articulations of deeper concerns; the right of the state to intervene in family life, the criminalisation of child abuse, and the concept of the moral order of society; that is, what is acceptable behaviour and who is entitled to judge it.

Throughout, social workers have continued to practise under these umbrella issues. The level of awareness for individual practitioners is a reflection of the relationship between policy and practice. Both feed from each other. For example, practice in Cleveland was influenced by practice and policy recommendations in Brent (Butler-Sloss, 1988), and that practice, in turn, had some impact in strengthening the notions of partnership with parents and parental responsibility which underpinned the Children Act, 1989. One practice repercussion is the involvement of parents in case conferences, which already seems to have had the effect of reducing the number of opinion type value judgements used by practitioners in decision-making (Frankel, 1989). Another, which is the concern of this book, is that practitioners need evidence on which to act, the strength of which is arbitrated by the legal discourse.

The pursuit of evidence has wrought a tremendous change in child protection practice over recent years. The document analysis in the child protection study rendered many examples of the shift. For illustration, I have selected one case, which is given in some detail, to indicate the measure of the change in terms of the issues outlined above: state and family, public and private, legal and therapeutic, crime and disease. Evidence, as it is legally formulated, is a central theme to the first of each of these pairings. This case shows how, in the past, evidence was a matter of finding sufficient grounds to justify some form of intervention, whereas now it is a much more systematic requirement and the foundation upon which most cases will rest. One point I want to stress is that this is not inevitable, and much depends on the theoretical frameworks that practitioners choose to adopt. They do not need to replicate the kind of relationship I describe above between policy and practice. That is, one where if practice goes wrong, policy responds and practitioners accommodate to it. In order to change this pattern they must, however, be aware of the pervasive nature of the legal discourse within which they operate.

## Case example

Initially, the case was referred in 1984 when the mother of a four-year-old boy contacted a social work agency because she was concerned about his possible sexual abuse by his stepfather. The record begins with a report of an interview with the mother of the child:

> [SW] then questioned mother about the incident which was alleged to have happened between her husband [name] and her first child [name] who is five years of age. Mother said that the incident happened approximately ten months ago when she was out one evening and her husband was baby-sitting, going on to describe that her husband was playing with [child's] penis then took [child's] pants down and was going to insert his penis into [child's] bottom when he stopped. She was insistent that there had been no penetration. Father had been to see a hypnotherapist twice at the cost of £20.00 per session to try to discover why he should try to sexually abuse his stepson but had been told by the hypnotherapist that it could take up to twelve sessions and he had decided not to continue this treatment.

Two weeks later the same social worker accompanied by a colleague visited the family and the stepfather was asked to describe the incident. She wrote that

He described in quite clear detail that the incident happened upstairs when he was in the toilet; it is the practice that they leave the toilet door open. He was playing with himself, saying that he was masturbating. His wife was out at the time and he was baby-sitting for both children. Whilst he was masturbating [child] who was wearing pyjamas came into the bathroom where father asked him to touch his penis. The boy refused to do this and went downstairs. Father followed the boy downstairs and told us that he was still in a state of sexual excitement, that he had asked [child] to turn round with his back towards him, had pulled [child's] pyjama bottoms down and had asked him to bend down and was on the point of trying to insert his penis into [child's] anus when [child] began to cry saying that it hurt. At this point father said that he suddenly came to his senses and he didn't actually penetrate [child]. When mother returned home he explained to her what he had done and mum herself said that she had examined [child's] anus and had noted no red marks, no injuries and everything looked okay, but he had not been medically examined. I said to both (parents) that I felt a medical examination was a necessity . . .

A medical was carried out ten days later and no injuries were noted. The police were not contacted and the focus of work shifted to the parents. The couple informed the social worker that they were considering a divorce:

I said that if the problems were marital then I felt that it was advantageous for either [SW] or myself to withdraw from this problem and I felt there was no need for two of us to be as deeply involved as we were at the present time. This was discussed at quite some length and the conclusions I came to were that I said I felt [SW] and myself should withdraw from the case until the divorce situation had been decided between the parents. I said that I felt that the incident over the sexual abuse from which we had originally come into the household could have been the result of many factors. I quoted these as [mother] being six months pregnant at the time and father was sexually aroused and [child] happened to come into the bathroom whilst father was masturbating himself and that [stepfather] appeared to be under pressure from work. It was decided at that point that the parents would contact if they felt there was need for further assistance.

The case was then closed. It was reopened three years later when a referral was received from another woman who was cohabiting with the stepfather who had, by then, left his previous family. The

referrer had a child to this man and also care of another 6 year-old
boy. The referral stated:

> Two days ago [child] complained to her that [father] took his
> pants down and made him bend over the settee and put his
> 'foot' up his bottom. When asked how he knew it was [father's]
> foot he said [father] had told him when it hurt. Two years ago
> a similar incident happened with [father's] wife's child.

On this occasion a social worker visited to check out the referral
information and then contacted the police. An investigation ensued,
during which the child was 'jointly interviewed', and the father was
interviewed by the police.

In 1984, the allegation and the parental response were taken at
face value, the presenting information — one incident — was the
information that was responded to. The child was not interviewed
alone, and the social worker's response focused on the parents. At
no point in the account is there any suggestion that anything other
than what was reported had happened. It was accepted that both
parents were telling the truth and that this constituted an account
of all the relevant details. Thus the focus on the child, and what the
child had to say was negligible and amounted to the fact that he was
in the same room as this was being discussed. There is no account
of what the child said to social workers, only of what this mother
reported him saying to her. The theoretical concept of 'disclosure'
was not employed. Furthermore, the account mentions that the
stepfather was baby-sitting for 'both children'. No reference is made
to the other child, and the possibility that she might have something
to say is not considered. The formulation of child sexual abuse was
one which framed it as an act with a reasonable explanation, rather
than more recent formulations of a predisposition with a social or
psychological pathology.

In withdrawing their contact, the social workers formulated the
factors, which they considered caused the incident, in a certain
way. This was that sexual abuse is understandable in certain
circumstances, and that these circumstances are related to the sexual
needs of men, the incapacity, in this case through pregnancy, of
women to fulfil male sexual needs, and the availability of children as
sexual objects. Sexual relations were constructed as family matters,
and only, solely, to do with the marital relationship, which was not
— if that was the only problem — the preserve of social workers.
These constructs are deeply rooted in the theoretical framework of
gender relations which has subsequently become more well known
(for example, Nelson, 1987; Driver & Droisen, 1989). There is an
acknowledgement of the pathology of sexual activity with children;
because it was referred in the first place and warranted a response,

and also articulated in the observation that it is treatable with 12 sessions of hypnotherapy. However, the resolution to this particular incident, having been formulated as a marital problem, was to sort out the relationship between husband and wife. Thus, the 'theoretical' formulation in the account has to do with the privacy of family life, and the responsibility of families to sort out their own problems where they can. The possibilities which one alternative analysis introduces reveal how social work can be restricted by its contemporary discourse and how it might alter.

> Through its analysis of incest as a sexual power relationship, the feminist literature has provided the tools to re-examine the family dynamics described in the family dysfunction and psychiatric literature . . . By linking the phenomenon of incest with the nature of the family and male–female relationships in patriarchal society, it can suggest intervention strategies that are social as well as individual. Waldby et al., 1989

I use this example to show how the discourse can change. Whilst there has been some acceptance of feminist theory into practice, it is still not embraced in a routine way. The approach observable in the materials from the child protection study reveal a legal, rather than any particular political, orientation.

In 1984, a medical was considered, but did not take place immediately, and the police were not contacted. In terms of 'theoretical' underpinnings there was no sense of 'disclosure' — that child sexual abuse is a difficult thing to talk about and that the child might have something more to say. No assessment is recorded on the child and his needs, what he felt about the experience, how he felt afterwards, and so on. The consequences were considered in purely physical terms. The mother inspected his bottom for damage and he was sent for a medical to see if her assessment was correct. This medical was not for 'evidence' since the kind of evidence now demanded in sexual assault cases would be the kind that could be obtained a short time after the reported event: forensic evidence, of semen or anal trauma, which would be unlikely to be present after 10 days. This is in part related to the acceptance of this incident as a 'one off', but also reflects the context of child abuse investigations at the time, which were predominantly set up within the framework of procedures for responding to physical assault. The focus was on penetration; it is reported that the mother was 'insistent that there had been no penetration' and the stepfather said he 'didn't actually penetrate the child'. As accountable features they represent the organisational relevance of the remarks, and suggest that penetration was the criteria for seriousness. The assessment is based on the physical abuse model; for example, the distinction between a 'slap', which would not warrant intervention and a 'severe beating' which would. Thus, almost getting to the act of buggery was not as serious as doing it. The crime was not committed, and the incident was never considered within a criminal framework, even though the option for indecent assault would have been available. The police were never contacted, rather this was a matter to be sorted out between the parties concerned. It was a private matter of parental responsibility, requiring a therapeutic not a legal approach. Consequently, there is no pursuit of legally acceptable evidence; the legal discourse, in this case is silent. The response three years later was characteristic of much of the material I will present in this book. That is, one that is dominated and framed by legal requirements and the pursuit of evidence. How has this change come about?

A significant event was the death of Jasmine Beckford which resulted in an inquiry reporting in December, 1985 (London Borough of Brent, 1985). As Nigel Parton (1991) points out, a major focus of the report was to locate social work in its statutory context. The social workers, it seemed, had not been sufficiently aware of the responsibility which the law had delegated to them. The practice implications were that social workers had to attend to their statutory responsibilities, and use their statutory powers to protect children. They had to situate their practice firmly within the law. By the time events in Cleveland began getting major public attention in 1987, these powers were being described as 'awesome' (Parton, 1991). Social workers were working within the law, but the law was acting as a 'rubber stamp' (Butler-Sloss, 1988). When the inquiry came to look at the evidence on which their actions were based they found it, by the law's criteria, to be lacking. A medical diagnosis could not stand as proof, children's statements were obtained in a context of pre-judging the issue, and the accused, the parents, had no apparent right to reply. It could be argued that it was Cleveland which gave final ratification to the dominance of the legal discourse, making it the discourse within which all others were interpreted. The resulting message was that children can only be protected on the basis of clear, legally formulated, evidence. If that evidence was lacking, it had to be accepted that the predicament of some children would remain 'unclear'.

There was a second strand which ran through the Cleveland Inquiry, the often-quoted notion that the 'child is a person not an object of concern'. I want to show how this concept interacts with the salience of gathering clear evidence, and suggest that, in practice, the two mitigate against each other. The potential conflict between them was not acknowledged in Cleveland. If the emphasis is on obtaining evidence, information that stands of itself as an account of an offence, then children as the subjects of the offence are the objects of evidence. In social work practice, this had considerable ramifications for the child protection process. The following example taken from the child protection study reveals the investigation process in 1988, post-Cleveland. A characteristic of cases investigated at that time was the pursuit of evidence, arguably at the expense of the child. Whilst this was the very criticism levied in Cleveland, in my materials it had a broader dimension. The children were not the victims of coercive disclosure techniques, they were the subject of a legal orientation which inevitably left their immediate personal and therapeutic needs as a secondary consideration — if considered at all. The case I use was on-going when the episode relating to sexual abuse began. Previous work focused on material help, financial support and care of the children, a boy and a girl. The social worker received a telephone call from the school expressing concern about a man whom the boy had said was staying with them. She continued contact with the family and established that the man was lodging with them. Later the school informed her that he was on a probation order for 'interfering with young boys'. After contact with probation it was agreed that the mother should be warned about allowing the man to stay. This was followed by a further referral from the school, that the boy had said 'he hated 'Max' — he rubbed his bottom'. A 'strategy meeting' was called and the decision to investigate was made. The record states:

> Discussed with Sgt Anderson CID — he felt there was enough to arrest Max if he was found in the house. [SW] and I arranged to collect Jos and his Mum — followed by police — and then to use NSPCC interview room.

> At NSPCC — I explained to Julie, while Jos was out of the room — why the investigation was taking place. She denies any knowledge of Max's past behaviour. Julie left the room with [SW] and interview began with Jos, myself and Sgt. Anderson. *Jos readily answered Sgt. Anderson's initial factual statements, but became very wary when asked if he remembered what he had told his teacher on Friday. Said that he didn't remember and became a bit flustered.* Suggested we had a play with the doll's house — spent a few minutes doing this in order to relax him. Sgt. Anderson left the room and returned to take up the interview. *Jos agreed with some of Sgt. Anderson's statements, but would not proffer any information himself. Attempts to use the anatomical dolls and drawings, while eliciting interest, brought no repetition of the allegations. Eventually the situation became too painful for Jos — saying he didn't want to remember and*

*asked for his mum.* Julie brought in and interview effectively ended. Sgt. Anderson informed us that Max had been arrested and would be remanded in custody overnight so it would be alright for Jos to return home. [SW] suggested that Jos be seen at school with the teacher to whom the disclosure was made in the hope that the allegation would be repeated. *Jos, once reunited with his mum soon settled down and was interested in the journey home — seemed very relieved to get home and rushed in.*

[Date; the following day]

Telephone call to Sgt. Henry police community liaison. Briefed Sgt. Henry on events of yesterday. Sgt. Henry agreed that he would be continuing with investigation today in place of Sgt. Anderson. Agreed that we would attempt to reinterview Jos today at school on the basis that Jos originally disclosed to his class teacher on Friday. *After the difficulties yesterday evening, it seems more appropriate for the child to be interviewed in the presence of someone he obviously trusts and who can see him through any reactions he may have.* Arranged to meet Sgt. Henry at school at 12.15 and that I would contact mum. Whilst I pointed out that we had no statutory reason to be involved we were dealing with a family who were very vulnerable, already had a social worker and whose mother had not been given the knowledge to protect her children from this man who had already assaulted them and was still in the house until last night. Telephone call to school spoke to head teacher Mr Green. He shares our concern about these incidents and agrees it would benefit Jos to be interviewed in school in the presence of Miss Solomon his class teacher. However, she cannot be available this afternoon until 3 pm. Also Jos is due to go to dentist 2.15, mum is calling for him at 1.30. After a lengthy discussion I agreed to phone Sgt. Henry to rearrange for later this afternoon and to see mum. Mr Green also said that Sandra, who is 11, had said this morning that Max had been touching her. So I asked that Sandra also be available for interviewing. Telephone call to Sgt. Henry. Arranged to meet at school at 3.15. Home visit to mum. Bob answered the door and told me that Julie had set off walking to school to collect Jos. Went off to try to catch mum. Met Julie outside school, had talk to her in the car and explained what was going to happen this afternoon. Julie agreed to be present for the interview and medical. She is very angry about Max and was threatening to physically assault him. Explained where court procedures were up to. Went into school to confirm with Mr Green. Julie, her co-hab and Max are all ex-pupils of school and known to him. He told me that Jos's behaviour had been deteriorating since Christmas (about the time that Max began lodging at their house). They had considered epileptic seizures as a possible explanation for this and Jos is undergoing investigations. School are aware of Max's past record and became alarmed when they heard of his association with the Smith family. Sandra is known to have been kept off school on occasions to have days out with Max. Took Julie home, Sandra also disclosed to her mother last night that Max had been touching her. She had taken our advice not to question kids too deeply yesterday. 3.15 pm. Joint interview school with Sgt. Henry and teaching staff. Julie was also present. First interview was with Sandra. *She was obviously reassured by her mother's presence and told us quite frankly that Max had put his hands down her underpants and touched her fanny. She also said that Max had licked her.* This description certainly fitted with Max's previous assaults on children. *It proved very difficult for Sandra to be specific about dates or number of times this may have happened. She could certainly recount the events of last Monday when Max had oral sex with her and seemed clear that she had been interfered with more than once. This problem was partly to do with poor concept of time and Sandra's low ability in general but also seemed to reflect a certain amount of guilt feelings that she had done little to stop Max from doing what he knew was wrong. Sandra seems to have achieved a certain amount of enjoyment out of the extra attention she got from Max who often took her to work with him and bought her sweets and so on. Reassured Sandra as much as we could that what happened was not her fault.*

Interview with Jos.

*Jos would not tell us anything directly but gave his teacher permission to tell us what he had said to her. Jos helped (teacher) with this and gained confidence as they went along. It was clear something had happened to Jos but he was very confused about the event and at one point said his mum and Bob were there when it happened. Jos could not differentiate between being in the house and in the same room plus 'knowing' and seeing were not clear concepts to him.* Sgt. Henry told us Max was pleading guilty to offences with Sandra but had not so far mentioned Jos. Julie was clearly feeling very guilty that she's had Max in the house and that when he stayed it had been in Jos's bed. Her anger and concern for her children was very positive and we all felt confident she would protect her children from Max in the future. However, the family's obviously vulnerable and

it was not clear how much support she would get from her
boyfriend Bob. He introduced Max to the family as a friend
of his and he was to be best man for their wedding planned
May. From what I have seen of Bob he seems of lesser ability
than Julie and whilst he has not opposed Julie's view of
Max so far he does not appear to have a clear view of the
implications. Sgt. Henry arranged for Dr Simon to examine
the children tomorrow. Julie insisted on being present at the
medicals and this was agreed. Sgt. Henry agreed to let [SW]
know the time of the medicals in case she wanted to be there
to support Julie.

There are several points to be drawn out of the record. The first
is that, whilst there is a lot of information here, most of it is of
the 'who said what, when' type; very little reflects on how the
children might be feeling and what the consequences of these
events might have been for them. It is important to stress that
this is not a complaint. What we are dealing with are the high
standards of practice motivated by concerns and understandings
of how to deal with child sexual assault cases. The auspices under
which the research was undertaken was a recognition of the fact
that practice needed to be changed, specifically to become more
child oriented than hitherto. Sections that pertain to describing
the child in the process have been emphasised. They show how
the child's feelings are articulated almost wholly in the context of
their status as objects of evidence. For example, Sandra's 'guilt
feelings' are only referred to once, as the possible reason for
distress or difficulty in remembering dates and times, and the
situation that was 'too painful for Jos' was to do with repeating
allegations. The primary focus is on getting the 'task' completed,
and the task is one of getting evidence. The social worker, rightly
or wrongly, already states that the children have been abused.
Thus, the only rationale for interviewing the children is to get
evidence of it. When it is acknowledged that the 'task yesterday'
was not completed, another strategy must be considered. It is not
an acknowledgement of the child's difficulties, the trauma he may
be experiencing, it is an acknowledgement that the investigators are
having difficulties.

The statement that:

> Whilst I pointed out that we had no statutory reason to
> be involved we were dealing with a family who were very
> vulnerable, already had a social worker and whose mother had
> not been given the knowledge to protect her children from this
> man who had already assaulted them and was still in the house
> until last night.

highlights a second shift. Events in Cleveland, and subsequently Rochdale and Manchester (see Chapter 10) show clearly that it is not acceptable for investigators to presume, prior to a court verdict, that children have been harmed or injured. Furthermore, their records have been, and with the greater use of pre-recorded video evidence almost certainly will be, called to account in court. Such a statement could weaken a case, particularly where there is no other corroborating evidence. In the future, practitioners will have to be more careful than ever that their records do not contain statements which could be construed as value judgements, opinions and presumptions of guilt. Recording of the interview itself will have to be much more detailed, and account will need to be given of planning. It is not clear from this record what the planning stage consisted in, what information was known about the child beforehand, there is no clear developmental assessment, decision about who would be the lead interviewer and so forth. Indeed, there is a change of interviewer for no accountable reason. Thus, the recording practices will have to change to take account of legal requirements.

Thirdly, whilst this intervention is designed to get evidence, it is unlikely that the interview would have been useful in a criminal court. In this case it did not matter, because the interview was not admissible and there was a confession from the accused. However, with the prospect that now all interviews could be used in criminal proceedings, their content must meet the stronger legal evidential criteria. What becomes problematic is that, if children are treated as people, with rights, feelings and wishes, and an entitlement to information about them, they can become tarnished as evidential objects. This was highlighted in discussions surrounding the *MOGP*, particularly to do with explaining the purpose of the interview to the child. It is advised that the alleged offence not be referred to, for the obvious reason that it could be seen as 'leading'; giving the child information about what could be a disputed fact. Thus, in the first instance, when talking to a child, it is not possible to tell them what others have said about them. It is also not acceptable to ask the child what they might have said to others, because of the hearsay rule. The way in which the child must talk is now guided by certain rules, and if they, or the people they are talking to, do not speak according to these rules, their talk can be edited out. In addition, the MOGP guides investigators to undertake only one interview wherever possible. In this case there were two, and, in the first, the allegations were put to the child. This would now serve to discredit the second. We also learn that the other child 'disclosed' overnight, and that, whilst the mother had 'not questioned the kids too deeply', she had been talking to them about the alleged offence. Such a statement could also discredit any further interview, opening it up to a challenge that mother had put ideas into the children's heads. Thus, the way in which children are responded to, even by their parents, is also to be guided by the legal process. These stand as examples of how the child can become, because of the emphasis on evidence, an evidential object, and further, how current practice might have to change to accommodate the *MOGP*.

The research interviews with children who had gone through this process revealed two further issues of relevance to prospective change at the initial investigative stage. First, none of the children I spoke to had any real understanding of what to expect. None of the files I examined gave an account of any planned and executed preparation of the child before the interview. Whilst there are constraints on what might be said to the child in evidential terms, it is important that the child knows why they are there and what they are expecting to encounter, whatever their age. Secondly, following the theme of children as evidential objects, it was clear that they were subject to organisational constraints; such as where they are spoken to, the timing of the interviews, which in some cases lasted from 2 to 3 hours. The guidance in the *MOGP* will, if followed, improve this situation. It gives clear advice about planning and encourages the investigating team to see planning as an integral part of the interview. However, the wider problem posed by the formulation of child protection intervention within the criminal legal discourse still remains. This issue is discussed further in Chapter 6.

## Conclusion

In this chapter I have used research materials to illustrate how investigative practice in child protection has changed over recent years. One key factor underpinning the shift has been the way in which the legal discourse has engaged with the child protection task. Whilst the remit for child protection has been situated in the legal discourse in the past, the legal discourse has now changed to accommodate the evidence, and the feelings and wishes of children. It has, however, done so according to its own rules, and these increasingly are becoming the rules of investigative practice. The behaviour of children is articulated in relation to their status as 'objects of evidence', which may have the effect of reducing the importance of other more individual and social needs. The introduction of the *Memorandum of Good Practice* develops on this by documenting the rules by which children's evidence should be gathered. If practitioners are not to get drawn into the evidential interviewing of children as a 'rule of thumb' they must first identify the strategies and focus of their present intervention, and question it in the context of the interests, feelings and wishes of the children and families they investigate.

# 2 Starting the process

Having established that the situation of child protection practice is within the legal framework, I want to turn to where the pursuit of evidence starts, and, in particular, to the decision-making process at the beginning of a case. The first issue has to do with orientation and whether a case becomes a case at all. An agency response which is formulated increasingly within the legal discourse effectively closes possibilities at an early stage, and the first part of this chapter shows how that might happen. The second part draws on the research and literature to establish why it is difficult for children to tell others about abuse perpetrated on them. Whilst this knowledge is generally accepted by social work practitioners and police officers, it is not wholly acknowledged by the law. However, the law does accept 'expert' evidence, and the research reported here can be used to inform that evidence in the task of making a case. Such knowledge begins to offer a bridge between the legal and therapeutic divide which is becoming characteristic of child protection practice.

One way of looking at the notion of evidence is to suspend, for a moment, the legal definition of what constitutes admissible evidence, and to interpret it in a day-to-day context. This broadening of application of the term evidence leads into an exercise in relationships between objects or events, understandings about what stands for, or represents, what in the every-day world. In relation to child protection cases, the beginning of a case is the point at which information is made known to an agency concerning a child: information which stands for or represents possible child abuse. The official term for this passing on of information is 'referral'. Thus the first exercise in broad evidential terms is to decide whether the information passed on warrants status as a referral, and what type of referral it is.

The outcome of 'making a referral' is a judgement: an achieved activity of the work. It is not just a matter of someone making a telephone call, or a visit to an office, and some other person taking this information. What eventually ends up as a referral — usually information on a form — is a methodically produced accomplishment of the participants to the activity. This might at first appear to be a very complicated way of looking at what most social workers consider to be a matter of routine daily work: picking up the phone whilst on 'duty', conversing with a caller, and writing down relevant information on a referral form; the work of 'taking a referral'. But it is important at the beginning to get an understanding of how this is an achieved matter, because the long path towards making a case begins here.

In order to make the salience of this statement clearer, I will begin with an example of 'taking a referral'.

> 11.47 am. telephone rang, Jane answered:
> 'Hello, can I help you?'
> A few seconds pass,
> 'Who is speaking?'
> Jane repeats the name given by the speaker and a few more seconds pass.
> 'em, yeah, em [short laugh] no, every man is not capable, every man does not abuse'
> [listens to speaker]
> 'Yes, in some situations, right, right, [pause] how old are your children? [pause] 10 months and 9 and a half years [pause]. There are various indicators, obviously we would know about the baby, but as regards the older child, a child of that age may tell you, but, having said that a child may feel threatened or frightened, 'I must not tell mummy because mummy will be angry with me', but you would notice if the child's behaviour changes, such as if s/he becomes very quiet, starts wetting the bed, won't eat, lots of things like that could be indicators of sexual abuse'.
> At least a minute passes in which the speaker is making a reply and then Jane says,
> 'Well, it depends on how open you are about it in your family'.
> Another long pause (over a minute) whilst Jane listens to the speaker.
> 'The important thing is to teach a child that her body is her own, that she has the right to say 'NO' if anybody whom she doesn't wish to touches her, however innocent, (stranger, or relative) that she has the right to say no, and you must teach her to tell you straight away'.
> Short pause while speaker talks:

'Who was abused as a child? [pause] Ah, and is grandad still around?'
Short pause while speaker talks,
'Well, at least it's someone to talk to, well, I think you would remember if you had been sexually abused'
Listens for over a minute:
'Ah, well we often try to block out unpleasant things from our minds'.
Listens for almost two minutes:
'No, often it is not a stranger in the park although that does happen too, it's more often a person that the child knows and trusts. You should teach your child about touching, what is good touching and what is bad touching, and about secrets, good secrets and bad secrets and that they don't have to keep secrets, they can tell mummy about secrets'.
Short reply,
'Yes, well it's the importance of teaching the child about touching and secrets [pause] emmm, well, thank you for ringing, good bye'
Jane puts down the telephone,
'That was very interesting' [sighs]
I asked her what it had been about.
'Just a mother wanting some advice on how to teach her child how not to be sexually abused.'
Another social worker in the room said 'Oh' and Jane said:
'Well, it was interesting in the end because she said that she became a mother when she was 13 and her sister was sexually abused by her father, and that even if she herself was sexually abused she wouldn't want to remember it.'
The other social worker said 'Ah, well, that's different'.
Jane replied:
'I think she may have been sexually abused by her father who is now dead, but that she doesn't want to say it.'
She then went on to talk about another referral received earlier in the morning. No further reference to this incident is made that day.

At the referral point, crucial decisions are made as to whether information stands as evidence of something having happened to a child, and about what action to take next. Referrals may prompt investigation, transfer (to another agency) or be designated 'advised, counselled and closed', and so on. The example given here fell into the latter category. It could just as easily have been an investigation. If, for example, this mother had presented herself to the school with this same information — concern that her child might be being 'sexually abused' — it is possible that the school would have made a referral and the likely response would have been for a social worker to investigate.

What can be seen from this example, and from all other 'duty' observations is the work of 'categorisation' as an activity for achieving meaning. The social worker is not just transcribing, unthinkingly, what is being said down the telephone. She is following a conversational structure, taking turns, answering questions and shaping her response in terms of the answers she, in turn, receives. One device for making sense of the information being relayed is the ability to employ categorisations to describe the world around us: 'doctor', 'patient', 'husband', 'wife', 'bad person', 'child', 'train station', 'wickedness', and so on, could all be 'categories' of information. This ability is part of our common-sense knowledge of the world and our practical reasoning about it. The term 'membership categorisation device' (MCD) (Sacks, 1966) has been used to denote the machinery by which we collect together certain categories into others and formulate descriptions of the world. One device, for example, is 'family' and the categories 'mother-child' may be heard as belonging to it. The concept is not intended to point to logical connections, but to 'grammatical' ones. If culture is thought of as a language, with rules and grammar, then categorisation work is about making grammatical connections. It is about understanding what goes with what, and what stands for what, and the concept of evidence itself has much to do with competent categorisation and the methodic ways in which we make sense of, see and hear, persons and events in the world around us.

Categories and their members have a 'cluster' of expected activities or behaviours, traits or characteristics associated with them (Jayussi, 1984). For example, doctors are expected to step out of a crowd at the scene of an accident, and if they do not, and it is known they are a doctor, it opens the question as to why they did not. This is one way that category-bound behaviours can be observed in every-day life, in terms of when someone's behaviour is questioned, when they do not do as they were expected to do. This is not to say that everyone who could be deemed incumbent of a category behaves in the same way. Rather, there are certain actions or behaviours which, if they were performed by an incumbent of a given category, would not be considered unusual; they would be appropriate. In the absence of any other information, there is a tendency to interpret the culture in these terms and 'hear it that way'. Sack's treatment of the phrase 'The baby cried. The mommy picked it up' describes the process (Turner, 1974). We hear this as not just any baby, but the baby of the 'mommy' who picks it up by utilising the categorisation device, 'family'. It can be expected that, when babies cry, *their* mothers do pick them up, not always, but not unusually. Whilst it would never be said that all babies cry, or that all mothers pick them up, or that this baby is the baby of this mother with all certainty, it would be heard that way until some other information might refine the interpretation. As competent members of our culture we require this ability to, on the one hand 'size up' what is presented to us, and, on the other, suspend absolute certainty. It is not a right or a wrong thing, rather it is a description of how presenting information can be oriented to for the purposes at hand. Thus:

> . . . the selection of a membership category by any member to refer to or characterize any other member (or even herself) could not be understood simply in terms of criteria of 'correctness'. Rather, it involves considerations of much greater analytical complexity, such as 'appropriateness', 'recipient design/recognitionality', 'implicativeness', *'orientation to already-used categories in the discourse so far'*, and so on. Jayussi, 1984, p.213. My emphasis

These are some of the features which underpin the construction of evidences for things and events; at the point of referral, during an investigation, a substantive interview and later in court. In the telephone conversation above, a decision is made about what sort of information is being presented. Categorisation work is observable throughout, for example:

> 'em, yeah, em (short laugh) no, every man is not capable, every man does not abuse',

Here the general category of 'every man' is deployed, and behaviour that can be applied to all men assessed in the light of it. Or:

> but you would notice if the child's behaviour changes, such as if s/he becomes very quiet, starts wetting the bed, won't eat, lots of things like that could be indicators of sexual abuse.

Implicit within this is a notion of what is expectable behaviour of the category 'child-in-distress', by which potential 'abuse' can be assessed.

The social worker is acting on the information given to her by using categorisations, which emerge, can be reassessed, and adjusted in the unfolding conversation. In trying to make sense of the information, she is formulating how the referral itself should be categorised. Is this a referral? Is it a serious referral, an 'advice' referral? How should the referee be categorised. Is she genuine? What motivation might there be for making the referral? What sort of a problem is being presented? These are crucial formulations at the beginning of making a case.[1]

The following statement, which occurs early on in the conversation, indicates how the referral is categorised.

> 'em, yeah, em (short laugh) no, every man is not capable, every man does not abuse'

The social worker does not say 'this is an advice referral', although that categorisation can be known retrospectively. However, the responses that follow from the statement show an orientation to the referral as one requiring general advice. It is a response to a question the content of which is here unknown. The worker has contexted the referee, and the referral in that statement as someone who does not have the same professional knowledge as she has about sexual abuse, if they did she would not need to say this. Similarly, it displays knowledge that this is not a specific allegation of abuse, for the purposes at hand, it is a general enquiry the response to which can be contexted in the general category of 'every' man. What follows displays an orientation to this already used category and results in the giving of general information up until the referee makes a specific comment when the question arises,

> 'Who was abused as a child? [pause] Ah, and is grandad still around?'

Confirmation that this is not a child in the present is displayed by her return to the initial orientation; general advice.

> 'Well, at least it's someone to talk to, well, I think you would remember if you had been sexually abused.'
> Listens for over a minute:
> 'Ah, well we often try to block out unpleasant things from our minds'
> Listens for almost two minutes:
> 'No, often it is not a stranger in the park although that does happen too, it's more often a person that the child knows and trusts. You should teach your child about touching, what is good touching and what is bad touching, and about secrets, good secrets and bad secrets and that they don't have to keep secrets, they can tell mummy about secrets.'
> Short reply:

'Yes, well it's the importance of teaching the child about touching and secrets (pause) emmm, well, thank you for ringing, good bye.'

Thus, the outcome for referral categorisation purposes is:

'Just a mother wanting some advice on how to teach her child how not to be sexually abused.'

That is, one that results in no further action. The crucial point here is not whether this was a right or wrong categorisation. It may, or it may not have been. What is clearly evident here, and elsewhere in the research materials is the 'fatefulness' of categorisation. Once a categorisation is achieved, then it is, to coin Sack's phrase, heard that way (Sacks, 1974). How information is framed is inherently consequential for the way it is responded to.

The agency in which my research was conducted officially displayed referrals of 'child sexual abuse' by ticking a box on the referral form. Of these referrals 37% were framed as relevant to child sexual abuse but were not treated as warranting an investigation. These were grouped for research purposes as 'other' referrals. A similar situation would hold for other types of child harm and injury within the agency. The two main groupings for 'other' referrals were those where adults requested support (12%) and treatment requests, including group applications, assessments and consultations (14%). The referral example given here would fall into the former grouping. Cases that were framed as requests for treatment, assessment and so on were responded to in a way which was appropriate to that categorisation. Once made, this became the orienting feature.

The following is an example of an 'assessment' referral which illustrates this point and shows the 'fatefulness' of categorisation. The referral form states:

> Request for assessment of family where 'F' (8) was s/a'd over a three year period by her next door neighbour — now has behaviour problems and sleeps with (brother) (10). See s/history provided by CPN'.[2]

A letter which initiated the referral explains how the CPN became involved because of the mother's depression, which had been attributed to difficulties in coping with the behaviour of the two eldest children. It continues with an account of an interview:

> '. . . at the beginning of the initial interview [date] [mother] went to some length to assure me that now their behaviour had improved since maternal grandmother had firm words with them. Gradually, however, she indicated that some problems did persist and that M was encopretic and had been for

approximately two years. There were frequent sibling fights and arguing and most interestingly F was markedly fearful of the dark. As a result of her fear of the dark she insisted not only in sleeping in the same room as her brother but also insisted on sharing his bed although she had/has her own bed. As [mother] relaxed more she informed me that F had been regularly sexually abused by a mentally handicapped 21 year-old son of the next door neighbour as a consequence of which the case had gone to court and he was no longer living at home. Retrospectively [mother] understands that the period of abuse [as far as I have been made aware consisting of genital touching and no insertion] had happened for three years beginning whilst F was aged 3 years. [Mother] realises now that F had on previous occasions tried to tell her what was taking place but she had never properly understood. Additional to F's previously stated 'problem' behaviour, mother had noted she was extremely 'fond' of males and would speak to them initiating conversations and both parents were fearful she may be easily abducted. Also F often c/o abdominal pains and yet more significantly F had apparently very recently licked a girl 'down below' and had stated if this girl should tell anyone F would 'kill her' this being said with her hands around the young girl's throat.?!'

The letter then includes information on the parental response which was:

. . . initially ambivalent but following further more directive counselling agreed that seeking expert help was the correct course to follow . . . [the] parents present as pleasant, caring, individuals whose marriage appears quite stable.

The file notes state that, at the next allocation meeting, the case would be taken on and arrangements were made for the CPN and the family to go to the centre. All the family came except the father who was having to work that day. Less than a month later a telephone call was recorded from the CPN to say that the family would not be coming for 'treatment':

He had been to see them the previous week to arrange for transport to the centre and they had told him that they didn't want any further help from us. We agree that there was nothing anybody could do at the moment, and it was a question of waiting for the next crisis to occur.

The case is then closed. Having been framed as a request for an assessment, the referral is oriented to in this way. It is stated that the child continues to display sexually explicit behaviour and has other problems, which in other circumstances might warrant referral for investigation. Of the 'investigation' cases, 47% were presented on the grounds that the child said something symptomatic, displayed sexually related behaviour or behaviour problems. However, the notion that this case might require investigation is not considered. There is nothing in the file information to indicate that the brother had been abused by the neighbour, yet he too is showing behaviour problems. Because of the assessment categorisation, and the subsequent non-co-operation of the parents which was oriented to, in an accepting way, under such a categorisation, these children were never seen. This observation has profound implications in light of the shift towards partnership with parents, parental responsibility and the rights of parents to make choices about the intervention they receive generated by the Children Act, 1989. It suggests that many cases could be accounted for adequately under organisational procedures, because of the way that categorisations are selected and oriented to. If a child died as a consequence, there would be recriminations. However, if a child continues to be the victim of secret sexual assault or emotional harm, who would be the wiser? For agency purposes, the case has been dealt with. This returns practice to a discourse in which only the most visible harms and injuries to children — only those where there is strong evidence — are attended to.

A similar approach is evident in the response to 'treatment requests'. One example was an application for group membership, which in itself would not stand as a warrant for an investigation. Through her group involvement, the girl gave further details about her own abuse, and also declared herself to be an 'abuser'. However, the worker involved from the group, while able to offer support to the girl, had great difficulty in invoking joint investigative procedures. In the case of treatment requests, one categorisation oriented to is that of 'previously investigated'. Treatment is viewed as a separate issue, and not a continuation of the investigation process.

Often this may be because the kind of information that evolves in treatment is of limited use for prosecution, because of the way it may have been obtained; by using leading questions, for example. A problem arises because children do not appear to demarcate in this way. Most seem unaware of the boundaries between what is usable, or relevant information, and what is not. Any information pertaining to the child is relevant to treatment. As a consequence, a much broader opportunity is offered to the child to give information, some of which may have been relevant to an investigation. The following case illustrates this:

Referral information: Parents were in the process of separating last year when P made allegations to mother that father was sexually abusing him. Mother immediately reported to solicitors who passed information to police. Probation officer [x] also involved. No prosecution of father took place but during custody hearing father withdrew his application on hearing mother's evidence. There is no access between Dad and P but the boy is showing signs of disturbance which he needs help with. He wanted his bedroom painted black and says his dad might haunt him when he's dead. Mum wants advice.

This referral is oriented to as a case for treatment and sessions are arranged. At the first session a fortnight after referral, it was agreed that two workers would work with the family, one with the child and one with the mother. The worker with the child writes:

I found P to be quite a likeable boy, easily able to talk although a little nervous obviously, but we did some drawing work and just a general introduction to get the feel of the place.

The next session was held over a fortnight later:

. . . I went through the abuse with P and he told me that his parents had divorced when he was about 4 or 5 years old. His dad had not made any sexual advances towards him at this time but P did complain that his dad never played any games with him. After the divorce he visited dad who was living with his own parents. P slept in a double bed with dad and they would watch video recordings, perfectly normal ones, and then dad would go to the toilet and return naked. He would then instruct P to go downstairs and tell his grandmother not to disturb them and then return to the bedroom naked. P then described mutual masturbation with his dad ejaculating. Dad had also lain across P who was on his stomach and had put his 'dick' against his bottom in-between his cheeks. He had not entered the anus. P did not show too much distress in giving me these details, he had obviously been over them with mother. I was wondering whether more had happened but was accepting when P said that actual anal intercourse had not taken place. I felt that he was being truthful about this. I gave P an opportunity to discuss his feelings about dad and actually to express them by using the male doll. He kicked the hell out of the doll and asked me to hold the doll up while he kicked him hard between the legs. P seemed to get a great deal of enjoyment out of this.

In this account there is a requirement that the details of the event(s) are made known and accepted as being a truthful account.[3]

This parallels the requirements of an evidential interview but, because the outcome is different, treatment/therapy as opposed to statement and court proceedings, the emphasis is altered. There is an acknowledgement of feelings about the events and an interaction which is aimed at displaying such feelings. It is the experience of workers involved in treatment that information about the abuse, which could have constituted evidence, can continue to be revealed for some time after the initial investigation period.

All the examples used so far show the consequentiality of categorisation for action that follows the giving of information, which was reviewed earlier. The latter two examples also show something of the difficulties attendant on reporting abuse and obtaining evidence for prosecution purposes. My own research examined features relevant to the initial report: how it was precipitated and how it was socially organised prior to the official referral. The available research on reporting behaviour is essential to expanding the possibilities acceptable to the legal discourse. At the present time, the fact that a report is not recent, or given voluntarily at the first available 'opportunity', is taken and used to imply that it might be constructed, malicious and false.

The issue of false reporting is a recurring theme in the child abuse literature (Besharov, 1986; Goodwin et al., 1982; Parton, 1989). None of this literature addresses the feature of categorisation as it might affect statistics relating to reported abuse, although one study (Everson & Boat, 1989) had the relevant finding that the disposition of the interviewer to believe the child had a significant effect on the number of substantiated cases. Yet all child abuse statistics are, amongst other things, the product of categorisation work. Instead, correlations are made on the basis of already oriented to categorisations to show that certain types of cases, those involving custody or access disputes, are more likely to be founded on false reports than others (Jones & Seig, 1989; Bentovim et al., 1988).

The fact that sexual abuse is under reported by victims has been well established by research. This can be substantiated in two ways: by examining the reporting behaviour of adults asked about their own sexual abuse as children, and by comparing outcomes of prevalence studies with national incidence figures. In his study of Boston families, Finkelhor (1979) found that, of those parents who were victims themselves, only 39% told anyone about it within a year of its occurrence. In a study of college students in which 19.2% of the women and 8.6% of the men had been sexually victimised as children, 63% of the women and 73% of the men did not tell anyone about these experiences. These figures suggesting the majority of victims tell no one, are supported by studies in the UK (Nash & West, 1986) and Australia (Waldby, 1985).

Prevalence studies in child sexual abuse vary in their findings as a result of a lack of methodological consensus. However, an estimate, taking all the methodological problems into account, has been made that 10% of the population will experience some form of childhood sexual victimisation (La Fontaine, 1988). Nationally co-ordinated referral figures to statutory agencies are not available. The only information on statutory involvement is the annual statistical analysis of the child protection registers. On the basis of these figures, 0.62 children in a thousand were recorded on the register under the category of child sexual abuse at the 31 March, 1991 (DOH 1992).[4] Thus, it can be seen that the disparity between estimated prevalence and registered cases is high.[5]

The reasons given for not reporting fall into two groups: those that account for not telling anyone, including mothers, friends and relatives, and those that account for not reporting the matter officially. Reasons for not telling anyone seem to centre on fear of blame and fear of not being believed (Nash & West, 1986; Finkelhor, 1979). Adult respondents in an Australian study gave the following reasons for not reporting: fear or anticipation of disbelief or punishment (29.6%), shame, guilt or social stigma (20.8%), intimidation or threats from the abuser (10.2%), not knowing who to tell (9.6%), fear of family breakdown (9.2%), denial and wanting to forget (7.5%) (Waldby, 1985).

With regard to official reporting in child sexual abuse, several factors seem to be relevant; the person who received the initial information and their response, the relationship of the alleged perpetrator to the alleged victim, the social organisation of telling, and the ability to categorise events or behaviours as abusive. There is very little comparable research for physical abuse and neglect in the UK or elsewhere (Parton, 1989). One American study gives an estimated incidence of physical abuse at between 3 and 4% of the population (Straus et al., 1980), which would suggest that physical abuse, like sexual abuse is under reported.

Mothers are most often disclosed to (Herman, 1981; Waldby, 1985), but their responses may not always be positive (Nash & West, 1986). The largest group of 'confidants'[6] in the Cambridge study conducted by Nash and West responded by being angry with the person believed responsible (25%) whereas, in Waldby's Australian study, this response was only reported in 4.7% of cases. Alternatively, 'comfort' and 'understanding' was offered as a response by approximately one-quarter of the Cambridge samples, and a 'positive, listened to, belief' response reported by approximately one-half of the Sydney group. The most probable reason for the difference in results is the focus on different forms of assault. Rather than decry this as a methodological problem in making adequate comparison, it presents interesting information on responses to incest in contrast to other forms of sexual assault. Whilst the Cambridge study did include cases of intra- and extra-familial abuse, over two-thirds of respondents were victims of assault originating outside the family. Thus, it may be that anger at the person believed responsible as an initial response is more likely where the assailant is not a family member, and that a positive response is more likely when the assailant is within the family.

This observation may point to a crucial variable in the reporting of cases, which would require further research. Namely, that in the case of intra-familial abuse, where the mother's response is supportive, cases might not be reported. Whereas in cases of extra-familial abuse, where parents are angry at the person believed responsible, they may seek to report as a form of retribution. If so, it could be expected that, of those cases that do get reported, cases of 'non-supportive', 'negative' reacting parents of intra-familial abuse victims, and cases of extra-familial abuse, where parents are angry, might be over represented. Previous studies based on reports to public agencies show that cases involving parents and known adults are in the majority (Burgess et al., 1978; De Francis, 1969; Peters, 1976; Creighton & Noyes, 1989). However, this does not mean, as Finkelhor (1979) suggests, that such cases are more likely to be reported, in itself. In order to make such a statement, it would be necessary to establish the true incidence of intra- and extra familial abuse, and also the true incidence of abuse by a known and unknown perpetrator, and to compare this to reported cases. This is not possible, as Finkelhor himself points out (1986), although his own study in 1979 suggests that children are more likely to be assaulted by a family member or an acquaintance. Thus, it is feasible that many cases of sexual assault involving parents and known adults are just as likely to not get reported. It has been suggested that reported cases are biased because they exclude a number of positive adult–child sexual experiences (Nobile, 1978), but, from the research evidence, and also from the data in the child protection study, the positive and protective response of a non-abusing parent would seem to be a more likely variable in reporting. The relationship between these features and how cases, especially in the case of negatively responding non-abusing parents, get reported, has yet to be explored.

Further insight into the reporting behaviour of parents and their children is given by Finkelhor's Boston study. Of the parents, 9% said that their child had been the subject of abuse or attempted abuse. Of the children, 39% who told their parents were boys, which is a percentage much higher than the official reporting rate would suggest. Overall, the children told their parents about a relatively high number of experiences with strangers. Only 10% of child reports concerned relatives. Finkelhor suggests that this finding might either result from parents who might withhold information about relatives, or that children may anticipate a crisis of loyalty and therefore not tell. Another feature of reported abuse in this study is that it often involved children, or young adults as the person believed responsible (PBR). Half the PBRs in the child report group were under 20 years. The suggested explanation of this is that it might be more comfortable to tell about a child than an adult, because the child fears retaliation or doubts that they will be believed. A little over half the parents in this study said they had reported the abuse they encountered. Reasons given for not reporting were: the parent felt they could handle the situation themselves; it was no one else's business; they considered the abuse not serious; or they felt sorry for the PBR. The variable that most differentiated reported, and non-reported cases, was the relationship of the PBR to the child. Where the PBR was a relative, none was reported, whereas acquaintances were reported in 23% of cases and strangers in 73%.

Respondents were also given a hypothetical case which over 75% said they would report. Thus, there is an incongruity between actual and predicted behaviour, which has some relevance here. If people think they would report, but in reality are less likely to, it may also be that, when cases are reviewed within the legal process, the judgement that they would have been reported by the victim at the earliest opportunity is also unrealistic. Finkelhor's research therefore suggests that assessments of the validity of allegations based on when, and how, they were reported could be tenuous, especially if they are taking account of the anticipated behaviour of parents. Finkelhor suggests that work is needed to educate parents on making it clear to children that they will be receptive and supportive, and that the benefits of seeking professional support should be emphasised. It is quite clear that, from events and media coverage in Cleveland, Rochdale, Manchester and the Orkneys, that the 'benefits' of seeking professional support in the UK, for both parents and children, are not self-evident, and this would be an obvious area for further development by child-care agencies in terms of their own public image.

There is some indication that professionals themselves are reticent about the positive value of reporting (Finkelhor, 1984; James, Womack & Strauss, 1978; NCCAN, 1981). The USA has mandatory reporting laws which between one- and two-thirds of professionals apparently do not adhere to. In Finkelhor's study, two groups stood out: criminal justice agency personnel and mental health professionals. He notes that both groups of workers may be distrustful of the investigation, and doubtful of its effectiveness. They may also be wary of interference in their own plans and the compromise to confidentiality that reporting seems to present. He also suggests that there may be reasons for under reporting in terms of research itself, and that experiences can be 'blocked' totally or partially, difficult to define or articulate, or not volunteered because of embarrassment. In a well-respected study, Russell (1986) found that unwillingness to disclose information about incestuous abuse was less related to a desire to suppress information and more likely to be related to 'unresolved trauma'. There is reason to anticipate that these features are likely to be parallelled in the real world of reporting. This is notable in victim accounts of their experience (see, for example, Bass & Thornton, 1983) and also literature which emphasises the secrecy element of sexual abuse. This factor is accounted for in many studies, but, for a particularly useful analysis, see Burgess and Holstrom, (1978). The child protection study found some indication of unwillingness to report by children, especially those children referred for treatment who go on to talk about further details of their experiences.

Reporting in research should not in itself be influenced by an often cited impediment to reporting (Berlinner, 1983; Waldby, 1985) that the victim may fear the consequences of the PBR's actions, especially where they, or those close to them, have been threatened with harm. Respondents to research can remain anonymous and should always be protected by rules of confidentiality; thus there should be no way of finding out about the victim's participation. However, whilst cases where the PBR uses force or threat are unlikely to be in the majority (Conte et al., 1989), it is clear from my materials that children are inhibited from talking because of a fear of the consequences which have often been articulated by the PBR themselves. There are many examples given in witness statements by children which have to do with a fear of breaking up the family, and people getting 'into trouble'.

There is a further factor which might impede reporting indicated in the CP study. It is an obvious fact that we do not just tell anything to anyone. There is a moral organisation to do with what we tell, to whom, tied up with patterns of social relationship and obligation (Sacks, 1966). Within our culture there are, for example, some topics which cannot be mentioned just anywhere. Many of these constraints are to do with matters of taste, polite behaviour, and so on, while others are more implicative as to character and/or reputation. Hitherto, no attention has been paid to the social organisation of 'telling' in relation to child reports, and also child abuse. However, some inference can be drawn on the basis of studies in other areas, such as death and bereavement. In his examination of the social organisation of dying, Sudnow (1967) reports on his observations of conversational practices surrounding the breaking of bad news. The research is replete with examples that signify that there is a shared cultural knowledge about the transmission of sensitive knowledge and also about appropriate behaviours and responses. For example:

> In one instance, a morgue attendant was observed to arrive at the nurses' desk to secure a deceased patient's belongings and addressed the nurse, asking where the patient's things were, while the relative was standing alongside the nurses' station awaiting the physician. The nurse managed, by eye signal, to alert the attendant to the bystander's identity and inhibit further references to his relative's body. This sort of possibility is maximized when the news of a death spreads within the hospital to those occupationally involved in such matters faster than it spreads to kin . . . p.126

This extract indicates the social order of telling as it is managed in a hospital setting. The point of it is that the social organisation is clearly visible in the behaviours described. In the case of death, doctors are the people who should break the news to relatives; it is not appropriate to overhear such news as occupational talk. The dead patient's doctor would have been socially, if not practically, identified as the first source of identification of death for certain. The relatives are treated as having an entitlement to that 'first-hand' knowledge. Thus, there is a sense in which it is known, and shared as known, that some people should be told before others and, therefore, that *until* those people are told, others should not be, or should not let it be known that they know. This has obvious ramifications for the social organisation of reporting child assault.

Confidentiality, and the imposition of it by children and parents on others, offers a means to handle the complex transactions surrounding information exchange (Hughes & Wattam, 1989). Children want to give information to teachers, for example, 'in confidence' and teachers hold it in confidence until they find a way to break confidence which accords with the informal 'rules' pertaining to confidential information. The rule-governed social organisation of confidential information is recognisable in the following extract from *Working Together*:

> Those in receipt of information from professional colleagues in this context [of child abuse] must treat it as having been given in confidence. They must not disclose such information for any other purpose without consulting the person who provided it. DOH, 1991*b*, p.11

Whilst this concerns professional information exchange, teachers show signs of treating reports from children about suspected abuse under the same rules. This can be telling the child that they are going to report the matter officially, or spending some time counselling the child to report themselves, or suggesting that someone else becomes involved on a non-informed basis to give general prompts about possible problems the child might be having (Wattam, 1989). Whatever the case, it is not a straightforward matter, and confidentiality is rarely breached without attendance to the 'rules', but crucially only where the rules can be enforced or breaches can be sanctioned. The person who is the first receiver of confidential information, known as such because it has been defined as confidential by the giver, is accountable. The official guidance is not given because people do not know the rules. Rather, it must be given because, much as in the hospital example, the transfer of sensitive information can be an occupational task, which has the effect of removing the accountability of the first report. The guidance reflects the need to relocate occupational information in the realms of the personal, largely because health professionals feared that social work and criminal justice professionals did not treat it so.

There is no reason to suggest that the case is any different for children, who may be the victims of assault of injury in secret, 'in confidence'. Because the 'rules' are social, children will be aware of them. Much of the preventative literature acknowledges this by accepting that children from a very early age understand the concept of keeping a secret. The task is to define what are good and bad secrets and thus to teach children when it is acceptable to break the rules (Elliott, 1985). However, much as official guidance will not prevent complex transactions around the social organisation of confidential information from occurring, instructions on good and bad secrets will not induce a child automatically to tell. The social organisation must be attended to. This is a key point in understanding when it is appropriate to take a different approach to interviewing a child under the *MOGP*. It may be that, in some cases, before a child can freely narrate about a potentially abusive event s/he needs to be freed from the socially organised constraints on the telling. If, for example, a child has not told her mother about her father's sexual assaults on her, she may find it difficult to tell a complete stranger, knowing that, as a consequence of that telling, her mother will have to know. Thus, the interview strategy should not focus, first, on 'what, if anything has happened' but on what might be the problems about telling. This strategy is incorporated into the SAGE approach which is outlined in Chapter 5. It should also take into account the difference between a report that something has happened, and the personal details of that report. So that, even if the social organisation of telling *that* something has happened is accommodated, the detail is a separate and further matter. To return to the death example, it is one thing to say that someone has died, but a different set of rules pertain to who properly should be the recipient of a full description of the death.

There are, therefore, a number of considerations to take into account when encouraging a child to talk. In addition to the social organisation and the order of telling, there is also the notion that children choose to tell only those they trust (Kelly, 1989). It is also the case that there are only a certain number of people children have available to tell. Diagram 1 Who do children tell, depicts the routes to the official report to the agency, where children could be identified as the original source of the report. Almost a third first told their mothers, the largest single identifiable group. The second largest group were school-related personnel, particularly teachers. Out of 92 children, only 7 came directly through to the agency without telling anyone first. The implications for practice are twofold in relation to the *MOGP*. First, the account given to the investigating team is unlikely to be the first, and secondly, because of the inadmissibility of hearsay in criminal proceedings, any previous reporting should not be directly referred to. This, again, presents the child with an artificial situation, the present solution to which is to inform the child of the constraining rules, or to guide her/him away from talk about what s/he has told to someone else. The latter is evidentially preferable because informing, before the child has given a report that anything has happened to them, might be viewed as prejudicial. I note the option here to show, once again, how the legal discourse restricts possibilities and one way in which it might change to expand them.

Telling and reporting are also linked to opportunity and provocation. A number of precipitating factors to the child's telling others were accounted for in the child protection study. As they are recorded, precipitating factors help to make sense and lend validity to the child's statement. For example the following referral concerning a 16 year-old girl:

> She told me that she had thought for a long time at the weekend, before ringing Childline, she had been at home in [town]. She had seen the TV programme and this had made her realise that she could talk to someone who understood about sexual abuse and had decided eventually to use this avenue to share her problems. She told me she had been sexually assaulted

**Diagram 1 Who do children tell?**

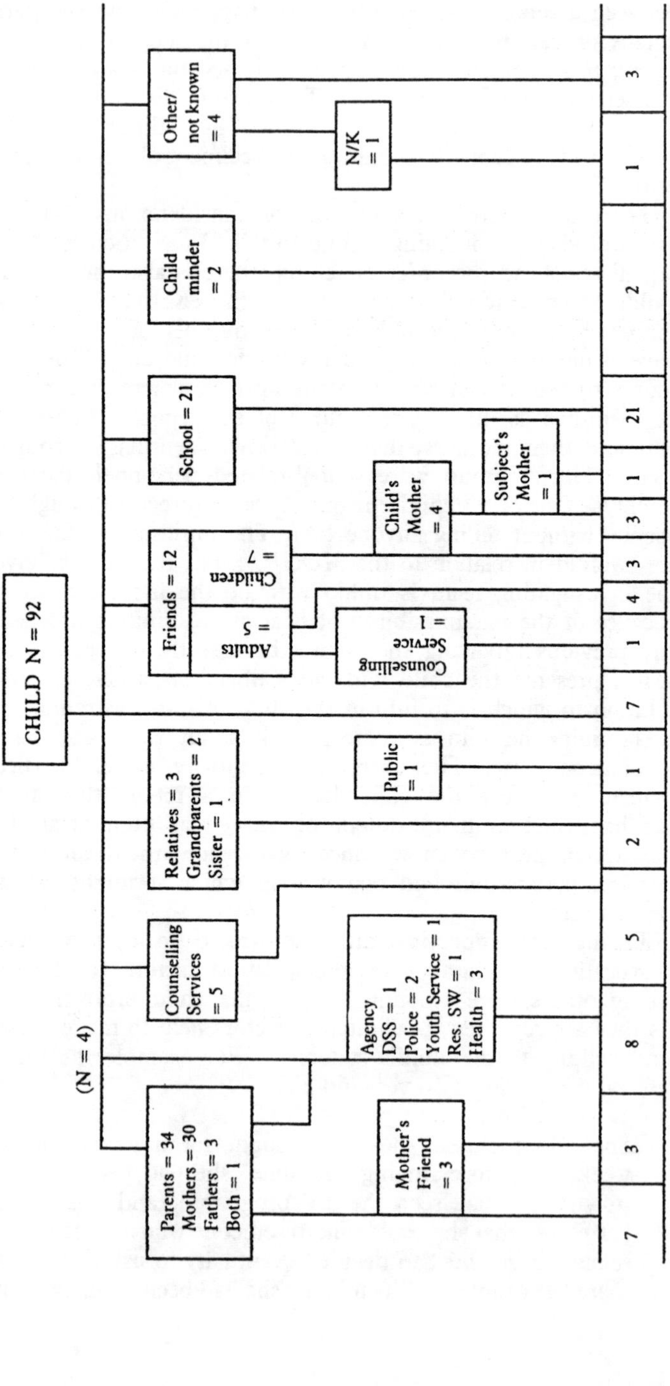

CHILD N = 92

(N = 4)

|  |  |
|---|---|
| Parents = 34 | Mothers = 30, Fathers = 3, Both = 1 |
| Mother's Friend = 3 | |
| Agency | DSS = 1, Police = 2, Youth Service = 1, Res. SW = 1, Health = 3 |
| Counselling Services = 5 | |
| Relatives = 3 | Grandparents = 2, Sister = 1 |
| Public = 1 | |
| Friends = 12 | Adults = 5, Children = 7 |
| Counselling Service = 1 | |
| Child's Mother = 4 | Subject's Mother = 1 |
| School = 21 | |
| Child minder = 2 | |
| Other/ not known = 4 | N/K = 1 |

Bottom scale values: 7, 3, 8, 5, 2, 1, 7, 1, 4, 3, 3, 1, 21, 2, 1, 3 since she was twelve by her father and this continues to the present day.

Described in this way, it is clear that what prompted the report was a television programme. This makes sense, yet a striking omission in many of the interviews of these children was that how a child had chosen to tell at the point s/he had was rarely referred to. This is an important issue, legally and therapeutically. Sgroi (1982) notes that it is a crucial question for children, providing a means for assessing the child's expectations and to consider whether they can be realistically met. Where physical symptoms provoke a report, for example, it can be expected that the child is worried about these symptoms, and that one expectation would be that the symptoms be dealt with. In addition to media coverage and concern about physical repercussions (particularly pregnancy), there were other precipitating factors. These included another child's account, where a child either in the family or peer group reported their own assault, and where this stimulated the subject child to report. Arguments were frequently cited as precipitators, for example:

> I asked X if she'd told her mother about the sexual abuse and she said that she had tried to tell her but she couldn't, she just told her boyfriend recently and a friend a couple of months ago. She had disclosed to mother on Sunday during an argument. Apparently mother had wanted her to stay in and X had refused, this ended up in an argument with mother locking her in. X said that she had broken down and mother asked her what was wrong, then had taken her out to talk . . .

It is important to understand and, if possible, during the substantive interview to clarify how an argument could stimulate a report. This is because, later, the motive for reporting might be construed as revenge, to do with the argument and not with the assault, for example, in the cross-examination of a child in court, the full transcript of which is given in Chapter 11.

> Defence: The first time you made a complaint was in a fit of temper.
> Child: Yeah
> Defence: Why were you in a fury with your mother and father?
> Child: Because she asked me to go to the post office.
> Defence: You didn't want to go?
> Child: No
> Defence: It wasn't anything to do with (the accused)?
> Child: No

Defence: Were you trying to upset your mum when you said these lies?

Child: They're not lies.

If the context of this disclosure in the argument had been talked about in the substantive interview, that is, this possible interpretation pre-empted by careful questioning, the frequent attempts to misconstrue motivation to report would be more difficult to maintain.

The law also tends to review a child's report in terms of opportunity, rather than provocation. That is, one method of assessing whether someone is telling the truth or not appears to be whether s/he reported the assault at the earliest opportunity. Some recognition is given to difficulties, in terms of presence of the accused, but, if the accused or the victim moves out of the situation, it can often be interpreted as an opportunity to report. This is a matter of observed practice rather than the formal rules of evidence, and it is possible that if a precipitating factor was located as a reason for telling — whatever the stimulus was — in the substantive interview, it would help to lend validity to the child's account.[7] For example, in the case of a 12 year-old it was not the absence of the accused but the prospect of his return that prompted the child to say something:

> Disclosure was made by the girl when the family was thinking of moving. The girl was not particularly enthusiastic about this and then . . . broke down in tears and told her mother 'I do not want to go back with him.' She said he had been 'touching her up'.

This reinforces the notion that a child's primary motive for reporting is to stop the abuse. Thus, if the PBR moves it is not necessarily likely to prompt reporting. Reporting can also come as a consequence of starting a peer appropriate relationship because the child either understands their own previous assault in another light, or feels restricted by on-going sexual demands within the family. Once again, this can be in the context of an argument, often under the guise of discipline and control. For example, the following referral from the child protection study:

> . . . [child] has spoken of father making her undress and parade around in front of him, though states no touching etc. took place, relationship very incestuous in nature. Parents separated some years ago but he spends a lot of time at home. Allegations came about when father complained about another man . . .

Finally, opportunity is not just a matter of absence of PBR, there are strong indications that opportunities for telling should be given. In a study of teachers, for example, one teacher had received nine reports whereas all other respondents (54) had received between none and three (Wattam, 1989). This teacher felt that her particular approach, which involved letting the children know when she would be available to talk, asking regular general prompt type questions of children she was concerned about, and responding in a non-judgemental way to whatever a child decided to tell her, encouraged children to come forward. Whether or not this is so, the child protection study had many examples of children who reported on being asked general questions, whether in therapy or adversity, for example, being interviewed by the police for running away from home.

In summary, the research indicates that child abuse is under reported by victims, parents and possibly other professionals. Reasons for not reporting tend to centre on fear of blame, and fear of not being believed, fear of the consequences of telling and wanting to forget or 'block' the abusive experience. A further factor, that of the social organisation of telling could be an important criterion in determining why it is that a child comes to tell others of her/his experience when s/he does. Knowledge of the routes to telling, the interactions and transactions that surround it, should inform the orientation to reports. Whatever the reasons for not reporting, it will be helpful if the topic of how the report came about can be explored in the substantive interview, both to pre-empt defence arguments and to find out, and where possible to meet, the child's expectations.

It is now more important than ever that legal and social work professionals take account of how reporting comes about, and the problems that this presents for children and families. Later in the book I will show how this becomes a crucial variable when scrutinising the testimony of children for validity, particularly in relation to recency of complaint.

## Notes

1   These formulations are the foundation of all statistics on referrals, since any statistics on the referral unit are dependent on the categorisation work that is done at this initial point.

2   Practitioners routinely use abbreviations, which are a topic of interest in their own right. They display what is expected to be known of the language in use of a social work team. The language of 'abuse' has been shown to be endemic in many settings, including social work in Western Australia (Thorpe, 1991).

It is also further evidence of categorisation work, with the same attendant consequentiality.

Here the abbreviations stand for:
s/a'd: sexually abused
s/history: social history
CPN: Community Psychiatric Nurse.

3    Not all approaches to treatment are the same, and further research is required into the effectiveness of various approaches. However, there does appear to be agreement about the therapeutic value of acknowledging the details of the abuse that are important to the child, whether or not they are the same details as those given in earlier statements.

4    This figure includes mixed categories, where sexual abuse is identified along with physical abuse and neglect. The rate of registration over the year is even lower, standing at 0.35 per thousand.

5    As the DOH point out, register figures should not be interpreted as a measure of the numbers of children abused. Registration criteria stipulate that

'Before a child is registered the conference must decide that there is, or is a likelihood of, significant harm leading to the need for a child protection plan. One of the following requirements needs to be satisfied:

(i) There must be one or more identifiable incidents which can be described as having adversely affected the child. They may be acts of commission or omission. They can be either physical, sexual, emotional or neglectful. It is important to identify a specific occasion or occasions when the incident has occurred. Professional judgement is that further incidents are likely;

or

(ii) Significant harm is expected on the basis of professional judgement of findings of the investigation in this individual case or on research evidence.

The emphasis is on further incidents or expected harm. Those children who have been harmed, and who are now considered safe would not necessarily be registered.

6    The relationship of confidants to the victim was not specified, although it is stated elsewhere in the study the largest group of confidants was mothers.

7    It should be remembered that the MOGP specifically guides interviewers away from 'Why' questions, because of their implicit suggestion of blame. Thus 'why didn't you tell before' is not advised, whereas 'how did it come about that you wanted to say something now' would be acceptable (given that the child has already said something).

# 3 Substantiation and risk assessment

This chapter represents the 'core' of the book. The research material is drawn upon to reveal some important features underpinning the decision-making process in the initial investigation of child protection cases. Hitherto, decision-making has been the subject of a great deal of research, but the emphasis has been on outcome rather than process. So that, for example, it is possible to know how many children end up in substitute care in a given sample, how long they might stay there, and the relationship between the length of stay and their chances of returning home (Packman, 1990). Decision-making is assessed in terms of a series of action outcomes. Alternatively, models are devised to aid decision-making such as Brearley's model of risk assessment. The application of such models are contingent on knowledge of risk factors, that is, information that might constitute a risk environment. Hitherto, this information has pertained particularly to the parents, and to such things as their age and maturity, experience of childhood abuse, levels of stress, marital status and relationship, social and economic living conditions, history of criminal behaviour and current state of health (Madge, 1983; Greenland, 1987). Once these factors are known, the 'dangers', 'hazards' and 'strengths' can be identified, and a decision reached (Brearley, 1982). One problem with this approach is that no risk factors are 100% reliable as predictive factors.

Research which has attempted to apply them to a sample of the population find that a number of cases are selected which do not result in the parents assaulting or neglecting their children (Lealman et al., 1983; Altemeier et al., 1984). This research, in conjunction with concern over the growing number of children referred to social work agencies, has prompted critical attention to the danger of 'false positives' — reports which are substantiated wrongly, such as may have been the case in Cleveland, and 'false negatives' — the children who are the victims of assault, yet their cases are not substantiated (Wakefield & Underwager, 1988). It has also stimulated research into risk assessment (see, for example, Browne et al., 1988) and the pursuit for more accurate prediction devices. Giller et al. (1992) note that social workers do not routinely use the research and literature on risk analysis in making their decisions. My own research would support this finding, and, in addition, reveals much about how they do achieve the decision-making through which cases attain the status of substantiation, or not.

Once a case has been reported, and its relevance to the agency determined, the investigative process begins. Each area child protection committee has its own set of inter-agency procedures concerning the investigation of child abuse. One common theme between them is the need to comply with the guidance given in *Working Together* (DOH 1988, 1991*b*). In that guidance, certain stages of work are identified, these are:

(i) referral and recognition;
(ii) immediate protection and planning the investigation;
(iii) investigation and initial assessment. p.27

The previous chapter addressed some of the issues to be borne in mind at the referral and recognition stage, in relation to making a child protection case. This second chapter, and the two that follow, report on the findings of the child protection study relevant to stages (ii) and (iii).

It has already been noted that, up until very recently, the only statistics on child abuse reported to statutory agencies in this country have been those of the 'register'. They have had a tendency to be treated as the outcomes of the initial investigative process, that is, as an indicator of substantiated cases. The criterion for registration is outlined as follows:

> Before a child is registered, the conference must decide that there is, or is a likelihood of, significant harm leading to the need for a child protection plan. One of the following requirements needs to be satisfied:
>
> (i) There must be one or more identifiable incidents which can be described as having affected the child adversely. They may be acts of commission or omission. They can be either physical, sexual, emotional or neglectful. It is important to identify a specific occasion or occasions when the incident has occurred. *Professional judgement is that further incidents are likely*;
> or

(ii)  *Significant harm is expected* on the basis of professional judgement of findings of the investigation in this individual case or on research evidence p.48 (my emphasis)

Thus, registration figures are a measure of professional judgements about future risk to the child of significant harm or injury. They are an interesting topic in their own right, but should not be misinterpreted as a measure of the numbers of children that the work concerns, or as a measure of reported child harm and injury. This observation begins to point to a matter of relevance to making a case in child protection. That registration, and substantiation of a case, is an achieved matter, which is not entirely contingent on what has actually happened to any particular child. Observations of how it is achieved in practice help to show the realities, rather than the theory behind risk assessment and substantiation.

Two recent research studies estimated that three-quarters of cases 'drop out' at, or prior to, the point of registration (Giller et al., 1992) and that approximately half the cases reported to a statutory agency are not substantiated (Thorpe & Denman, 1992). In the child protection study it was very difficult to identify what constituted a substantiated case. Many were characterised by indecision, and comprised various versions of events such as those given by parents who consistently denied anything untoward, children who were saying things which could be variously interpreted, and teachers or other adults who were convinced something was wrong. Social workers and police officers had to weigh up all the information and rarely accounted for cases as substantiated or not, rather they couched their accounts in terms of the *probability* that something may, or may not, have happened. It is, therefore, not surprising to find that cases which were resolved one way or the other, that is substantiated or unsubstantiated, are in the minority (17%). All but one of these cases reached this outcome within the first month. Thus, in the case of alleged child sexual abuse, the initial investigative assessment is of crucial importance to making, or breaking, a case.

The majority of cases in the sample were undecided in some way. They do, however, fall into two groups: those where involvement continued because there was sufficient information to warrant concern, and those where involvement ceased. Where there was no further involvement this did, in 14% of cases, amount to an unsubstantiated case, one where with some degree of certainty a decision was reached that the report was wrong. However, a further 13% of cases were discontinued because the evidence was lacking, and because it did not appear that future involvement would render any further evidence. This does not mean that something, or nothing, has happened, but rather that whether it has or not cannot be proved or disproved. This finding reveals the crucial role that evidence plays, even in the early stages of the process. The findings are represented below in Tables 1 and 2.

These findings suggest a very different picture to that available from research in the USA where it is estimated that 65% of all reports are unfounded, with 'no reason to assume that it is different for child sexual abuse' (Wakefield & Underwager, 1988). In Besharov's study (1986) which concerned all forms of child abuse reported, of the 35% remaining reports, approximately half were later not substantiated. In the table above it can be seen that, after a 6-month period, only one case was considered unsubstantiated. Involvement ended in 11% of cases, but this was as a result of protective action, either from the extended family or because of alterations in family circumstances which decreased the element of *risk*. Because of lack of evidence, 5% were terminated and involvement continued in 25%. The continuing involvement group comprised those children who were in substitute care (18%), out of the home in some other arrangement (2%) and/or receiving treatment, or where involvement in criminal proceedings was still continuing (5%). Thus, it could be said that these were

**Table 1. Initial outcome after referral (at one month)**

| Outcome | Frequency | %Total |
|---|---|---|
| Unsubstantiated | 15 | 14 |
| Lack of Evidence | 14 | 13 |
| Further Involvement | 44 | 42 |
| Substantiated (NFA) | 2 | 2 |
| No further action after initial consultation | 29 | 27 |
| Not known | 2 | 2 |
| Total | 106 | 100 |

**Table 2. Outcome after 6 months on further involvement cases**

| Outcome | Frequency | %Total |
|---|---|---|
| Unsubstantiated | 1 | 1 |
| Lack of Evidence | 5 | 5 |
| Continuing Involvement | 26 | 25 |
| Involvement Ended | 12 | 11 |
| Total | 44 | 42 |

substantiated cases. However, it could equally be said that they were not, since many did not result in a prosecution.

The danger of 'false positives' has been used to undermine social work practice in the press ever since Cleveland. Whilst it might be that some cases are reported mistakenly, and substantiated mistakenly, the arguments on which such a claim rest are tenuous. To be able to say, with 100% certainty, that nothing has happened is extremely difficult in allegations of sexual assault, though less difficult in cases of physical assault. This is an interesting state of affairs. If, for example, it is alleged that a child has been severely beaten by his father, the investigating team would look for bruises. In the result of the discovery of bruises, which can be identified (medically) as being caused by a beating *such as the one described in the allegation*, it might be possible to say the allegation is founded. If, however, the child has bruising which is inconclusively linked to adult acts, then it might be said there is a possibility of assault. If the child has no marks whatsoever, it could conclusively be stated that s/he had not been subject to the action which was alleged. The model is relatively simple: allegation — investigation which consists in matching the allegation to the evidence — result. Thus, in terms of assessing probability of risk, a matching process is going on, between information describing an event and signs which might corroborate that event. In other words, the investigation is about finding signs, evidence for, the allegation. This is not entirely as a consequence of the legal discourse in which child protection investigations are situated, it has much to do with the way that any person might routinely assess presenting information for its validity. Now, the same model is applied to sexual assault, only there are rarely overt signs of sexual assault, so the evidence is contingent on what the child has to say. It is a case of matching accounts, rather than matching an account with a definitive sign. This is why a false positive in the case of sexual assault is so difficult to determine — as is a false negative. The process of matching accounts is complex, and becomes a matter of versions, and deciding which version is correct. Thus assessment that something might have happened to a child, and might happen again, that is, of *risk* in cases of child sexual assault is tied to methods of assessing 'truth', authenticity, and credibility, and crucially, not to some medical diagnosis of a definitive physical consequence of a harmful action. Of course, cases are rarely clear-cut and, in many cases of alleged physical assault, there will be the problem of versions as there is the problem of medical symptomology in some cases of sexual assault. It is, in all cases, however, the activity of 'matching' one thing (the allegation), to another (the evidence), which underpins the assessment of future risk.

The following extract is an example of how the false allegation issue has been presented. What most practitioners will know from their own practice is that there are rarely certainties. Yet, the debate about false positives continues to propose that there are. The following is an example, written at the time the Rochdale and Manchester cases concerning 'ritual abuse' were being reported in the press:

> These reports confirm my own clinical experience that in cases of Satanic Abuse the proportion of false allegations and fabricated allegations is much higher than is normally found in other cases of sexual abuse. It is now well recognised that not all allegations of sexual abuse are accurate and that false allegations occur regularly. In large published series of cases the proportion of true to false allegations is fairly high (at about 10 to 1). In certain circumstances the proportion of false allegations seems to be much higher. These circumstances are well known and include:
> (a) allegations made by one parent against another during the course of hostile custody proceedings
> (b) allegations which arise as a result of repeated and faulty interviewing of very young children
> (c) allegations which are made on the basis of an incomplete evaluation of the evidence for or against sexual abuse
> And finally in my experience a new category:
> (d) allegations that children have been involved in sexual abuse in the course of Satanic Rituals. Weir, 1991

This example is characteristic of other false allegation proponents in that it (a) makes general claims of a quantitative nature, as above 'In large published series of cases . . .', 'It is now well recognised that . . .', 'These circumstances are well known . . .' without backing the claim with any reference, (b) uses research material obtained in one context and links it to another context, which may not be appropriate, here linking research material on false allegations with the case of 'Satanic Abuse' (c) fails to make the distinction between false allegations made by children and parents, and those made by third parties, and (d) seriously misrepresents the figures when they are cited (Westcott & Davies, 1990; Westcott, 1991)

The 'research' often used to back up this side of the false allegation debate is that of Besharov (1986), who, as stated earlier, gives a figure of 65% of all reports being false. There are several problems with Besharov's writing, which are not dissimilar to the observations made about the above citation. First, this 65% figure is given in the USA where mandatory reporting laws exist, and where many reports are not necessarily allegations, but expressions of concern by professionals. Secondly, this figure concerns all child abuse reports. In the case of child sexual abuse, Jones and McGraw (1987) found a much lower rate of 2% false allegations stemming from children and 6% stemming from parents. Subsequent studies have confirmed the lower rate (Everson & Boat, 1989). Thirdly, 'unfounded' reports are described as those that '*are dismissed after investigation*'. This reveals nothing about the process of investigation and the way in which practitioners routinely decide on what an 'unfounded' report is in the first place.

A similar observation could be made in the UK since no distinction is made between cases that 'drop out' of the system and 'unfounded reports', yet the two are very different. Cases can be dismissed after investigation for a variety of reasons, not necessarily because the report is 'unfounded'. In general, these have to do with an assessment that the child is not at any future risk, or that the case cannot warrant further involvement because the signs, the evidence, do not corroborate the allegation. The question then is not whether something has happened to a child, but whether there is sufficient corroborative information on which to 'found' a report's validity.

More recently, interest in criteria based statement analysis (see, for example, Kohnken, 1990) has led to research which seeks to validate this method of testing the reliability of children's testimony. Much of this research has been dependent on selecting a sample of 'false allegations', and comparing these to a sample of proven cases (Raskin & Esplin, 1991). Various criteria are decided upon to identify false allegations, and, from any given sample, a proportion can be designated as false allegations by using these criteria. For example, the rate of successful prosecutions, the consistent denial of the person believed responsible under lie detection tests, the lack of any medical or forensic evidence, and the denial of the child when the allegation is made by a third party. The proportion of false allegations are then examined in order to enable predictive factors to false allegation to be identified. One salient factor identified as most predictive of false allegations, and thus underpinning false positives, has been that of custody and access disputes (Jones & Seig, 1988; Bentovim et al., 1988).

None of these criteria is sufficient to predict adequately whether an allegation is false. For example, there are rarely physical signs and symptoms in cases of child sexual assault (Royal College of Physicians, 1991). Only a minority of cases proceed to prosecution, whether or not an assault has occurred. In the majority of cases in both samples of the present research, initially at least, the person believed responsible strongly denied the alleged offence. Finally, all the work on cognitive distortion and justification with sexual offenders (Wyre & Swift, 1990) would suggest that a negative lie detector test could be the norm, depending on how questions are phrased. Perpetrators do not always see their own behaviour as 'abusive', harming or injuring; they construct their behaviour with positive connotations, such as nurturing, loving, educating and meeting the needs of their victims.

In order to transform a false allegation into a false positive, someone must decide that the case is substantiated. This 'faulty' reasoning generally has been laid at the door of social workers who are accused of taking a 'believing' stance. It is particularly symptomatic of criticism in child sexual assault cases, and less likely in others, mainly because it is largely child sexual assault cases which have the unique characteristic of the possibility of being dependent on the child's testimony alone. Where there is physical evidence, the notion of believing the child has been less problematic.

In Cleveland, Manchester and elsewhere, social workers have been castigated, publicly and privately, for starting off from the position of 'believing'. However, there are two strands to the 'believing stance' which have become confused, and it is the label of 'believing' which has become discredited, and has resulted in both strands being called into question in evidential terms. One strand is 'believing the child', the other is believing that 'abuse' has occurred, whatever the child or alternative evidence might suggest. The whole notion of 'disclosure' was scrutinised on this basis in Cleveland. In legal terms, one cannot be seen to pre-judge an issue, the facts should speak for themselves. Yet, as the previous chapter indicated, the need to be accepting of the possibility that a child has been sexually assaulted is a concept which has been founded on clinical practice and research which suggests that children find it very difficult to talk about sexual abuse perpetrated on them for numerous reasons, and that their statements about it are minimalised (Sgroi, 1982; Summit, 1983). The task for practitioners is to convey an accepting stance (Biestek, 1957) whilst retaining the legal, and practice requirement of objectivity. This is hard to do, and the difficulty of it should not be under-estimated.

It has previously been noted that cases referred with similar presenting information can result in different responses. In order to understand the debate about false allegations, and false positives better, it is important to deconstruct the process of decision-making in investigation and substantiation, to see how it is that some cases achieve this outcome and others do not. There are two further reasons for this; first, it is always important to reflect on the decision-making process in order to ensure that it is operating as effectively as possible, and secondly, in terms of making a child protection case, the situated moral reasoning which achieves the outcome of substantiation and registration provides the resources for legal scrutiny, and it is important to understand how these operate.

Two explanations for differences in outcome have been proposed. The first attempts to identify the 'rules' that operate in the process; the 'rule of optimism', whereby practitioners use the devices of 'natural love' and 'cultural relativism' to explain what might, under different circumstances, be interpreted as abuse (Dingwall & Eekelaar, 1983). The 'rule of optimism' is further evidence of categorisation at work, and suggests that substantiated cases must seriously breach what could be broadly construed as 'normative' expectations before they achieve the status of substantiation.[1] The second has to do with what could be defined broadly as value judgements (Higginson, 1990) and moral judgements (Thorpe, 1991) whereby certain decisions are based on opinions about such things as parental competence, moral character, drug and alcohol use, and so forth. Moral judgements are founded on categorisation work. They are performed in the context of cultural knowledge, and, for professionals, the context of professional knowledge which includes assessment of risk factors. There is a real 'chicken and egg' problem here, which suggests that recently identified risk factors, based on traits detected from reported 'abuse', are, in fact, those very same factors which might predispose people to report in the first place, to do with judgements about moral character. To exemplify this, the *NSPCC Annual Report* from 1901 categorises 'child-abusing' types as:

> The drunkard, the devil-may-care and idler, the married and estranged, the married and unfaithful, the unmarried, the tramp, the better and gambler, the speculator in child life insurance, the avaricious and greedy. NSPCC, 1990

These are not so dissimilar from more recently proposed attributes, for example, those identified by Greenland (1987), which include young, unmarried parents, poverty, unemployment and deprivation, history of criminal behaviour, alcohol and/or drug abuse. Is it the case that the correct group of people have been identified for the last century, or is it the case that, because of categorisation and moral judgement, certain people are predisposed to being reported? The state of the research literature and activity on risk assessment is, sadly, still in its infancy, and cannot answer this question. It is, therefore, unwise to suggest that practitioners should base their decisions upon it, and, to this extent, it is clear that the law as arbiter is a form of safety net on moral judgement. The fact that someone is an alcoholic, drug user, or young unmarried parent could not stand as evidence of her/his propensity to assault children, in law. The danger would be where, so-called, 'scientific research' begins to endorse these characteristics and the law enlarges the legal discourse to accommodate them. The policing of families within the moral order would be complete.

There is a further dimension which attends to the structures, rather than the subjective content, of the decision-making process (Wattam, 1991). Wherever one looks at the process, at whatever point, and in all its different formal and informal contexts, it is generally possible to identify one or more of the following structures in reasoning about a case: specificity, motive, corroboration and categorisation. Earlier, I referred to the process of substantiation as one in which there was a matching activity between one piece of information (the allegation), and signs, or absence of signs, that the allegation is valid (evidence), and the way in which the absence of physical symptomology in child sexual assault cases acted to focus significance on behaviour. I now want to turn to the signs as they were observed and articulated in the child protection study. I refer to their use in terms of structure, because the information was structured by, and around, them. The process of 'matching' was a matter of 'corroboration'; looking for, and deciding on, what stood for the information contained in the allegation. The issue of corroborative evidence appeared in the files, though not always, or very often, as an explicitly legal and court matter. It had to do more with the process of decision-making, and with what kind of evidence practitioners use to reach and justify the decisions they make. Deciding whether a report was founded had to do with interpreting and making judgements not only about what the child said but how they said it. For example, the following was offered as a conclusion to an 'inconclusive' interview, and illustrates the structure of corroboration. The allegation concerned the child's father who had been charged with indecent assault after his daughter's friend complained to her own parents that he had taken her knickers down and fondled her, and that he had done the same to his daughter.

> 1. [Child] has quickly become fairly relaxed after doing a drawing. When she moved over to the dolls' house it was she who raised the idea of playing naughty games but then refused to describe their nature and refused to talk about [friend who made the allegation]. She very quickly moved into a rather defensive mood.

It is known by this social worker that children can refer to such activities as 'naughty games', often because this is how they are formulated by the adult concerned. Thus, when the child starts to talk about 'naughty games' the social worker takes this as a possible sign which matches to, and is potential evidence of, the allegation's validity. She then notes:

2. [Child] indicates that she will talk about the games only if the WPC promises that she can see dad, and mother can remain in the room. She clearly fears that talking about the games will mean daddy will not be able to come home and when the WPC says if [child] tells the truth everything will be alright [child] replies 'it wouldn't'.

A relevance between 'games' and her father is drawn by the child, and the fact that she states things wouldn't be alright if she told the 'truth' is taken to indicate a fear of talking about that. The reasoning behind such an assessment follows:

3. One would normally expect a child to be happy to talk about the games she plays in her family and certainly one would not expect a child to associate such conversation with separation from her father. It may be (*a*) that she had connected the two events from hearing adult conversation in respect of other children complaining of games daddy plays which led to his remand (*sic*) from home. (*b*) that she has been told not to talk about the games because daddy will go to prison. This would of course mean there is indeed something to hide . . .

The 'evidence' is founded on devices which draw on every-day knowledge, and professional experience, such as: a refusal to talk, being defensive, an association between talking and what will happen to daddy, an acknowledgement that, if she told the truth, it wouldn't be alright, and their relevance is founded on what one could normally expect of children. The social worker knew that this kind of evidence would not stand up in a legal context, thus she concludes:

I do not believe that this interview provided any evidence of sexual abuse of [child] by her father and it would be ill advised to draw firm conclusions from it. However, it is clear that [child] is a highly defended little girl on this particular subject and that in itself might be cause for substantial concern and even suspicion.

Thus, there is 'concern' but no more at this stage. The allegation is neither substantiated, nor unsubstantiated, and the outcome of this interview is inconclusive either way. The activity of corroboration is pervasive in the assessment of risk, and this is dependent, in part, on the other structure of categorisation, particularly on an orientation towards the normal and expectable. There is also what might be considered a continuum along which the value of corroborative information is assessed, so that some forms of corroborating information are stronger than others allowing a more conclusive outcome. A second example shows how this can occur. The referral states that:

> Over last weekend a man called [name, address] uncle was baby-sitting. [Child] alleges he sexually assaulted her and from her description of the event and her action in running out into the road in her night clothes there is little doubt in police minds that her allegations are true . . .

The validity of the allegation obtains from 'her description of the event and her action'. A description of this is given on file:

> [Child] complains that [a man] aged [XX] had touched her indecently on her chest and genitals. Shortly after this [he] was arrested. He was very drunk and awkward. The following day he was interviewed but refused to answer any questions on the advice of his solicitor. [Child] was interviewed and said she had been playing with her friend at [address] and asked if she could stay overnight. This was agreed by the family. At 7.45 [friend's mother] went out to her work in a pub. By 10.15 the children were ready for bed but continued playing upstairs. [The man] then separated the children, leaving [child] on her own. [Child] said [the man] had been drinking whisky. Ten minutes later he came back upstairs, went into her room and touched her on her chest. [Child] told him to leave but later he returned and this time touched both her chest and genitals. He used the flat of his hand and never actually touched her vagina . . . He returned to [child's] bedroom for a third time and asked if he could spend 10 minutes with her. She refused and he went away. After he had gone she crept downstairs in her nightdress and ran home. He seemed to be asleep in a chair drunk.

There is a sense of corroboration, not sufficient for proof beyond all reasonable doubt, but in a practical sense, in that the child is reported as describing the man as drinking whisky and when he was arrested he was described as 'very drunk and awkward'. In addition, and this is remarked upon as validating the allegation in the referral, the child ran home in her nightgown. The referral was made by the girl's parents who could corroborate that they received her home in that state. But there is more here. The police think the allegation is valid on the basis of the child's description, and thus it can be asked what, about the above account, corroborates its validity? The description is quite *detailed* in terms of time and action. The child is reported to talk in terms of minutes, and is very *specific* about what is touched; there is a distinction between chest, genitals and vagina. There is also an account of how she was touched, with the 'flat of his hand'. The features of detail and distinctiveness which give *specific* information, are those which are relevant to the allegation, and point to a further structure — that of specificity — through which and with which information is assessed. Its salience as a structure is derived from corroboration, since there must be things and events to corroborate, the more specific they are the more available to corroboration they are. Whilst many specific details are not open to corroboration, or are not corroborated when they are offered, their specificity indicates their availability for corroboration, if the corroboration were possible, and thus lend the allegation validity. So that the specificity of information, of and in itself, becomes a corroborating device.

One further structure was identified in the decision-making process about validity, and that was the structure of motive. It was a structure because it underpinned the interpretation of information through and through (Wattam, 1989, 1991). If a motive, other than a desire to help a child, could be detected at referral, this information acted as a filter through which other information was interpreted. In the case of a mother, separated from her husband, for example, who alleged sexual assault to her children whilst in her husband's care, this was interpreted in the context of their estranged relationship. Whilst the children did show some behaviour, and physical symptoms, that could have been associated with sexual assault, and under other circumstances may have led to continued surveillance or a different outcome, this investigation ended as 'inconclusive', and the following record made:

> Eventually, [police officer] challenged [mother] as to her motivation for making this complaint. [Mother] admitted that it was her intention to make trouble for [father]. [Mother] is particularly upset at the impending marriage between [woman] and [father] and the thought of her children calling [this woman] 'mum' . . . Police decided they would have to treat this as a malicious allegation and no more.

There were many cases like this in the sample, though it is not the numbers of cases that are important here. What can be seen throughout this case, and others, is the way in which the motive for referral structures the interpretation of any subsequent information, and how the case ends once the motive is clearly established, irrespective of what has happened in between.

Thus, it can be said that, if information about an allegation is detailed and specific, it lends validity. If a motive, other than disinterested concern, can be identified, it detracts from validity. If information can be corroborated, by any means, and at any level, it lends validity to that information — whether it be towards substantiation or against it. Finally, persons and information as I have shown in the first chapter, will be categorised and oriented to according to the expected behaviours and events contingent on that categorisation.

All of these structures are resources for making sense, devices for practical reasoning. As structures, they are to some extent unavoidable. Cases are made and unmade by them, future risk is assessed by them, and on occasions they may not be the most appropriate structures. In such cases, it may be necessary to show how things can be interpreted as they are, and why they might need to be considered differently, using the research evidence available. Because custody and access disputes have been identified as the most likely cause of false allegations, I will use this to show how the structures underpinning the decision-making process may potentially mislead decision-makers. Custody and/or access was a feature in 14 of the 106 cases in the child protection study. Three of these cases warranted further involvement, four were found to be unsubstantiated, six failed to proceed because of lack of evidence, and one warranted no further action for an unstated reason. Thus, on the face of it at least, it would appear that 13 of the 14 cases were investigated fully.

The outcomes of these cases were founded on the structures I have identified above. In terms of categorisation, in the case of custody and access disputes, it is expectable that parties to the dispute will say things which incriminate each other and further their own respective chances of getting custody of the children. A level of animosity is anticipated, and it is well known that children can become pawns in the game between their separated parents. A conflictual context to referral is a salient and orienting feature which must be accounted for before the allegation of abuse is substantiated, or not, as is more often the case (Wattam, 1989, 1991). Thus, for example, a social worker who receives a report from a mother who complains about the behaviour of her ex-husband and makes a 'vague' allegation about possible sexual abuse, orients towards the categorisation and category-incumbent behaviour of 'divorced parents' in order to context the allegation. This is closely related to the structure of motive, since, if the motive can be broadly construed as one of possible revenge, it must also be accounted for in the investigation.

Once oriented to, information obtained in the investigation is used to corroborate the initial categorisation, so that, when the mother admits that there was an element of revenge in her allegation, this corroborates information which has been obtained through the original orientation. Despite indications that something could have happened to a child, it is not the indications that are oriented to but the 'element of revenge'.

All the children in cases where custody and access were a feature were aged below nine. Given that, in the overall sample, this age-group had the highest percentage of unsubstantiated cases, and that only 23% of children under nine warranted further involvement (compared to 63% of children over ten), this might indicate that younger children are more vulnerable, either to unfounded referrals, or to abusive relationships that are difficult to substantiate. In terms of the structure of specificity, younger children are less likely to give as much detail as older children, and, in the case example I use here, the children were also described as 'vague'. Despite this, there was a statement that something 'rude' had happened, talk of 'bathrooms' in connection with 'secrets', and potential medical signs that were not followed up officially. It is not possible to know how these structures of categorisation, motive, specificity and corroboration operated in the research undertaken elsewhere on false allegations. However, until such an analysis is reported, it is premature for anyone, expert or otherwise, to say that false allegations are more likely in custody and access disputes or any other context. It may have much more to do with the knowledge of custody and access as it operates as a variable in the decision-making process.

The question remains as to what can be done by practitioners to improve the quality of decision-making. My intention has been to describe the process, so that the reflective practitioner might inform her/himself. However, I will conclude this chapter by drawing out some of the implications for building a case in both civil and criminal proceedings. From the file analysis in the child protection study, it became clear that the experience of investigative assessment for the children concerned was not primarily an accountable matter. Records themselves contained different types of information; accounts of events, short entries that said who did what and when, such as:

Thursday, 10th September: Attended case conference at [town] Social Services. Case remains closed.

Occasionally there were what could be described as self-reflective accounts, where practitioners write about their feelings on a case, for example:

> I am not sure what the next move will be, I suspect there will be further concerns expressed by the school and I feel that my role is to build up a better relationship with Mrs Brown. On a more positive note, she did listen to me today, she did not get as aggressive as she has on previous occasions, and I feel that there are benefits to me going to the house on my own.

Until certain features of the work become accountable, such as ascertaining the feelings and wishes of the child, it is possible that they do not get attended to in quite the same way. Thus, one way of building a case in child protection, is to record practice with what is accountable, and with what practitioners feel should be accountable, in mind. Much of the discussion about a case takes place outside the records, and the record acts as a gloss of that discussion. Now, more than ever, recording practices must be attended to, since records concerning planning and strategy meetings, case conferences, the investigative interview and contact with the child and family may be used as evidence. Knowing this, there may be a tendency to use records as the official gloss of the discussion, interaction, or contact. It is therefore crucial to take stock of what is left out, and begin to view records as being open to the kind of legal scrutiny detailed in Chapter 10. What might be the day-to-day fodder of social work decision-making, such as an argument between mother and daughter, can later become central in the process of proving or disproving a case. Thus, practitioners must begin to record their knowledge in a way which can be described as 'second guessing' the defence. This means identifying the way in which a case has been oriented to, from referral and through the initial investigation, and scrutinising that orientation by examining what has been used to corroborate it. Very often, cases can proceed on the basis of a general sense of concern which is not, at first sight, based on any kind of 'factual' status. But, in the same way as research materials can be analyzed, it is important to ask how we know, to identify and look at what has been taken to stand for what, and to account for it in recording about a case. This does not diminish the importance of any given sense of concern, but does allow critical scrutiny of its foundation. It also affords the opportunity to collate as much evidence as possible, evidence which, on its own, might not stand in a legal context, but contributes to the formation of a case. In an example alluded to earlier, and given in detail elsewhere,[2] a structural break down of the case reveals how an initial allegation is discredited. By using this method, of asking what stands for what at any decision-making point, it can be seen that the outcome of the case is not just an interpretation, or re-interpretation of the 'facts'. Rather it is an orientation to certain 'facts', such as motive underlying complaint, and their salience above others which results in outcome. The task for practitioners in recording will be to counteract the orientation by detailed accounts of how they decide whether a case is, is not, or might be, valid, as an on-going matter. To illustrate this, reconsider the file entry given in the Introduction concerning the 13 year-old child:

> . . . She had witnessed white, sticky stuff and that it had hurt her. She also advised that there had been threats made upon her to keep silent. It appears that most of the incidents took place in his bedroom. The policewoman interviewing the child then began to discuss the subject of lie telling and whether or not [child], whose mental age is only 8, understood what telling lies involved. I considered that this process of the interview was unduly lengthy, and it appeared to me that [child] had been subjected to considerable questioning about the validity of her story, however, she did maintain the story throughout. Times and events did alter, and at one time she did retract but then reiterated the original story . . .

Records do not represent a complete version of the events they describe. They record only relevant aspects at the time the record was compiled, aspects which in the light of future events, may be reappraised. Garfinkel (1967) stated that any investigator would encounter 'troubles' in reading files:

> . . . if he consults the files in order to answer questions that depart in theoretical and practical import from organisationally relevant purposes and routines under the auspices of which the contents of the files are routinely assembled in the first place.

A crown court clerk, or lawyer, reading the case cited above would have different questions to ask of it than those for which it was originally compiled. The final sentence would be of crucial relevance for legal scrutiny, since consistency is clearly a criteria upon which children are judged. Thus, if this practitioner had been 'second guessing' the prospective use of the record in court he might have also described how it came about that times and events did alter, and how it happens that some children do retract, and give possible explanations for these features. It is, of course, not possible to record everything; however, it is important to broaden our perception of 'relevant' evidence and comment upon this in the files wherever possible. In making such matters explicit, it also enables practitioners to account for the decisions they take,

and to reflect upon them, particularly in relation to the structures
I have identified here.

## Notes

1.  Dingwall and Eekelaar were writing before the events in Cleveland, and very
    little of the work reported in their study pertains to child sexual assault,
    which appears to have been treated somewhat differently. It could also be
    argued that a greater awareness of child sexual assault within the family,
    and the prevailing 'addiction' model of child sexual abuse, have shifted
    the focus away from working with parents who may be implicated, and
    onto the child as client. This shift has been underpinned by the findings
    of inquiries into child deaths, particularly the Jasmine Beckford Inquiry
    and could possibly be viewed as engendering a 'rule of pessimism'. The
    implications for the implementation of the Children Act, 1989 which stresses
    the paramountcy of the child, but also the importance of partnership with
    parents are significant.
2.  Readers who want to know more about the methodology involved in
    'deconstructing a case' are referred to Wattam, C. 'Truth and Belief in the
    "Disclosure" Process', *Policy, Practice and Research Series*, NSPCC, 1991. In
    Chapter 4 of that paper, I apply the methodology to identify the structures as
    they are articulated in a case concerning an allegation of child sexual abuse.

# 4 Medical and forensic evidence

The second chapter made some reference to events in Cleveland and the issue of believing the child. A further key issue in Cleveland, and subsequently, has been the status of medical evidence in child protection cases, particularly those involving allegations of sexual assault. It is no coincidence that child abuse in its most recent construction began as a medical issue, detected initially by radiographers who were concerned about abnormal bone X rays (Pfohl, 1976). The notion that, if a child has been the victim of avoidable harm and injury, there will be medical evidence of it is long standing, and has dominated the statutory response in child protection investigation. The development of expertise in detecting non-accidental harm and injury has been particularly symptomatic of assessment in physical abuse. The importance of the medical detection of 'abuse' has been underlined throughout inquires into child deaths over the last 20 years (DOH, 1981; DOH, 1991a) and close inter-agency working between medical and social work practitioners has been consolidated by government guidance (DOH, 1991b). In addition, an intrinsic feature in preparation of cases of assault, both adult and child, is the obtaining of medical evidence concerning the injury incurred. The depiction of abuse on which this approach is founded is one of an act with physical consequences, which will be detectable by medical expertise either because of the recency of the act, or its severity, as in the case of healing fractures. This formulation of child abuse does not allow for the possibility that children may be harmed without observable physical consequence, either because the harmful actions are not recent, are committed in a way as to disguise their physical manifestation, or have no physical manifestation, as can happen in many cases of sexual assault. The pressure to obtain medical evidence in order to make a case is strong, and thus, rather than accept that, on occasions, the lack of medical evidence may be, in itself, corroboration of the type of harm incurred by a child, the absence of medical evidence is seen as a deficit. This chapter examines these issues to do with what medical evidence is taken to stand for, to represent, in the investigative assessment and legal process. It will be seen that, in the absence of clear guidelines, the decision to obtain medical evidence, and the ways in which it was used, were strongly linked to situated moral reasoning and the structures outlined in previous chapters, particularly those of categorisation and corroboration. This finding is helpful in determining just what the medical evidence is standing as evidence of, and I conclude with some recommendations for practice in the light of it.

Of the 106 children in the child protection study who began as potential subjects for investigation, a medical examination was noted on the files in 28% of the cases. The results of these medicals are outlined in Table 1.

An inconclusive outcome is one where signs were present but these could not definitely be attributable to sexual abuse. A negative outcome was one where no signs were present, and a positive one where the medical examiner stated that the child had signs consistent with the allegation made about them. Medical substantiation in sexual assault is an area fraught with difficulty (Hobbs & Wynne, 1989) and it is problematic to define what constitutes a definitive sign. However, it is possible to illustrate how positive, negative and inconclusive outcomes are recorded.

On the whole, in the child protection study, medical examinations and their outcomes are only reported briefly in the files. The weight given to the outcome varies from case to case, though it does not seem to be consistent with the type of symptoms or medical observations made. In other words, it is not the case that a particular physical symptom, such as the absence of a hymen, in an allegation of sexual assault, is routinely taken as evidence of that assault. For example, in one investigation concerning two girls under the age of ten, the children denied any sexual contact

**Table 1.  Outcome of medical examination**

| Outcome | Frequency | %Total |
|---|---|---|
| Inconclusive | 11 | 10 |
| Negative | 11 | 10 |
| Positive | 8 | 8 |
| No medical | 76 | 72 |
| Total | 106 | 100 |

in the interview although the eldest child had told her mother that something had happened at their grandmother's house which had made her sore. The youngest child said nothing. The mother, herself a childhood victim of sexual assault, was convinced that the children had been 'interfered with' and made a referral to the social services department. After a lengthy interview using dolls and play materials, in which nothing of any further relevance was obtained, the children were medically examined. The soreness on the older child was confirmed, and could have been caused by an infection. The younger child was found to be without a hymen. This was considered by the police officer and the doctor as significant and thus warranted further investigation. The case which I describe in some detail below has similar medical symptoms, but they are considered quite differently.

Some medicals were carried out by the child's general practitioner, although the majority were carried out by the police surgeon. It is acknowledged by most practitioners that the police surgeon is the best person to do the examination, but some parents insist on the medical being carried out by their GP. Many GP's are not trained in the particular requirements of forensic examination, and may misinterpret signs, or misunderstand their significance. The acknowledged expertise of the police surgeon is a further example of the construction of evidence. It is not the case that a medical sign is *in itself* evidence, given that two doctors might interpret the same sign differently. Work must be done to achieve a sign's evidential significance, and police surgeons are generally skilled in this work.

The case example used here has been selected because it highlights many features in the decision-making process which have been identified previously, concerning corroboration and orientation. In this case, it reveals that medical evidence might apparently be interpreted inconsistently because it is used to corroborate both the possibility that something may have happened, as in the case cited above, or as evidence that something need not have happened, as in the following case. There was a very clear impression from reading the files, and field observations, that signs are interpreted not for what they consist in per se, but in terms of their corroborative value. It is this corroborative value which renders the outcome: positive, negative or inconclusive, not the signs themselves. However, if the use of medical evidence as corroboration of the already 'oriented to' categorisations is examined, then its use is consistent. There is, for example, nothing intrinsic about the absence of a hymen, or a vaginal infection which allows it to stand as a sign of sexual abuse. If the referrer can be categorised as someone who has a motive for 'making trouble' then the sign can be oriented to in the context of that categorisation (Wattam, 1991), and can be reconstructed as an expectable, or normal, physical condition. Where there is no other possible orientation, then the sign might be considered as symptomatic of assault. This issue of orientation and medical signs, even in the context of physical abuse, is crucial to understanding the decision-making process and how things might go wrong. Jasmine Beckford, for example, was examined by a school doctor only a matter of months before her death. Thus, an understanding of the relationship between orientation and interpretation of medical evidence, in practice, and the development of a methodic approach to identifying such a relationship, may result in more accurate assessments of child harm and injury, both in the investigation and the courts. At the present time, ambiguity or an absence of signs can, under certain circumstances, be used as evidence in defence of an alleged offender, both by the courts and by her or his family. Not only can this have the consequence of undermining the child's account, and confirming the fear of not being believed, it can also result in children remaining in high-risk environments.

The case used here to illustrate some of these points had a substantial amount of corroborative evidence in the form of the mother's account, but there is no support to the allegation given by the children in interview. The children were aged 8, 5, and 3. The mother originally contacted social workers anonymously, and some time was spent getting her to reveal her identity. Her concern stemmed from various incidents: she had heard the sound of her husband having an orgasm and found the eldest daughter and her husband in bed together, but her husband said he was reading. Later her husband accused her of interfering with their son. On another occasion, the mother walked in on her husband getting changed and her daughter holding on to her nightie. The daughter looked 'startled'. On another, she observed her husband in the garden shed. He had his hand down his trousers and looked as if he was masturbating, the daughter watching him. She later asked the daughter about this, and she 'became very agitated about it' and 'began to cry'. On another, the mother overheard her husband with his daughter saying 'up and down', and later she heard her son using the same words whilst holding his penis. Other incidents replicated those already detailed. In addition, her daughter thought she might be pregnant.

The children were interviewed. It was reported that the daughter's answers were 'detailed', thus the structure of specificity which has the effect of making an account appear more valid was present. The record also stated that the children would give no indication of sexual abuse, and, crucially, in the same context, it is reported that they loved their father. In terms of categorisation, it is normal, and expectable that children will love their fathers, and it is not expectable that they will do so if they are being abused by them. The GP examined the children and found the son had a 'radians around the anus', which could have been an infection. The eldest daughter was described as a 'normal' 8 year-old (categorisation/orientation), whose hymen was absent and the anal region was larger than 'normal'.

The middle daughter also had an absent hymen and the vaginal opening was inflamed. The doctor felt

> . . . the girls were nothing other than normal young girls. He felt it was not abnormal for there not to be a hymen and the redness could be caused by worms [corroboration of orientation]

When the father was interviewed, he denied doing anything untoward against the children but admitted to being sexually abused himself as a child. The mother had also talked about her own experience of child sexual abuse. The father claimed that he washed the children in a way that might have caused the absence of a hymen. The GP had discussed this case with his colleagues, and it was recorded that none of them believed the allegations of sexual abuse. In defence of the father, and his admission of washing the children in a certain way, the GP suggested that the father's definition of a vagina was not the same as a professional definition. He went on to state that the 'evidence was circumstantial and there was no scientific evidence to support the allegation'. The police observed that:

> . . . the concern in this case, as in many of these cases, is the lack of evidence. In this case there was no evidence at all from any of the children. There were only sketchy instances given by mother and the doctor's statement. [Police officer] had been told that a lack of hymen could be hereditary and the redness could be the result of an infection. The problem was that, at the time of the examination, no swabs had been taken. When tests were asked for, time had passed and it had cleared up . . . .

Later it is recorded that the father admitted to masturbating over his daughter's leg and the police described this as 'obviously strange behaviour', but also stated that this case had 'the least evidence of any that he had dealt with. There was nothing to put before the courts'.

The crucial missing factor in this case was a statement from the children with which to corroborate the other evidence. Without a statement from the children, there was only the mother's account to corroborate. This account was questioned during the conference. Her credentials as an objective witness were weighed in the context

of her own abuse, her previous behaviour in relation to the medical
practice — she was described as having 'attached herself' to GPs
quite 'quickly' over a period of years, and also inconsistency in
her story — she denied knowing about something which later she
admitted to knowing. This construction of the mother as a victim
and possible help-seeker makes motive for complaint available for
scrutiny. Thus, with only the medical evidence standing, and
this, in itself, having already been discredited, there became no
case to corroborate and only 'sketchy evidence' if there were.
This is not because the medical symptoms in themselves were
'sketchy'; the interpretation made of it hinged on its corroborative
value. In another case, where the child has given an account of
penetrative sexual abuse for example, these symptoms might have
been considered strongly corroborative.[1]

This case also indicates a failure to make a distinction between
the medical and forensic aspects of an investigation. Sexual abuse
has no definitive symptom in a medical sense. On rare occasions,
the physical consequences of sexual assault can be independently
corroborated forensically, such as where semen is present. It is
important to consider this distinction since the case above, and
others, indicate that it is not always made. There are at least two
separate purposes to a medical examination, and the two should
not be conflated for evidential purposes. One is the retrieval of
forensic evidence of a physical phenomenon which can corroborate
the child's statement, the other is an examination for medical signs
to ensure that no damage or harm is done, and that, if it has been, it
is appropriately treated. The forensic aspect was minimally attended
to in the above case, pointed to in the police officer's reference to
'swabs', and by the fact that they were not taken at the right time.
However, and this is a matter of some consequence, the evidence
was treated in a forensic way, as standing for, or corroborating,
whether or not something had happened.

This feature of treating medical evidence in a forensic way, as
opposed to treating forensic evidence in a forensic way, can lead
to the kind of outcome described above; that no medical evidence
means no forensic evidence and thus, in this case and others, no
case, whereas in many cases forensic evidence is a rare event (Royal
College of Physicians, 1990). An absence of forensic evidence in
cases of child sexual assault is not unusual, and could therefore be
considered as, if anything, consistent with an allegation. Lack of
forensic evidence could rarely be sufficient proof that an allegation
is unfounded.

Bearing this in mind, I want to return to the point made earlier
that absence of 'medical', and notably not forensic, signs can be
used to acquit an alleged perpetrator, both by legal practitioners

and also by his own family, and serve to undermine the child's account. The following case is an example:

> [child] gave a detailed account over the past two years of sexual interference by her father . . . . Oral sex appears to have been a significant part of this, but [child] felt her father had stopped short of full sexual intercourse. On occasion he had made attempts, but as [child] protested that this hurt, he evidently desisted . . . .

Arrangements were made for the child to be examined by the police surgeon:

> Dr A concluded no evidence of sexual intercourse, although [child] appeared frightened and disturbed when he made his examination of her genital area. [Child] otherwise appeared in good health.

This conclusion is reported immediately after the examination, thus no forensic testing of swabs and so forth could have taken place. The following day the social worker writes:

> We met two detectives leaving as we arrived. They have been questioning [father] who is steadfast in his denials. With no medical evidence forthcoming they feel they cannot hold [father] much longer . . . .

The child was interviewed again when it was noted that the child's story 'appeared to be as intractable as her father's denials.' The mother was not sure who to believe, and all the children in the family were taken into care because of misgivings about her ability to protect them. The police later informed a case conference that the father had been 'reported', but, in view of the 'minimal' evidence, it was unlikely that he would be prosecuted. In a later report, compiled by an 'expert' for the purposes of civil proceedings, it is clearly stated that all the professionals involved with the child thought there was some foundation for the allegation. They included teachers, barristers, solicitors, guardian ad litem, social workers and foster parents. There was not one dissenting voice, and yet apparently nothing could be done about the person believed responsible on the basis of lack of, not forensic, but 'medical evidence'.

In this case, as in many others, lack of forensic evidence would have corroborated the child's story, and should not, in itself, have been a reason for not proceeding with a prosecution. In general, the CPS are the final arbiters of whether a case is sufficiently strong to withstand the prosecution process. In the CPS study, I asked to see all the 'pre-process' advice cases, as well as those that went through.

Within the time frame (6 months) and area constraints imposed, there appeared to be only three such cases. This finding implies that there is a decision point about prosecution taken early in a case by the investigating team, and particularly by the police. I would put it at no more than an implication, but recommend that agencies examine the 'drop out' points and circumstances surrounding them in their own areas. With the introduction of the *Memorandum of Good Practice*, this might alter, with the CPS having the potential to be involved at the earlier stage of the substantive interview. Furthermore, of the 43 sexual assault cases proceeded with in the CPS sample, less than a quarter had supportive medical reports and seven cases had inconclusive or non supportive reports. In the remaining cases, no medical reports were available. This did not, however, appear to prejudice the result in any systematic way with the majority of cases resulting in guilty pleas.

There is a substantial amount of forensic evidence that could be sought in cases of alleged child sexual assault. The dominant orientation in the investigation of such cases, which is also visible in the *Memorandum of Good Practice*, is that towards a sexual event, or set of sexual events. In the cases where forensic evidence was sought in the child protection study and given in the CPS study, it is done so when it is directly associated with the sexual act and its evidences, such as stains on underpants and bedding. This, however, is also only sought occasionally, and not as a routine matter. A question remains as to how often forensic evidence is sought routinely to corroborate other details of the child's account, which could contribute to a case and certainly develop it. For example, the case of a 6 year-old who alleged that sexual acts of indecency always took place in the bedroom of the person believed responsible. He denied her ever having been in this bedroom, but the room was never checked for fibres, hair or other possible forensic evidence.[2]

Pursuit of medical evidence is also related to the feature of 'taking things at face value'. Thus, where the child's story does not imply that there would be medical evidence, it might not be sought. For example, in a case where the person believed responsible allegedly got into bed with a child on regular occasions, but where the child stated he did not touch him 'sexually', this was accepted and no medical was carried out. Similarly, the case of the child who specifically described being touched on the vagina by the 'flat of the hand'. There were some cases, however, in the child protection study sample where no medical was considered and the reason is unclear. For example, the case of a young child who said her bottom was sore because 'Daddy put something up it', or the 2 year-old who alleged boys had been doing 'rude things' to him, or the 4 year-old who said a boy had 'interfered' with her, or the 5 year-old who was trying to put his penis into his sister's vagina, and so on. A further group of cases in which medicals did not appear to be carried out, or routinely considered, in the child protection study were those which had a medical context to referral, such as when a case is referred by a health visitor, or school nurse. For example, the case referred by a health visitor of a mother who had presented herself at the clinic with her baby saying the child had a bad nappy rash and she wondered whether the child had been sexually abused. The doctor checked the nappy rash and advised referral to a social worker. On receiving the referral, the social worker telephoned the health visitor and discussed the case. She recorded the following:

> [Health visitor] asked [mother] why she thought [child] could be interfered with and mother said she just wondered as it was being talked about a lot, meaning TV. [Health visitor] told mother that she had reported it to the NSPCC and mother asked if the NSPCC needed to come because several families on [street] where men had been sent to prison for sexually abusing their children had their windows broken . . . [Health visitor] feels that mother didn't really understand the implications of what she had said.

The social worker took no further action. The case highlights a feature, found in others, that where a medical professional has been involved and has examined the child in some context, this appears to preclude the question of an 'investigative' medical. It also reiterates the features of treating information at face value and conflating medical and forensic examinations. Treating information at face value is arguably the most overriding issue in the decision of whether or not to subject a child to a medical examination, in practice. Where a child gives an account of an event which would not 'at face value' allow forensic corroboration, medicals do not seem to be carried out. The following case acts as an illustration:

> It took us quite a long time before we got [child] to say anything at all about X, but eventually he did say very clearly that X sucked his wee-wee while he pulled his penis out and said that 'he had done it to that'. [child] was getting a little tired of the interview and we agreed to break off and try again on [day].

> [date and time] picked up (mother) and [child] for interview with [police officer]. Spent well over an hour with [child] conducting an interview which once again was videoed. Unfortunately [child] had had quite enough of this and although

he said that X had orally abused him on one occasion and perhaps two, he began to retract such a story and said that it had never happened — he had made it up. I felt that we could not pursue the case any more and it was left with [police] deciding to take a statement off mother during an interview which she is to conduct tomorrow. She then intends to interview X and see whether he makes any admissions. She will keep us informed.

I took [mother] and [child] home and she was asking me what might happen. I told her that it was now largely dependent on how the police interviewed X and whether he actually admitted that he had committed some offence. At this stage all we can do is wait for the police to inform us of what has happened, and then as far as the [agency] is concerned this case can be closed.

There is no further information on file, and it can only be assumed that the police did not get back, or if they did the outcome was not worth recording. There does not appear to be consideration that anything more might have happened to this child, or that what happened could be corroborated in any forensic way.

Taking things at face value has a further dimension in the case of medicals and evidence. Where a child says something quite specific, that might be substantiated with forensic evidence, such as 'I've just been buggered', absence of evidence can mean the end of an investigation, especially where there is no other corroboration. Thus, it can be the case that there is little acknowledgement of how children might explain events differently from some adults. For example, some children might say they have had intercourse, when in fact they have experienced 'dry' intercourse.[3] Both these examples were given by teenage children and are quite specific. Much attention has been paid in the professional literature on interviewing, to using language appropriate to the child's own use of it, but the emphasis has generally been on the younger child. When children start to use adult terminology, as young adults, there appears to be a danger of assuming they mean the same things, perhaps, in part, because they indicate an adult awareness of other relevant matters, such as names for parts of the genitalia.

The conflation between medical symptomology and forensic evidence may be a problem of inadequate recording practices, rather than the examination itself. For example, in the following case a child alleged she had been assaulted by another child who 'poked her finger in her bottom'. The child was examined and the following recording made:

[child] had been examined by Dr C who said she had not been interfered with sexually but there was a torn part at the back of the anus, possibly caused by constipation.

The relationship between what is actually said by a medical examiner, and the recording and interpretation made of it by practitioners, is one for further exploration. It may well be that the doctor was, on this occasion, attempting to make the distinction between forensic evidence and physical signs. That is, there was no 'forensic evidence' which might have been recorded as 'not been interfered with sexually', but there were physical signs which might also be consistent with constipation. During the research, police officers and social workers were heard to say 'there's no evidence', when they were actually describing a situation where there was no forensic evidence.

Records of investigative practice may well constitute documentary evidence. On the whole, medicals are recorded in social work records in terms of arrangements and outcomes, for example:

Arrangements were made for the child to be examined on Wednesday [date] at our offices. Although I was not involved in this, I understand that the child was in fact examined by [police surgeon] and there was no evidence of anal penetration.

In both short arrangement/outcome entries, and in longer discussions of medical evidence, the account and outcome was never observed to be challenged. Questioning the interpretation made of observed physical symptoms is not an accountable matter. The authority of the medical practitioner as a commentator on child abuse has been noted elsewhere to do with their status and role in case conferences (Hallet & Stevenson, 1980). But, whilst medical practitioners are viewed as the sole arbiters of physical symptomology, attention is not paid to how they practically reason to decide what stands for what. From the case I outline earlier, medical evidence was being used to corroborate the assertion that nothing untoward had happened to the children; that they were nothing other than 'normal' children. Yet, in another case the same symptoms are seen as cause for concern and warrants for further investigation. This suggests that another element, other than an ability to diagnose a physical symptom is in play, and that this could be up for inter-agency scrutiny.

There is also what can be described as a 'recency' effect in the use of medical and other forms of evidence. The most recent explanation appears to be the candidate version which supersedes all others, even though they might contradict, and their points of contradiction have not been noted. In other words, it does not

appear to be the case that new evidence points to a contrary
explanation but rather that the most recently recorded account
is the most salient. For example, in the most recent account
of the case above, it was stated that it was difficult to know
when the 'reddening' had occurred, and it was noted that 'there
was no time at all' — this is once the case had been oriented
to as one which involved the 'normal'. Yet, previously recorded
information indicates a number of opportunities during which the
alleged acts could have occurred. A similar example, though not
about medical evidence, is where practitioners account for their
certainty in the files that a child has been sexually assaulted, on
the basis of the initial interview. Shortly afterwards, the same
practitioners can accept the account of the person believed to be
responsible for the assault, as one of complete innocence. This can
be accounted for with just as much certainty, but not with any
reference to the first version given by the complainant. The effect
is to leave two alternative versions of the same event intact, but the
most recent appears to stand as the strongest indicator of future
intervention. This feature is not observed in all cases, particularly
where there is medical or forensic evidence, or eye witness accounts
which compete. However, it is symptomatic of cases which rely
on verbal evidence alone, thus particularly affecting child sexual
assault cases and should underline the importance of understanding
what an 'unfounded' case actually consists in, and the recording or
measurement of such cases.

There is an issue here about recording practices, which on the
whole, in the sample I examined, would not have withstood
evidential scrutiny. The early stages of an investigation are crucial
in making a case, and matters which might not seem relevant at the
time can become so later. Hence the recommendation in *Working
Together* that:

> The importance of recording at all stages of the child protection
> process cannot be overemphasised . . . . Records must be
> accurate and clear, and contain all the information known
> to the agency about the child and family. Records need to
> reflect all the work which is being done by the worker(s) within
> the agency and they should also indicate working arrangements
> with staff in other agencies. Good quality records are essential
> to inform the work . . . and they should contain clear details
> of the investigation, assessments, the decisions agreed, the basis
> on which they were made and the plan on which work is based.
> p.26 DOH, 1991*b*

What must also be borne in mind is that what is relevant, accurate
and clear are all decidable matters. Attention needs to be paid to

recording so that it consists less of a series of organisational 'glosses', as in the case of 'no evidence', and more in the accurate detail that is obtained from other sources to make up that 'gloss'.

Finally, a further way in which lack of medical and forensic evidence might mitigate against the pursuance of a case in the early stages has to do with non-validation of an allegation, and the effects that this has on the family. The following example shows how lack of medical evidence can be treated by a disbelieving mother.

> When she was told that [child] had said what had happened to her, [mother] said she didn't believe her, that [step-father] wouldn't do anything like that. [The police officer] then told her that [step-father], whom he had spoken to earlier, had admitted doing it to [child] . . . we advised that the two girls should be medically examined and mother agreed to this. She was present when Dr X medically examined the children and both children were found to be sound with no evidence of interference . . . . After the doctor's medical had shown that there was nothing wrong with the girls, [mother] again reiterated that she didn't believe [child] and that [step-father] couldn't have done such things to her.

For some children, their family's failure to believe them, and to side with the person alleged to be responsible, is distressing and has long-lasting consequences for future relationships. It is indicative of how information about medicals should be cautiously disseminated, especially in cases where there is no parental support for the child.

This practical, and emotional, requirement for some kind of physical proof of harm or injury is also symptomatic of the way in which cases of offences against children are routinely processed by the Crown Prosecution Service, but, crucially, medical evidence is used in much the same way as it is by those originally investigating the case. That is, medical evidence is considered to strengthen a case if the witness account indicates to the lawyer that the evidence might be present: it is used to corroborate a verbal account. Of the 65 cases examined in the CPS study, concerning all types of offences against children, approximately half (34) were accompanied by some form of medical evidence. This was either supportive (27), inconclusive (3) or non-supportive (4). Only one of the non-supportive cases rendered a not guilty verdict, the other three resulted in guilty pleas. All of the cases involving physical assault contained medical evidence, and the remainder were sexual offences. However, as I noted earlier, the majority of sexual offences had no medical evidence yet still proceeded.

The *Memorandum of Good Practice* states that sufficient time must be allowed before the substantive interview for a medical to take place. Each case should be taken individually, and it may be that the relevance of a medical does not transpire until after the interview. The planning and consultation phase of an investigation must include some discussion about when, and whether, to conduct a medical examination. This, however, does raise the issue of parental and child choice, which should be considered in all cases. There are two points here; first, that taking account of the child's wishes and feelings may prove organisationally difficult (Wattam & Barford, 1992). For example, where a child clearly expresses a wish to be examined by a female or male doctor and there is no one easily, or immediately, available, or where the child does not consent to the medical. There were no cases in either sample where the parent or child did not consent to a medical examination. It is, therefore, difficult to know how absence of consent, either by the child or parent, will operate as an evidential variable.

A further issue to do with consent is the way in which the child is informed about the examination and the purpose of it if the medical is conducted prior to the substantive interview. Care must be taken not to explain the reason for the medical in terms which might prejudge that something has happened to a child. Attention should also be paid to the way in which the examination is recorded. It is not unusual for children to talk spontaneously about who has touched them, and where, in response to a doctor's enquiries. The information can then be developed, in a non-leading way, in the substantive interview.

This raises the question about when to do the medical. The *Memorandum* suggests that medicals should be carried out before the substantive interview. There is a danger, however, that medicals could become a routine part of the investigation.[4] In practice, much will hinge on when a referral becomes a complaint, an issue I address in Chapter 6, and the time and resources available. A general rule of thumb would be to consider the timing of the medical examination at the strategy or planning meeting, and to conduct one prior to the substantive interview if the allegation and information obtained at the planning stage suggests that medical or forensic evidence might be obtainable. It is better to enter the substantive interview with some evidence already established (although its explanation should not be pre-judged) than to have none at all.

To conclude, a clear distinction needs to be maintained, for the purposes of recording and compiling evidence, between medical and forensic evidence. In practice, this distinction was not observed, and conclusions were drawn about the lack of forensic evidence — which is rarely found, and medical symptoms — which are diagnosed occasionally but are, in themselves, inconclusive. Consideration should be given to:

(a) the purpose of doing a medical or forensic examination in each respective case. The full context of the allegation needs to be taken into account, not just what the child, or referrer, has said.
(b) the timing of the medical examination in relation to referral information, for example, if the complaint is of non-recent assault is an immediate medical necessary?
(c) previous medically related contact and how this relates to the present investigation. For example, has the child been appropriately examined or not? Do not assume that s/he has.
(d) cases where the medical examination does not corroborate the child's account. This is a topic for further exploration in the substantive interview, and should not automatically be assumed to mean that nothing has happened.
(e) the recording and dissemination of the results of a medical, particularly in relation to prospective use as documentary evidence, and also by the child's family.
(f) further development in the pursuit of forensic evidence, shifting the focus away from evidences of *sexual acts*, and on to the corroboration of other elements contained in the child's account.

## Notes

1. The practitioner involved in encouraging the mother to report this case clearly believed that these children had been abused. It is not my intention to speculate on 'good' and 'bad' handling of cases, though many readers will probably have drawn their own conclusions here. My task is to display how such outcomes are achieved, in the hope that explicating the process will enable those involved in decision making to appraise their decisions in the light of such structures, and not on the content alone, as has more traditionally been the case.
2. Resources are an obvious problem here. In the report of the research to the ACPC it was thought impossible to investigate anything but a small minority of allegations in this way. That, however, is an important point to note in itself. Is it the case that cases fail to proceed because of lack of evidence, or because of an inability to pursue evidence because of a lack of resources?
3. This refers to an act whereby the penis is inserted between the legs at the top of the thighs and the child is instructed to keep his or her legs tightly closed.
4. There is a major question concerning privacy and children's rights connected with this issue, which I cannot enter into here. However, the type of medical examination associated with sexual assault is detailed even in its least contentious format, to be possibly construed as abusive in itself by some parents. This issue of the 'abuse' potential of investigative practices has also been considered in the use of anatomically complete dolls (Westcott, H., Davies, G. & Clifford, B., 'The use of anatomically correct dolls in child witness interviews'. *Adoption and Fostering*, 13, pp.6–14)

# 5 The practice of interviewing children on video before the *Memorandum*

When Judge Pigot was commissioned to look into the admissibility of pre-recorded video evidence in criminal cases, it was suggested that one factor which required consideration was the influence that the 'prospect of use', of videos in court, might have on the making of them. The Home Secretary wrote:

> Immediately attractive as this idea is, we have had some doubts about whether it would actually have the effect of making things easier for the child victim, and can see grounds for fearing that it might make matters worse. If the accused contested his guilt, the child would not be spared having to give evidence again at the time of the trial, since we could not contemplate removing the right of the accused to have such a crucial witness cross-examined at his trial. There could also be problems over editing the tape, which may well contain material which would be inadmissible for other reasons, and it is not altogether clear what effect the prospect of *use in court would have on the extent to which the original interviews served their main purpose of aiding the police and caring agencies.* Home Office, 1989 (my emphasis)

The concerns expressed here about cross-examination and in-admissibility are dealt with elsewhere in this book. In this chapter, I want to use the materials from the child protection study to show how substantive interviews were conducted prior to the *Memorandum of Good Practice*, and, in doing so, to raise questions about what the main purpose was so far as the police and caring agencies were concerned, and further, to ask whether this purpose was achieved. These questions are crucial to understanding the process of interviewing children and obtaining evidence to make a case. They are also central to the decision-making process in terms of selecting routes for child protection case plans.

The years covered by the child protection study were 1986 to 1988, thus video-recorded evidence was not admissible in criminal proceedings. It was, however, admissible in wardship and care proceedings, and could be used by the police as a resource when interviewing a suspect. At the time, it was generally thought that video interviews were also conducted for therapeutic purposes. Whilst this was undoubtedly the case in one or two areas (Great Ormond Street for example, Bentovim et al., 1988) the child protection study suggested that, elsewhere, a different process might be in operation.

The 'Bexley' experiment (Metropolitan Police and Bexley Social Services, 1988) was widely accepted as a prototype model for the investigation of child sexual abuse. Following this approach, a social worker and a police officer would jointly interview a child in an attempt to combine the roles of investigation, prosecution and child protection, and the interview would be video recorded. Prior to Bexley, and similar attempts at joint investigation elsewhere, a child protection referral would be investigated by the agency to which it was referred, usually the social services department in the case of child sexual assault, and that agency would alert the other if it was considered relevant after the investigative assessment. The aim of joint interviewing was to combine protective and investigative tasks, and primarily to reduce the number of times the child had to give their account, by combining the police and social work roles within the interview. However, it was clear from the materials in the child protection study that, in initial assessment interviews, where videoed, these aims were not achieved. The various routes to referral usually meant that the child still had to tell of her/his experience more than once, and, rather than combining roles, it was more often the case that the interviews were conducted with the evidential requirements and legal restraints as paramount considerations. This was probably a result of two factors: first, their potential admissibility as evidence, and secondly, because they involved and, in many areas, were led by police officers who are accustomed to interviewing under the rules of evidence. Thus, there was information on how the prospect of use in court influenced both the investigation and the child. Whilst the Advisory Group did consider the issue of cross-examination, and editing, it did not examine how the adherence to legal requirements might affect the child, and crucially, the quality of information obtained for child protection purposes. The findings of the child protection study, and also early observations of the *MOGP* in pilot (Wattam, 1992), suggest that legal requirements may actually prejudice the type and amount of information obtained with the consequence of weakening cases and leaving children vulnerable.

When this finding is placed in the context of the increasing dominance of the legal discourse in child protection practice (Parton, 1991), it can be seen how interviewing for evidence can also have the effect of reducing child protection intervention. Given that up to 75% of cases 'drop out' of the investigation process prior to, or at the point of, the case conference (Giller et al., 1992), questions must be asked about why this occurs. It will always happen that some referrals do constitute unsubstantiated cases, but this is unlikely to account for 75% of all referrals. My own study indicates that one important factor in determining whether cases proceed or not is the presence or absence of evidence, and the prospect of court action, civil or criminal. The organisational response appeared to be predisposed towards an investigative framework, and particularly to the pursuit of evidence, once the grounds for action in a case were established. Less than half the referrals incurred further involvement after the initial investigative assessment, and only a quarter of all referrals had continuing involvement at six months. Whilst 73% of cases did involve an investigation, in contrast, very few children (less than 10%) were offered treatment post-investigation, even where the investigation substantiates the allegation (Wattam, 1991; Thorpe & Denman, 1992).

The structures for building cases, those of specificity, categorisation, corroboration and motive, operate at the initial interview as they do in other parts of the investigation. There is some indication, however, that their importance is related to stages of the investigative assessment, so that, as we have seen in Chapter 2, motive is salient at the point of allegation making and later, in Chapter 4, that corroboration is strongly relevant to medical and forensic evidence. The structure of specificity appeared to be more closely connected to perceptions about the child's credibility, which, in practice, turns into a focus on detail, and was most relevant at the interview stage. In the first part of this chapter an example of a video interview highlights the way in which the search for detail is conducted[1] and shows how it might happen that interviews may not render good evidence and result in a case being dropped. A second reason for focusing on the fact that interviews pre-*MOGP* have been conducted with a view to evidential requirements is that something can be learned about how, and why, evidential requirements are difficult to meet in practice. I therefore use this example to begin to indicate some of the more problematic areas for change, bearing in mind the requirements of the *Memorandum of Good Practice*. The second part of the chapter takes the analysis further by utilising a framework derived from a sociological tradition of examining conversational practices. Looking at the interview in this framework shows how the process might be difficult for children, how it mitigates against getting further information, and what improvements in the interview can be made in the light of it.

Whilst undertaking the child protection study, I interviewed a number of social workers, some of whom had worked with both adult and child victims of sexual abuse. One worker made a comment which seemed to contradict a presumption that children will be willing to talk about the details of their experience:

> [Adult survivors] all have something they want to get off their chests. It's a bit like when people are dying, they want to talk about some dark secret they'll go to hell for. It's very difficult when it might seem so trivial. Adults, when they get 'that bit' out in the open, they start to heal. A lot of it is to do with the actual physical description of the abuse. They seem to want to tell the details so it's not in their heads, their memories, and they've handed it over . . . . We don't always let children talk about details, but they're usually not able to do it. Of all the kids I've worked with I can think of just four that could give nitty gritty detail. But adult women can. Children don't seem to have the emotional capacity to deal with it, it's only in adulthood that they are able to recognise it.

She went on to give an example of a woman who had been abused as a child. From that example it is clear the details to which she was referring were very specific matters. The example cannot be given here because these are the kind of details that thoroughly personalize the experience, make it very much *that* person's experience, and thus, very difficult to share. These are, however, also the details which would be considered important in evidential terms for the 'truth value' or credibility of accounts. Whilst the comment above does only represent one practitioner's experience, it is notable because it cuts across an assumption often made in legal settings. That is, the more detailed a child's account is, the more likely it is to be true. This is based on a further assumption that an abusing event will be memorable and traumatic for a child and they will therefore be able to recall it in detail (Undeutsch, 1990). Such an assumption does not take into account levels of trauma during the experience, blocking, reframing the experience as non-abusive, or even not knowing the experience was abusive in the first place.

However, the search for detail was omnipresent in the interviews I observed on video tape. The following is an extract from an interview with a 12 year-old girl:

MPO  = male police officer
FPO  = female police officer
C     = child

MPO '. . . If you can start, the thing is to start from the beginning, that's the main thing, alright?

C It first happened when I were about 7, I'd been ill, I was sick and got in like me Mum's bed, me Mum and me Dad, and a while later I couldn't go to sleep and then me dad started to kiss me and everything and then he started like rubbing his hands up and down me and I went to the toilet and was sick and got back in my own bed and he came out to me and he started kissing me and that, and I told him I didn't feel well and goes 'Oh well, we'll have to do something tomorrow' and eh, and then he left me and then if me mum went out or anything he'd start like kissing me and everything.

MPO Can I just stop you there, can we just go back to what you were first saying, you weren't feeling very well. What was wrong with you?

C I were just ill

MPO Just sickly ill?

C Yeah

MPO Oh right, and you were in your mum's bed and your dad started kissing you. Is that wrong, there's nothing wrong with that is there?

C No, but

MPO I mean I kiss my children

C Yes, but kissing like wrong do you know what I mean?

MPO Can you explain to me what you mean?

FPO More detail than that.

The child offers an account of what happened to her in terms of 'everything' or 'and that'. Whilst this would be sufficient in some contexts, sufficient to know something had happened, it is not here accepted as an adequate account. The reason for this is not that it is an insufficient account in order to help the child, clearly something is happening to her that the child considered to be 'wrong' which has to do with the way her stepfather touched and kissed her. At this very early point in the investigation, if the team were going at the child's pace, it might be considered appropriate to accept that this was all the child was prepared to say at that stage. However, the team press for 'more detail'. One framework for making sense of the quest for detail is that of

evidential requirements. The team want the child's account to stand
as evidence in itself of a crime committed. This child, and many
others, found talking about 'the nitty gritty' very difficult. Part of
the problem was understanding what it was they should be saying
— after all 'everything' can be seen as adequate, as could 'kissing
like wrong'. That statement is focused on and the child is asked
to clarify it more than once. She then offers 'like me dad kisses
me mum', but this too required clarification. Eventually the social
worker intervenes and asks a more specific question which the child
readily answers.

> SW: '. . . whereabouts was he kissing you?
> C: Like on me lips and all round me face and everything
> SW: Anywhere else?
> C: And eh, no but he were like kissing me wrong, do you know
> what I mean?
> SW: (Yes) were they sort of like longer kisses not just pecks on
> the cheek?
> C: Yes.

It is clear that the perceived evidential needs are here being
juxtaposed with the child's needs. The social worker is trying to
help, without using leading or closed questions, but in fact does
end up using one. All three adults are in an artificial situation,
in which they have to account for their apparent inability to
carry out 'business as usual'. That is, to know the things adults
should know about and display this as known in the course of an
'ordinary' conversation. Because of this they resort to the following
explanations of why things are 'unordinary':

> 'We know what it means, but it's got to come from you, OK?
> Do you understand, you're alright, just relax?'
> and
> 'How do you mean, you see we've got to be careful we don't
> put words into your mouth. We don't want to say things for
> you, you've got to say them yourself, do you understand?'

Both of these statements point to the way in which this interview
was constructed for evidential purposes. But the interview also
stands as an example of the perceived evidential requirements by
these particular people.

The problem which faces practitioners who must get children to
talk in an evidentially sound manner is that it is not always possible.
Not because practitioners are not skilled, not because they make
mistakes (although both of these can occur), but because children,
by and large, don't know the rules. Children are unaware of the

ways in which familiar adult–child interaction is transformed into
'interaction-for-the-purpose-of-obtaining-evidence'. Relevant to this
is the different way in which the child's own story can be presented.
This can be illustrated with a research interview with one of the
children from the child protection study. On reading through the
transcript, I began to ask why, in the context of a research interview
on telling others about her experience, this girl had elected to say
all the things she did. A large part of the interview seemed, in
that immediate context, irrelevant. She talked at length about her
relationship with her stepfather (X), in terms of what they did, what
he said, what she said, where they were at the time and so on. The
following is an extract from that account:

> Well X said to me last year, well I was going round with this
> lad, well I wasn't going out with him just sort of a friend, and
> he worked for X and (  ) I mean, I hardly ever go out with
> boys you know, I'd known him for ages and he was just sort
> of a friend and (I wanted to see him), not every night, once
> a week perhaps and X knew that I was seeing somebody, he
> didn't know who, it was because [name of boy] rang up our
> house to ask X if he could borrow the van, and X said 'I've
> a list of six names here who [have been] talking about him'.
> Anyway on Thursday, it was the week before I came to work
> up here, and he said, X came upstairs, and he said 'do you want
> a cup of coffee' and I knew that he knew that I was seeing [name
> of boy] and I said 'no thanks, I'm not bothered', and I said
> 'but I'll have a cup of tea' and he said 'right, but come down
> then', so I went downstairs, he said 'let's go outside then', so I
> got outside [and lit a] cigarette and he said 'it's [name of boy],
> why haven't you told me?' I said 'well I didn't think it was any
> of your business' and 'where you've done it, in the back of his
> car, in my shop?' he said, 'cheeky little sod and cheap tart'. I
> said 'no X, actually I never have done it', 'well' he said 'look
> A I'm only trying to save you', 'SAVE?' I said, 'Oh God' and
> X said 'Do you remember (  ) I'm only trying to save you like
> you saved me' and I wanted to scream (  ) 'And you saved me',
> he said 'I'd be in prison now if it wasn't for you' he said 'I'm
> just trying to save you"
> Interviewer: How did you save him?
> Respondent: Well, I don't know what he was talking about,
> probably if I'd ever told (my social worker), do you know what
> I mean?'

After looking at this again and again, and the pages of similar talk, I
realised that this was an account of how telling, or not telling others,
surfaces in all its relevant detail for the child concerned. I have also

looked at statements, and the above is neither characteristic of these
or the type of interview from which the first extract was taken.
These other formulations are generally less articulate, less fluent
and, crucially, they are focused on the required details of *sexual
acts*. This girl talked around sex, and this is the way that sex is
talked about as 'a rule'. Sacks noted that:

> . . . to put it in a slightly paradoxical fashion . . . that
> the proper literal way to talk about sex is to talk about it
> allusively . . . so that if you talk about sex literally you're not
> talking about sex properly, you're talking about sex 'frankly'.
> That is to say, what would otherwise be ordinary talk about
> some other topic, talked of in the same way for sex it's
> 'talking frankly'. What would be for some other topic talking
> about it allusively is talking about sex, in effect, literally. So
> the language for talking about sex, and the language for
> talking about a variety of other things is specifically allusive.
> Sacks, 1971

Talking about sex allusively being the proper way in which sex is
talked about, is a known-in-common feature of our culture. It is not
assumed that people who talk this way are avoiding the real topic
of sex; rather they are pointing to it in the way that talk about sex
is socially organised. Thus, in talking around sex, in alluding to it,
children are talking about it, but without the detailed event focus
that is required by the investigating team. Given the objectives of
an investigation, to produce evidentially sound material, allusive
talk about sex is rarely sufficient, although it may be sufficient to
make the child appear credible. What is required is a decidable
definiteness as to what has happened, in terms of details, times,
verifiable instances, and so on. However, if one of the criteria
for credibility in our ordinary conversation about sex is that it is
not talked about in terms of the minute physical detail of sexual
acts, that feature which is *thought* to lend credibility will be missing
from evidence presented to the courts. Hence, it is crucial that
children should be enabled and facilitated to talk about anything
and everything that they perceive to be relevant, freely and without
interruption. The free recall stage in the recommended interview
protocol of the MOGP is there for that purpose. Interviewers must
be careful not to frame the interview in terms of details of acts,
rather, they should attempt to obtain the child's relevance whether
it be the washing up, eating an evening meal with the accused, or
whatever.

The interview from which the first extract was taken can be
reviewed in terms of what can go wrong because of immediate
practical considerations. Such a review indicates some of the areas

which the *Memorandum of Good Practice* has sought to address, in principle. The features highlighted by this interview are drawn out to illustrate the importance of guidance contained within the *MOGP*, but also to show how the context and situation of the substantive interview predisposes it to certain actions, and how it is difficult in practice to do otherwise.

Firstly, no one was introduced to the child. The cameras began working when the child was sitting in the room with one of the interviewers. They were 'chatting' about school. This lasted for approximately 2 minutes when a social worker and another police officer came into the room. At that point, the conversation stopped and the social worker inquired as to where she should sit, the police officer said 'sit next to her if you like', pointing to the child. One reason why no one was introduced was because everybody already knew of each other. The referral, which had been made the day before, had resulted in the child being seen and taken into care on a temporary order. The investigation was already in full swing, and all these people had been involved either from the outset, or well before the videoed interview. However, the assumption that a child knows who people are, and more importantly, what they do, and why they are there, cannot be made. Children state that, despite knowing people's names, and even jobs, this does not adequately explain for them who is involved, at what point, and why (Wattam & Barford, 1992).

This also points to the importance of handling the pre-interview stage carefully. The *Memorandum* acknowledges the need for some initial questioning, to establish whether there is a need to consider criminal investigation. The operative word is 'whether', and not in detail 'what'. It can be decided on the kind of information that a child might give freely that something bad has happened, that my Dad's been kissing me 'wrong' and so on, without probing for further detail, that there is an indication that something may have happened to a child which requires investigation. Some children will say a great deal more than this. In such cases, the *MOGP* directs practitioners to listen to the child, rather than question, and to note the discussion in detail. In certain cases, the need to afford the child immediate protection under an Emergency Protection Order, will necessitate interviewing the child. However, even in these cases, it is important for practitioners to know where to stop, and that decision can only be made with reference to the purpose for the interview.

Secondly, the 'rapport phase' consisted of a 2 minute talk about school before everyone was present, and approximately three minutes of questioning on family names, addresses, household details and favourite subjects at school once they were. This was not uncommon. The *MOGP* notes that the aim of the rapport phase is to help the child relax, but that there is an additional function of providing information — about the child's developmental level, communication skills and so forth — with which to assess information already gathered at the planning stage. I would suggest that there is a potential third function to the rapport phase, that of familiarising the child with the way in which s/he is expected to give an account, which is discussed in more detail below. Whatever the case, and for these reasons, the MOGP states that:

> The rapport phase should not be omitted even if the child has had significant previous contact with the interviewer.

At some point during this phase, the reason for the interview should be explained, without referring to the alleged offence. In practice, this is a very difficult task to accomplish. In the interview above, it was just stated to the child 'You know why we're here'. Because of the previous contact in this, and in many other cases, the explanation for the interview has often been given prior to the interview taking place. However, whilst that is expectable, it is not satisfactory evidentially because it indicates that discussion about the interview has already occurred, and opens the interview up to criticisms about coaching and pre-judging the issue. Each case will need to be considered in the light of individual circumstances. It is permissible for the interviewer to say that

> he or she wants to talk about something the child has told to someone else.

although the substance of any previous disclosure should not be referred to, since this is hearsay. Where there has been no previous disclosure, it may be possible to context explanation for the interview in terms of an explanation of who the interviewer is, for example

> Hello, my name is . . . . I am a social worker and one of my jobs is to talk to children. Sometimes children tell me good things about themselves, and sometimes they tell me about things that upset them. I have been asked to talk to you today, do you have anything you want to tell me?

It is best not to frame explanations just in terms of unhappiness, e.g. 'something seems to be making you unhappy', since this could also be viewed as pre-judging the issue.

There is an element of dishonesty here, in that none of these examples constitutes real explanations for the interview. The interview is not just about finding out what might have happened to a child. It is also about providing evidence, which is why it is on video. This brings up the issue of informed consent, and whether children are able to consent to something they do not fully understand. The *MOGP* advises that formal written consent is not required, but states that the consent of the child should be sought where appropriate. It is important to acknowledge that the way in which the issue of consent is dealt with at the interview, and throughout the investigation, is a matter of professional judgement and one which needs consideration at the strategy meeting. Discussion could be focused around the question of how the purpose of the interview is to be explained, bearing the following criteria in mind: Do not couch the explanation in any way that a) pre-judges what might be said, b) is dishonest, c) makes promises that cannot be kept. Do consider a) the child's age and ability to consent b) the issue of parental consent (see Chapter 6).

Thirdly, whilst the child is no longer assumed incompetent,[2] it is still recommended that it is established that the child understands the importance of telling the truth. In this interview, the issue was covered with 'the main thing is to tell the truth, alright?' which clearly would not display the child's understanding of what telling the truth consists in. One obvious way is to give the child a false statement and to ask whether it is true or a lie. The important thing is to do this in a way which does not imply that the child might be lying. In order to avoid intimations of lying, it is also suggested that the issue is covered in the rapport phase, and not subsequently. If the question of whether the child knows what the truth is, or not, comes up during, or after, their account, it may leave the child feeling s/he is being doubted. It does not have to be a long and complicated discussion; in one case observed, the interviewer ended up in a lengthy debate about the difference between 'telling lies' and 'telling tales', but sufficient to show the child understands what telling the truth means.

Fourthly, there are three adults present, all of whom ask the child questions. In this interview, the social worker had her arm round the back of the child and it was not possible to see body contact. Because of the camera angle, and number of adults in the room, it is not possible to see all the adults fully, and thus what they might be doing. This would, in itself, disqualify the interview under the *MOGP* because it would not be possible adequately to display the circumstances under which it was made. In addition, the *MOGP* recommends that only one person leads the interview and asks the questions, and that, if two people are doing the interview, one should make notes about possible questions to come back to. When the child begins her account, she is stopped. Thus, there is no 'free narrative' stage. The child can no longer tell her story in her own words. Initially, the questions are for clarification. Under the *MOGP* these should be noted and returned to once the child has finished talking.

The interview example above was carried out to obtain evidence that would satisfy a court. It may never have gone to court, but one overriding purpose of conducting the interview, and constructing it in this way, is that it might have done. Hence, the participants cannot have an 'ordinary' conversation, they must, whether they like it or not, 'breach' what is usually taken for granted as shared-in-common knowledge. They cannot be seen to take certain things for granted because, at some later date, it might be alleged that the interview had been pre-judged. In a legal context, that would be interpreted as a shortcoming of the evidence and proof, or disproof, of a whole case could rest on the interpretation made of it.

In making this statement I have used some terms which require clarification. The first of these is 'ordinary' conversation. By ordinary, I am not here referring to the topic of conversation, such as who will pick the children up from school or what the weather is like, or some other 'routine' matter. Ordinary conversations are denoted by their structural qualities; those of turn-taking, question and answer, leading into, and out of, topics and so forth. We may have ordinary conversations about special topics or mundane topics. The point is that people are capable of doing so because they are, on the whole, familiar with the expectable 'rules' of conversation within our culture. Conversations could be considered 'unordinary' where there are imposed alterations on the structure, such as where some form of ritual is in force, for example, church services, or formal interviews, in other words, those where different or additional rules are operating, such as the rules of evidence.

Garfinkel (1967) outlined some essential features for ordinary conversations. He observed that, without these features, conversations would be difficult to carry out in the form in which we know them. In order to demonstrate this, he asked students to report on a conversation. On one side of a page, the students had to write down what was actually said. On the other, they were asked to write what they and the co-conversationalist understood they were talking about. Predictably, what was said could be elaborated on; there were many matters which were mutually understood that were not articulated. If it were necessary to explain in every detail how it has come about that conversationalists are able to say each and every particular expression, conversations would never get completed. So, one point about ordinary conversation is that it takes certain things for granted; namely, that there is an amount of shared-in-common knowledge about the means, the 'methods' by which conversations will be sustained throughout their course. Garfinkel refers to these as the 'sanctioned properties of common discourse' and they include:

> The anticipation that persons will understand, the occasionality of expressions, the specific vagueness of references, the retrospective–prospective sense of a present occurrence, waiting for something later in order to see what was meant before . . . p.41

These are known as 'sanctioned' because, when people attempt to hold a conversation, ignoring them they get into difficulties. Furthermore, conversationalists can 'sanction' each other for breaches of these properties. These sanctions can come in many forms, including amusement, anger, bewilderment, distress, and even a refusal to converse further.

Without information to the contrary, children will anticipate that the conversation they are about to have in a 'substantive' interview will be an 'ordinary' conversation. They will not know that the rules are different. Thus, we can anticipate that they will frame what they are saying using the features Garfinkel outlines. In the interview above, the child anticipates that the interviewers will understand what she is talking about, that the meaning of her expressions is given in the occasions on which they are offered. For example, when the social worker asks '. . . whereabouts was he kissing you' she anticipates the child will know that this refers to the previous occasion of talking about kissing in the conversation, and when the child answers 'Like on me lips and all round me face and everything' she anticipates that the 'everything' will make sense in terms of what preceded it, *and will add sense to what preceded it*. This is her attempt to explain, and it will be hard for her to know just in what particular way her statement is inadequate.

There has been growing research interest on the trauma associated with court testimony. One criticism that was levied in the literature has to do with the anecdotal nature of existing evidence, and possible bias in the research (Goodman et al., 1988). The feature of 'unordinariness' was massively evident in the interviews I observed. By taking examples to display it, I am not picking one case that happened to be like that. All the interviews, and certainly all 'substantive interviews' in the future, must be conducted under the rules of evidence, and these are not entirely the rules of ordinary conversation. As a consequence, it is likely that some children will continue to be 'thrown and helpless', and might find the experience 'painful' (Wattam, 1991). In others, talking about abusive experiences may be difficult in itself. However, account does not seem to be taken, and opportunities sought to rectify, the un-ordinary situation in which children find themselves. The effect is a situation pre-disposed, by its very structure, to make the child feel doubted and confused.

Having made the point that interviews represent un-ordinary situations, the very fact that the participants are conversing at all shows that certain features of ordinary conversations are retained, so that, on the one hand, the rules are attended to, for example, the child is asked a question, she anticipates she should reply, the child asks a question and anticipates a reply and so on. On the other, they are breached, one answer is not adequate, nor a second, nor a third. More and more detail is required at a point where the child might think that these adults must know what she is talking about (especially if she has been through her experiences with one of them before). The interviewers do not say why things have to be this way. Children, and also adults, need to know what, in particular, is being asked for out of a whole host of things that could be talked about. In this case, the child's first attempt is one which she considers adequate. Her use of 'everything' and 'and that' says it all. What more do they need to know? The ensuing conversation makes an attempt to explain what more is needed. However, she is clearly still not able to meet the interviewer's requirements, what more must she say then? This, I suggest, is one reason why many children can appear confused, frustrated and angry, both in these interviews and in court. Without knowing why, and, crucially, without knowing what the rules are, they must inevitably draw their own conclusions. One conclusion, even where interviewers comment to the contrary, is that they are not being believed.

It might be said that these features are not really that con-sequential in the long run. After all things can be talked about, and explained at a later date, possibly in a therapeutic setting. In terms of damage to the child, they are potentially quite minor matters, that can be put down to the discomfort of misunderstanding. However, it is necessary to consider what the consequences might be in terms of the process as a whole. First, a frequent reason children give for not reporting abusive experiences is that they fear disbelief. If the style in which they are interviewed must inevitably reinforce that they might be doubted, it is likely to reinforce their original fear. A consequence might be retraction, refusal to give any more information and minimalising the amount of information given. In short, it may well have the consequence of stopping the process altogether. Secondly, if it is not possible to facilitate children using the tools of ordinary conversation, it is likely that some information may be left unsaid, so that, in practical terms, interviewers are not going along the best route for information-gathering.

The problem remains that practitioners are bound by evidential constraints. One way to get round this is to find a means of informing the child of the different rules, without prejudicing the evidence. Earlier, I suggest that the rapport phase can be used to familiarise the child with the requirements of the interview. As King and Yuille (1987) point out, children who are placed in the artificial situations induced by experimental research are generally prepared by familiarising them with the task at hand. In a similar way, it is possible to identify the attributes required to give good evidence and make some attempt to familiarise the child with them early in the interview. 'Good' evidence is generally credible evidence, and, as I have already shown, credibility is achieved through the structures of specificity, motive, corroboration and categorisation. Thus, one key factor is the amount of detail recalled without prompting from questions, and another is the confidence of the child (Davies & Noon, 1991). Some suggestions about preparation for the interview which give the child an indication of what is expected, and therefore seek to minimise the distracting effects of 'un-ordinariness', are given in Chapter 7.

The rationale for joint interviews given earlier needs to be reviewed in terms of the observed practice. Was the main purpose to find out what if anything had happened, or was it that the investigating team already had some idea of what had happened, but they needed the child's explanation of it on video? In my initial discussions with team members during the child protection study, there was concern that practitioners often came out of the interviews with the same amount of information as they had when they started. There was also an acknowledgement that there were things said to children which were considered to constitute a form of secondary abuse, such as the child who was asked 13 times whether she was lying. These two observations begin to point to the implications for present interviewing practice and decisions about diverting from the *MOGP*. Interviewing for evidence should only be pursued if it is compatible with the child protection purpose, which is to ensure the child is safe. If it is not possible to do an evidentially sound interview, then so be it. The *MOGP* can give guidance on what such an interview should consist of, but it should not be followed at the expense of protective action. This may seem like quite an obvious statement; most practitioners would not willingly leave a child at risk just because there is insufficient evidence for a court. However, it needs to be clearly stated, and seen, that the whole investigative process is pre-disposed, right down to the selection of words used with any particular child, towards getting evidence, and that risk is determined within the context of that. It is therefore important to see how the nature of what constitutes evidence needs to be broadened out to include information relevant to the child.

The prospect of use of these videos in court has had profound effects on the process for children. First, interviewing under perceived evidential constraints can limit the kind of information obtained. In particular, it pre-disposes towards a focus on a sexual event, and discourages talk about people and experiences which might be relevant to the child's experience. Breaching the rules of 'ordinary' conversation might have the effect of leaving the child feeling doubted or confused, (one of the key reasons given for not reporting in the first place), and feeling unsure of what is expected of her/him and the kind of detail that is required. There is, therefore, a danger that the pursuit of evidence can interfere with, or jeopardise, a protective emphasis.

## Notes

1. Other structures are in evidence throughout the interview, and, in the extract given, the use of categorisation is also clear. However, this is an analytic point and will be explored further elsewhere.
2. Before the Criminal Justice Act 1991, children were considered incompetent unless the court was satisfied that they could distinguish the difference between telling the truth and telling lies, and understood the importance of telling the truth.

# 6 Making the decision to interview

This chapter will examine decision-making in relation to the pre-interview stage within the framework of the Children Act, 1989, *Working Together under the Children Act*, 1989 (DOH, 1991*b*) and the *Memorandum of Good Practice* (Criminal Justice Act, 1991) on interviewing children for criminal proceedings. The attempt to combine these three documents will be the practitioner's lot, and, as this chapter will show, not an easy one. Laws and procedures provide the organisational framework and rules, but rule-following is an achieved matter subject to interpretation and application under practical circumstances (Bittner, 1965). In showing how rules are applied, it begins to be possible to reflect the complexities of investigative practice and to enable informed decision-making on the basis of understanding it.

Under Section 47 of the Children Act, 1989, the local authority has a duty to investigate allegations of child abuse. This entails making enquiries to enable it to decide whether action is required to safeguard or promote a child's welfare. In particular, enquiries should be directed towards deciding whether application needs to be made for a court order, or whether any other powers invested in the local authority under the Act needs to be exercised, and where the child should best be accommodated. *Working Together under the Children Act, 1989* (DOH, 1991*b*) endorses the principles which underpin the Act and are relevant to investigation. These are a focus on the welfare of the child, parental responsibility, partnership with parents and other family members, and support of the child within the family wherever possible.

The main purpose of the *MOGP* is to guide practitioners in making video recordings of child witnesses for criminal proceedings. The advice contained within it is about talking with the child in a way which is evidentially acceptable. The principles underpinning evidential requirements have to do with not pre-judging the issue, and allowing the facts to speak for themselves. Thus, in the *MOGP*, evidential requirements are paramount, and, in the Children Act, the child is paramount. This would not matter if the civil and the criminal, the two processes of protection and prosecution, could be kept distinct from each other. However, with the advent of joint investigation and the pairing of protection and prosecution issues at the very beginning of a child protection investigation, it becomes a matter of some consequence.

Because the purpose of the *Memorandum of Good Practice* is to encourage best practice in obtaining evidence from children, there are what might appear to be some contradictions. These contradictions stem from the inherent conflict between legal and therapeutic intervention. The following extract from *Working Together* is symptomatic of that divide.

> Where the police are undertaking a parallel investigation which may lead to prosecution of an alleged abuser, there are important issues to be considered about the need for the child to receive appropriate counselling and support and the need for the child to appear as a credible witness in court. p.28

At the centre of the conflict are the interests of children and the interests of justice. They are not mutually exclusive, but, in the course of an investigation, it is police officers and social workers who must balance these two interests, and decide when one does act against the other which one should take precedence. Hitherto, this professional decision has not been acknowledged in the aims of joint working. Rather, the anticipated benefits of a joint approach have been given as:

(*a*)   A reduction in the number of occasions children are interviewed;

(*b*)   Establishment of a clearer understanding of individual worker's roles;

(*c*)   Increased co-ordination in the delivery of services;

(*d*)   Establishment of group support for difficult decisions;

(*e*)   Increase in effective communication between professionals. Conroy et al., 1988

Better decision-making about which route to follow is, at a hazarded guess, intended as an outcome of these aims. However, as Kelly and Regan (1990) point out, even if it can be shown that the stated aims are achieved, it cannot be shown that joint working results in better decision-making, and better outcomes for children and their families.

There are at least two issues in relation to the *MOGP* which, if not carefully considered at the early stages of an investigation, are likely to emphasise the evidential focus to the detriment of the child. The first is related to the status of the interview, the second to joint working and the difference between a referral and a complaint. Given the already oriented to response of getting evidence before, or instead of, offering help, it is important that these issues are highlighted and understood if a child centred approach is to be the practice.

The 'substantive' interview to be conducted under the *Memorandum of Good Practice* is intended to take the place of 'evidence in chief'. This means that the child still has to go to court, but that s/he needs only to be there for cross-examination on the evidence s/he has already given on video. Whereas, in the past, children have had to go through their original statement concerning the allegation again, sometimes several months later, now they should not have to.[1] The video stands as evidence of their first account, and thus, in principle, this should be easier for the child. However, whilst, before, the evidential standards were those which applied to civil proceedings, and were generally less strenuously interpreted, now the standard required is much higher — hence the need for the *Memorandum*. This also means that the conditions of the interview, from the child's point of view might, in some cases, be more difficult. The effect of giving evidence, in chief, at the beginning of the investigation is that criminal justice criteria are being assessed in, and are being used to assess, a child protection context. As the *Memorandum* states:

> The questioning by the police officer or social worker, in effect, replaces examination of the child by an advocate in open court.

The intention of the *Memorandum* was to make the evidential interviewing of children of a higher quality, a most laudable aim in the context of Cleveland, Manchester, Rochdale and the Orkneys, and, as my own project showed, potentially many more areas as well, where cases of 'well-intentioned' but evidentially flawed interviews acted to undermine cases in court and potentially leave children at risk. However, in aiming to improve matters it has had some consequence which was less intended: Criminal justice criteria have been thrust to the very forefront of child protection investigation. This has at least two quite serious potential repercussions; the first is that the child's immediate needs may, in practice, take a secondary place, and the second is that cases in civil courts could possibly be weakened. Social workers have a strong role to play in making strategic decisions about when, and whether, to conduct a substantive interview under the *MOGP*. With increasing emphasis on the expertise of the police in evidential interviewing, the social-work role must be highlighted, strengthened, and very clear, if practice is to be child-centred.

Stone (1990) made a similar observation about the nature of child protection work in general and suggested that the perceived conflict between a 'humanistic' and a 'control' model was a consequence of a confusion about who was the client and the nature of child abuse, which has traditionally been operationally defined as a familial problem. The 'humanistic' approach was characterised by 'a non-punitive outlook', whereas the 'control' model was symptomatic of 'punishing' (Gelles & Cornell, 1985). If the child is the client, the dichotomy between compassion and control diminishes: the model selected should be the most appropriate for the child concerned. There is no point in going to court unless that strategy is part of an overall child protection plan, or unless it serves the needs of justice and is not to the detriment of the child. Stone suggests that social workers do not fit happily into the criminal justice system and that there are tensions which derive from:

1) The social workers' understanding of the causes of child abuse.
2) Their corresponding perceptions that these causes are not remedied by putting offenders in prisons.
3) The knowledge that prisons have not proved effective in deterring other offenders, or in preventing other types of crimes.
4) The belief that the law and the criminal justice system, is, by and large, the wrong response to the question of child abuse.
5) The investigation and criminalisation of people, whatever wrong they have done, is not a motivation for becoming a social worker; and is at odds with social work values which emphasise the capacity of human beings for growth, learning and change. p.51

These attitudes, once again, reinforce the dichotomy between punishment and compassion. There are clear indications that the criminal justice system does not deal well with child harm and injury, particularly intra-familial uncorroborated child sexual assault. However, there are no clearly agreed criteria by which the effectiveness of alternative therapeutic interventions can be judged, and nothing which states that such interventions cannot be accommodated by a criminal justice system. However, if the dichotomy continues to be reinforced — if social workers interpret their role as *either* extending the policing function of child protection *or* working outside the criminal justice system with alternative approaches, the effect could well be to the detriment of the child. The first puts an unhealthy emphasis on detection and investigation. One interpretation of the *MOGP* could be to reinforce that function, since the majority of referrals have a potential criminal aspect, thus all referrals might be candidates for evidential interviewing under its guidance. The second effectively takes away a child's right to compensation and justice. Social workers, involved from the beginning of this process, now have an obligation to ascertain the child's feelings and wishes, and a professional duty to act to protect the child from further significant harm and injury. They are the key players in deciding whether anything untoward has happened to any particular child, and in devising a plan which will protect them. A child protection plan must consider evidential interviewing.

As Chapter 2 displayed, referrals can often be ambiguous. Of the child sexual abuse referrals which I examined in the child protection study, 15% concerned something which had been said by the child, and 32% concerned sexually related behaviour, both of which could have been considered as possibly symptomatic of sexual abuse. An example would be the following:

> Mother concerned about possible sexual abuse to her 8 year-old daughter by her father. Daughter admitted to her and husband about MGF's[2] 'tickling' ?sexual abuse. She said this had happened more than once when she had been in his home and whilst other members of the family were there. It took the form of touching and tickling.

Is this case appropriate for a 'substantive interview' under the *MOGP*? Under past procedures in the area of my research study, the police child protection team would have been contacted by the social worker after this referral had been received. Given the ambiguous nature of the information, it is likely that one of the investigating team, and probably the social worker, would have seen the child, in this case with her parents. On the basis of the information obtained, a 'joint' interview, that is, one involving the police and social services, would either be set up or dismissed. Part of that information would be based on what the child had said. Further research (Wattam, 1992) indicates that, even where the *MOGP* is being applied, the need to see the child and family before the substantive interview is still a consideration, and, in practice, it is more likely than not.

The introduction of pre-recorded video evidence as evidence in chief, brings with it an expectation that it is a recording of the child's first account, and implicitly, the child's first account to the investigating team. If it is discovered that a member of the investigating team has seen the child before the interview, there is a danger that this might be exploited at some future date by the defence. For example, it might be alleged that the social worker had put ideas into the child's head before the substantive interview. However, when the 'substantive' interview is the first occasion of getting the child's account, as we saw in the previous chapter, evidential constraints take priority. This means that a child's first point of contact could be one of legally restrained scepticism.

Ultimately it is a matter of professional judgement, and one for the strategic planning meeting to take into account. Certain things can be done to minimalise the possibility of the later exploitation of a child-centred approach by the defence. Good recording practices, careful listening rather than questioning, strategic use of reinforcement which gives the general impression of accepting what a child is saying, rather than obviously biased statements such as 'you're being a very good brave girl for telling me this', and so forth. However, the recommendation from *Working Together*, cited above, suggests that practitioners must strike a balance between the needs of the child and those of criminal justice, and it may be that it is decided, in the interests of particularly very damaged and reticent children, that the criminal justice route is inappropriate in the short term. Some might consider this to be unfortunate, since these children are likely to be the victims of the most serious assaults.

In the field, and at the initial investigation stage, the interests of children and criminal justice are represented respectively by local authority social service departments and by the police. The organisation of joint working is subject to variation across the country (Moran-Ellis et al., 1991) although there is broad agreement that cases should be investigated jointly wherever possible. The Bexley model was the first to be published and subject to evaluation, although other forces and areas were practising some form of joint working. Bexley is often viewed as a prototype when, in fact, it was more of a consolidation and exposition of a developing style of inter-agency working which had developed out of the police response to sexual assault cases (Kilkerr, 1989).

In the Bexley model, referrals were processed and co-ordinated by the Central Child Abuse Service. Following the referral stage, a joint police officer/social worker team would be appointed to carry out the investigation. Whilst it was acknowledged that all investigations vary, there were a number of areas that were relevant to most: interview referrer, visit the family, plan the medical where appropriate, seek consent for interviews and use of video, consider removal of the child where consent is refused, interview the victim, interview any witnesses, and interview the suspect (Metropolitan Police & Bexley Social Services, 1987). One criteria which distinguishes the Bexley model from other arrangements is that of having a central referral point. Whilst the specialist assessment teams (SATs) advocated by the Cleveland Inquiry (Butler Sloss, 1988) had some similarities with the Bexley model, a distinction was made between intra- and extra-familial abuse, the latter being presented as a police matter, which might be referred to the SAT if the child is subsequently assessed as being in need of protection. This, and any other requirement to decide on what sort of 'child abuse case' any particular case is, and in whose domain of responsibility any case rests, is potentially problematic. It also relates to a further practice issue to be considered in the planning of an investigation: that of when a referral becomes a complaint.

The area of the child protection study had joint working arrangements. However, no specialist assessment team and crucially, no central referral point, had been appointed. The police had established a child protection team, which was largely an extension of what used to be known as the 'juvenile bureau'. Social services had their own 'child-care' teams which covered a wide range of child-care related referrals, including child protection. A joint training scheme between police and social services was in operation, but those who trained together may not necessarily work together. When a referral was received by each respective agency, decisions were made about whether it was appropriate to invoke joint working arrangements. If a joint investigation was decided upon, the relevant agency would be alerted. A national survey reinforces that this approach is characteristic of service provision across the country. Nearly three-quarters of both agencies initially assessed referrals before taking investigative action. Much depended on the categorisation of the referral,

> We found that allegations or suspicions of sexual abuse, from whatever source, were not necessarily treated as a referral needing joint investigation. They may be categorised, for example, as 'suspicion only' or 'vague information', in which case they would be handled differently. This categorisation process, which was based on a number of factors and operated somewhat informally, had the effect of gatekeeping entry to the joint investigation system. Moran Ellis et al., 1991, p.8

The decision to involve the 'other' is founded on what is thought to be relevant, or necessary, by one agency about the other one. There is no opportunity for the police to say — at the point of referral to social services — 'this is a case for us', or vice versa. Theoretically, if there are good relationships between the police and social services, and a clear understanding of each other's roles and responsibilities, this should not present a problem. However, problems do occur where these relationships are tenuous and strained, and where workers have little respect for either the role or the incumbent of it. In general, relationships between social workers and police officers are good, but, in my study, there were some undercurrents and, informally, each would, on occasion, criticise the other. As relationships have developed, so has confidence in, and awareness of, the respective agency roles. In the team to which I was attached, it was customary to involve the police in referrals concerning child sexual assault, if only to share the information, and allow the police to say how they want to be involved. However, there is evidence of some misunderstanding of what certain things mean to respective workers. For example, 'planning' an interview can be a well-thought-out, organised process which involves a meeting of the participants prior to the interview. The subject matter for planning would have to do with organising the interview itself, deciding on what information is necessary prior to the interview, and who will attempt to obtain it, making contingencies for alterations, working out what information is required from the child, and how this will be sought in the light of the child's particular circumstances, and so forth. Alternatively, planning can be interpreted as a 10-minute chat just before the interview to confirm that the right child has been brought and the referral information is correct. There were indications from my own research, both in the child protection study and in the evaluation of the pilot of the *MOGP*, that some police officers had a tendency towards the latter interpretation, and felt that social workers took too much time. Thus sources of difference might well have to do with different interpretations of particular tasks, and these basic ground rules need clarifying outside of the investigative process.

Relevant to this point is that a referral is not the same as a 'complaint' to the police, or at least would not have been prior to joint working. The emphasis on joint working, however, has had parallel significance for the child protection investigation as has the introduction of criminal justice criteria at a very early stage. That is, the police are involved from, or almost from, the outset. So that, when a member of the public makes a referral concerning a child sexual assault allegation to a social worker, they are unwittingly making a 'complaint' to the police. To some extent, this may be considered, certainly according to official guidance, to be no bad thing. It is this assumption, that joint working is a good thing for collecting and constructing evidence as a means of effecting better child protection that I now want to examine.

First, in relation to the number of times children are interviewed, a reduction is viewed as positive. This is because there is a practice recognition that giving an account of an abusive experience is difficult, and children should not have to give it repeatedly. The evidential requirements of criminal proceedings give an additional reason for this; that a fresh account is likely to be more convincing than one which has been through repeated tellings, and also that it is likely to give more information. The literature and research reported in Chapter 2 reinforce the proposition that giving an account of an abusive experience is difficult. It is difficult for a number of reasons: a fear of being disbelieved, a fear of the consequences — particularly the separation of families, a fear of blame, breaching the social order of telling, and talking about intimate and uncomfortable experiences which are not, in general, talked about. These difficulties should not be under-estimated, and it may take several months of careful counselling before a victim is ready to give an account which is adequate for evidential purposes. Thus, s/he may need to go through many interviews prior to the substantive interview. These need not be interviews directed at getting the same 'story' every time, they may just concentrate on particular 'chapters' or 'episodes' in the experience. Victims need to build up trust to feel they have some control (Children's Society, 1991; Kelly, 1989) over the consequences of telling — this is one reason why children's helplines were needed, and are used by thousands of children annually.

If a child opts for the helpline route and is eventually persuaded to inform the social services of her/his situation, some of this counselling work has been done. Once the referral is received, statutory procedures and joint working will be invoked and a 'substantive' interview will be carried out as soon as possible. If, however, a child's mother, or other third party, contacts social services about alleged sexual assault to her child, the child will receive the same response, without the benefit of counselling. Which of these two routes is likely to give the best 'substantive' interview? Of course, we cannot know. For some children, in certain circumstances, it may make no difference. We can know that, for others, it will, because of the experiences of children in therapy, who continue to give details of their accounts long after the initial investigation. This is also relevant to the assumption that a 'fresh' account is more likely to be better in evidential terms. The assumption is derived partly from the research literature on memory, which clearly shows a 'recency' effect. It is also linked into value given to a recent complaint in law (see Chapter 9). For those children who have had recent experience of limited duration of an abusive experience, the 'recency' criteria might be applicable. However, some children will have experiences which cover months and even years of harm, injury or neglect. The research also points to the tendency for children to recall 'scripts' of repeated experiences, rather than accurate detail of one event. Thus one interview concerning the most recent event may not be accurate, or appropriate, in order to give detailed evidence which adequately reflects the offences committed against a child.

A 'blanket' procedural response of one interview is inappropriate for all cases; children and circumstances vary. Any response which aims to get the best evidence must be able to take this into account, and not assume that one joint investigative interview is the optimum achievement in all cases. The majority of referrals to professional agencies come from parents, other agencies (such as schools) and the public — they do not come from the children themselves. This is something that a joint investigative approach must be able to accommodate. Why should children who have their 'disclosure' route selected for them be penalised in a way that children who select their own route are not? A partial answer to that question has to do with the fact that, if a child is referred by someone else, the allegation may not be true, whereas, if they refer themselves, it is more likely to be so (Bentovim et al., 1988). Hence the initial investigation stemming from a referral to a statutory agency is directed not at finding out what has happened, if anything, to any particular child. Rather it must, in practice, first be directed at finding out whether the allegation has some substance. Once the validity of an allegation is established, then it could be said that the referral has achieved the status of a complaint. But who is the complainant? Technically, and legally, it is the victim. The status of complainant in other crimes presumes the act of making a complaint. Child abuse is complicated by the fact that a child might acknowledge that they have been the victim of a potential crime, but they may not wish to become a 'complainant'. The question is, do they have a right to not make a complaint in the face of evidence which suggests a crime has been committed against them? The arbiters of this decision are the joint investigating team, and one prime consideration in determining whether a 'substantive' interview on video should be conducted must be about when a child has the right to consent to the process. Not only is it now necessary to take account of the child's feelings and wishes, it has also been suggested that a child should not have to go to court unless they wish to do so (Home Office, 1989). The difficult task for practitioners is to balance this issue of the child's rights and consent, the child's immediate therapeutic and protection needs, and the benefits of a longer-term strategy which includes prosecution and possibly protection through the courts. Each of these bears relevance to an assessment of when to do the interview, and pre-interview work.

Finding out what has happened, if anything, to a child is the next step after referral, and the best way to do that might not be through a 'substantive' interview in the first instance. It may be to build up a relationship of trust with the child. Statutory agency workers need to be freed to do this work without fear of recrimination at a later date, by prosecution or defence personnel. One way in which such recrimination can come about is where the child reveals at some future date, whilst open to legal scrutiny, that a social worker told him or her that X was the case — that she was 'a good girl for telling', that 'lots of people are hurt by their parents, so she might have been too', and so on, that is, told the child something which could later be said to pre-judge the issue. If a counselling relationship is developed to build up trust, this is an entirely different approach. So long as practitioners bear in mind that whatever they say should be evidentially acceptable, rather than orient their whole approach towards obtaining evidence, there appears to be some rationale for gently bringing the child into the process outside of joint investigation and interviewing procedures, as already occurs through the helpline route. If the criminal justice system wants to act in the interests of justice, and punish those who are guilty of offences against children, it needs as much good evidence as possible. It will not get it if the attempt to do so is made too soon in certain cases. These cases are likely to involve the most seriously damaged and traumatised children, and the rationale for taking such an approach can be made to a court using the child's health and well-being as the central concern.

The two case studies which follow highlight some of these themes, and suggest appropriate routes for practice decisions.

## Case 1: James

James is 12 years old. He has recently taken two overdoses. After the first he refused to return home from the hospital and was admitted into care. Shortly afterwards he took the second overdose, and whilst in hospital, some letters were found in his bedroom indicating an intention to commit suicide and suggesting that his uncle had caused him to try to take his life. A strategy meeting was called. The police, social worker, family case-worker, team-manager, officer-in-charge and residential key-worker were present. The team-manager opened the meeting and asked the key-worker to relate the circumstances so far. He explained that, after James' second suicide attempt, some letters had been found. The key-worker suggested that they looked as if they were meant to be found, they were so obviously placed. The letters were explicit in stating James' desire to die, and his distress at some of the acts perpetrated on him. The meeting had been called out of the designated time since it was felt there was no urgent child protection issue because James was now in care. The key-worker went on to say that, because the strategy meeting was not held until Wednesday, and James had been discharged on the Monday, the interim period had been difficult. It was obvious that James had wanted to talk about what was going on. The letters had gone and he must have noticed, but the key-worker had been told not to discuss this with him.

The decision taken by the meeting was that a joint interview would be arranged after James had been seen by his key-worker and been informed about the strategy meeting and the need for a 'substantive' interview.

Subsequently, James was seen by the key-worker but he refused to say there was any problem with his uncle. He became very angry about his letters being taken and snatched them back and ripped them up. He was very upset that other people, the police and nominated worker, had been involved and he refused to say anything to them.

The protection issues in this case centre around James' suicide attempts, and the fact that he could be returned home if he or his parents requested it, thus putting him back into a high risk situation. The parents did not believe James and continued to allow the uncle to live in the house. The prosecution issue has to do with obtaining evidence with which to charge and prosecute the uncle. The two converge on this point, since, if James' uncle can be removed from the home, the risk is reduced. However, it is not obliterated. James' behaviour is disturbed and, at the present time, potentially life-threatening. Thus, there is a separate protection issue to do with his own mental health. In order to ensure James' safety, both must be considered, and they cannot be dealt with at the same time. James' suicidal behaviour needs careful therapeutic intervention, which might involve talking about his uncle and the alleged sexual assault. James wants to talk, and makes several attempts to do so. He is denied this opportunity and, having been denied it, refuses to take the option of talking, subsequently, to people he neither knows nor trusts. The outcome is one of inadequate protection and, possibly, no prosecution.

This case, whilst extreme, is not exceptional in the sense that it highlights the serious end of child harm and injury. Those children who have been most seriously assaulted, that is, have suffered the most significant harm, are likely to be the most damaged. They may not all try to commit suicide, but other life-endangering behaviours are characteristic, such as running away from home, self-mutilating behaviour, sexual promiscuity, withdrawal, depression and so forth. Yet it is these cases which are the most likely candidates for prosecution because of their very serious nature. Thus, the impetus to retain evidential requirements at an early stage is strong, as it was in James' case. However, if the key-worker had been given permission to respond to James in the way he had wanted, to talk to him when he wanted to talk, would the evidential requirements have been jeopardised? The *MOGP* acknowledges the possible need to talk to the child before the substantive interview. It suggests that the child should be listened to, rather than directly questioned and that a careful note should be made of the discussion. It does not rule out the possibility of answering a child's questions and suggests that this is the point at which a child can be informed of a substantive interview so that the child's willingness to co-operate can be assessed. If the child is not willing to go through a substantive interview, there is little point in taking this route, since s/he is not likely to say much of value. Where it is known, or thought strongly probable, that a child has been the victim of a criminal offence because the child him or herself has made the allegation, then the purpose of the interview is two-fold, and cannot be explained legitimately to a child as for finding out whether something, if anything has happened. It is already known by the child, and known to be known, that 'something' has happened. The aim of the interview is to find out what, in detail — thus the interview can be explained in terms of needing to know more. This need to know more must also be contexted with the potential use of the video. The reasons for video can be explained to an older child in terms similar to the information sheet contained in Annex H of the *MOGP*.

> I am making a video recording of my interview with . . . because I think it will spare him/her from having to go over the same ground with my colleagues. If there are any legal proceedings, it could be played in court to spare him/her some of the ordeal of criminal proceedings.

However, it must be acknowledged that some children may require counselling to get to the stage where they are prepared to give more information, and that this should be distinct from, and shown to be distinct from, coaching. So long as the worker does not say anything which appears to pre-judge the situation, and does not 'lead' or say things which could be construed as 'putting ideas into the child's head' the danger of allegations of coaching are minimised. Most importantly, all such contact must be carefully documented. In such cases, whatever happens in prosecution terms, this approach is more likely to afford the child protection and support.

Whilst acknowledging that there is a need to secure the immediate safety of a child, *Working Together* (DOH, 1991*b*) also states that:

> The balance needs to be struck between taking action designed to protect the child from abuse whilst at the same time protecting him or her and the family from the harm caused by unnecessary intervention. p.27

and that:

> In some cases courses of action other than a formal investigation will be decided upon following the consultation process. p.27

Thus the remit to examine alternative approaches in the interests of the child are contained within this guidance.

## Case 2: Shelley

Shelley, 9 years old, had been displaying explicit sexual behaviour towards her 4 year-old brother. She had been seen by mother, undressed, with her brother's clothes off, simulating intercourse. The mother told the health visitor who passed the information on to an educational social worker (ESW) who regularly visited the family. The ESW saw Shelley with her mother and asked her about this behaviour. She said she had seen other children doing it at school. However, on checking this out, the school thought it was highly unlikely. On a return visit the ESW discovered that the whole family had been watching a video, supplied by a relative. A description of the video stated it contained detailed information about sex, reproduction and childbirth. A strategy meeting was called and it was decided to interview the relative who introduced the video, and also to see Shelley again with her mother about the source of her sexual knowledge. The interview was to be carried out by a social worker; the police wanted more evidence before they became involved.

This case is symptomatic of many cases where sexual behaviour is observed rather than any disclosure made, and is further complicated by a possible explanation — that the behaviour is modelled on something seen elsewhere, either in school or on video, or possibly both. The overall strategy decision in child protection and prosecution terms, is to get more information, in order to assess whether there are grounds to warrant further intervention. However, in this case, we do not have the appearance of a child seriously traumatised by abuse — not yet, at least. Thus, this would be an ideal case for a 'substantive' interview. If the child says anything about the source of her sexual knowledge, it would be on video tape. If she does not, nothing is lost. The interview guidance in the *MOGP* is specifically geared towards just this sort of case, where it is not known what, if anything, has happened, and where the child can give his or her first account. The purpose of the interview is exploratory, and should be explained to the child in these terms.

In this case, the child has already been interviewed by related professionals. This is not atypical. Teachers are often involved before the social services, as are health visitors and ESWs. Inter-agency procedures often direct education, health and other workers to alert social services at the earliest opportunity, in order to avoid duplicate interviewing. In the child protection study, there was some evidence to show that information had to obtain a status of some certainty before it warranted referral to a statutory agency (Wattam, 1989). In that study, a further complicating factor had to do with the transmission of confidential information. Where teachers, or others, have been placed in a confidential relationship with a child by virtue of their relationship, they had difficulty in breaking confidentiality. This was partly to do with an assessment of the possible consequences of reporting and highlights the need for clearer information and training for other professionals about the requirements of the investigative process, particularly in relation to the Criminal Justice Act, 1991.

In conclusion, the duty to investigate does not imply a duty to conduct a substantive interview on video. This must be a planned, strategic, decision founded on the best interests of the child, which will include an assessment of her/his emotional and physical state, her/his entitlement and ability to informed consent, and the nature of the allegation.

# Notes

1.    The option to give a statement in written form is still available.
2.    Maternal grandfather.

# 7 Interviewing children under the new guidelines

The *Memorandum of Good Practice* (*MOGP*) began its life as a Code of Practice. The switch from 'Code' to 'Memorandum' is a significant one: it emphasises the status of the document, which is voluntary. With the change of name there was also an acknowledgement that the methods it recommended should not be considered as the only, or the best, methods in all cases. The interview framework contained within the *MOGP* is founded on the 'stepwise' approach. In this chapter I want to examine the rationale for the stepwise model, and discuss some of its implications. I will then go on to present some alternative approaches which might be considered in particular circumstances, and discuss the evidential implications of doing so.

Over recent years and especially post-Cleveland, attention has been paid to what is variously entitled the 'investigative', 'formal', or 'assessment' interview. These terms refer to the interview of the child conducted soon after a referral has been made to an official agency, which is now the 'substantive' interview in the *MOGP*. Pre-Cleveland, the term 'disclosure interview' was frequently used to describe the same kind of exploratory, evidence-seeking, interview with the child. Since then the term 'disclosure', as applied to the initial interview has been discredited because it pre-supposes the child has something to hide and thus pre-judges the issue (Butler-Sloss, 1988). However, it remains a useful therapeutic device which acknowledges that some children's experiences are difficult to talk about, and that presenting information may be indicative of further significant harm and injury. The 'substantive interview' is not and, we are told, should never be referred to as a disclosure interview. This is because the information it contains should stand on its own as evidence that something has happened, and as I have noted earlier, it cannot legally be pre-supposed that the child has something to hide. Furthermore, disclosure interviews are often associated with techniques which are designed at getting to the 'undisclosed' information; such as hypothetical questions (Bentovim et al., 1988) and these techniques are difficult to accept within a legal setting because they can appear suggestive and leading.

In a recent review of interviewing models (Vizard, 1991) it was noted that most recommend a staged approach. 'Stepwise' is such a model, containing four stages: rapport, free narrative, questioning and closure. Stepwise has been used in Canada (Yuille, 1989) as a model founded on research and evidential requirements. King and Yuille (1987) make suggestions as to how the interviewing of children might be improved in the light of research on children's testimony. Younger children were seen as a particularly difficult case since they appear to need help with recall, but also to be more vulnerable to error if direct questions are the sole technique used for extracting information; this is probably because of sensitivity to context and their dependence on social cues (for a review, see Spencer and Flin, 1990). Davies and Flin (1988) note that the quality of children's memory is a reflection of retrieval competence and cognitive development. They suggest that younger children are not necessarily less capable than older children in terms of their memory, though may need help to retrieve details. Overall accuracy does not appear to be very different from adults, although adults can generally recall more. Like adults, children are better at recalling details of central events, and not as good at description of persons or incidental detail. There is some research to suggest that children's memories are enhanced and affected by their understanding of an event (Cohen & Harnick, 1980), which would suggest that comprehension of the acts perpetrated on them may assist children to disclose those acts. Their understanding need not be the same as an adult's, but, clearly, if adults are looking for a similar significance of event quality, that is, one which would make it sufficiently significant to recall freely in a 'substantive' interview, this may not be the case. Some research suggests that 'context induction', prior to questioning about the critical incident is helpful (Davies, 1986; Davies & Flin, 1988).

In clinical interviews, the rapport stage sets the tone for the whole interview, and is important for building trust and a relationship with the client in order to move on to what might be difficult information to talk about. Its aim, as stated in the *MOGP*, is to:

build up a rapport between the interviewer and the child in which the child is helped to relax and feel as comfortable as possible in the interview situation.

This stage also has a number of additional functions; it supplements the knowledge gained at the planning stage, so that, if the child appears less, or more, able than was thought from the pre-interview information, it allows the interviewer to adapt his/her approach. Furthermore, if the child does not respond well to the person selected as lead interviewer, the other team member could step in at this point.

It was noted in Chapter 5 that these interviews present very 'un-ordinary' situations for children. Recalling and giving information is a skill which children cannot be expected to know without some guidance. The assumption that underlies the way in which the legal system approaches children's testimony is that, if something has happened, children will tell you about it. But, as I have already argued, it is very difficult for children to know in some cases just what it is they should be saying, and to have the confidence to say it. Thus, there is a third function to the rapport stage, which is to set the context of the interview, in order to prepare the children for the way in which they will (implicitly) be required to talk. For example, a neutral topic could be selected, such as cleaning teeth, catching the bus to school, and so on. Care would need to be taken that the topic was not related to the allegation, since each of these examples could be under certain circumstances. Once the topic is selected, it would be talked about in a general way. The child could be asked to tell the interviewer everything s/he can remember about the activity of say, picking a flower. The cognitive interview strategies of sequencing and perspective, discussed later in this chapter, could be applied. Information could be asked about detail, smells, taste, and other sensations. Discussion of truth which should come towards the end of the rapport phase could be a natural part of this conversation. This establishes a reference point so that, later in the interview, it would be possible to refer back to the ways of telling about the neutral activity to explore information about the allegation; for example, 'Do you remember how we talked about cleaning your teeth, all those different ways of remembering as much as you could, can you try and do that about (what you have just told me)'. In addition, it will clearly display, for all to see, further information about the child's developmental level and abilities.

There are some things to avoid at this initial stage of the interview. First, the alleged offence cannot be referred to, because this might be seen as 'leading', pre-judging the issue, and, at that stage, it could also constitute hearsay in many cases. Secondly, it is best to steer clear of any topic which might be associated with the alleged offence, for similar reasons. Boggs and Eyberg (1990) suggest some useful communication skills for rapport, some of which are applicable throughout the interview. They consist of verbal and non-verbal behaviours that acknowledge the interviewer is listening, and understands what is being said. Such actions range from simple statements and body movements — for example, nods, smiles, 'ah', 'I understand' to 'descriptive statements'; non-evaluative comments that describe the situation, for example, 'I can see you know how to play this game' or 'that is a drawing of a house'. Boggs and Eyberg give examples such as 'it looks like you're a little nervous about being here today', and 'you look like you're thinking hard about that question'. These are not entirely non-evaluative, they are the descriptor's opinion, and they suggest an interpretation to the child which might colour the interview and therefore they are not recommended. However 'you look like you enjoy drawing pictures' would be alright because it is not about a potentially central topic. Describing is helpful to show you are engaging with, and accepting of, the child.

Reflective statements are another useful device, where the interviewer repeats what the child has said. This not only acts to reinforce their words, but can also be used to further information in the required direction without leading. This can be particularly useful towards the end of the free narrative stage. For example, the child says 'I like going to Nana's house, but not when Robert's there' and the reflection could be 'when Robert's at Nana's house you don't like going there'. However, it can be used to great effect in the rapport stage to reinforce that you are listening, and understanding what the child is saying. Summary statements can be used to review what the child has said, and can be used in a similar way to focus the interview. These statements are referred to again in the closing stage of the interview. Praise statements indicate approval and should be restricted to neutral topics in the rapport stage, such as 'you've drawn a really good picture there'. Praising the child later in the interview can be seen as reinforcing and possibly suggesting to the child that there are some things you want to hear about and others (those that are not praised) that you don't. Thus an allegation could be made that this was a way of leading. Commands can be used strategically in the rapport stage to introduce praise. For example, 'draw me a picture of your favourite animal' can be rewarded by praise, so long as the activity commanded can be viewed as neutral.

Questions on neutral topics can be used in the rapport phase, for example, about hobbies, the journey to the interview, favourite games or TV programmes. 'Why' questions are to be avoided throughout. The *MOGP* suggests that 'why' questions may lead the child to attribute blame. This is because 'why' questions are generally used by adults to children in a negative context, such as, 'why did you do that?' referring to bad behaviour, and may be perceived by children as requiring them to account for, or justify, what they have done.

Play is acceptable at this stage, but genitaled dolls should not be used. Despite research to the contrary (Westcott, Davies & Clifford, 1990), it is still a widely held belief that such dolls might be suggestive, and thus could be construed as 'leading'. The rapport stage is a lead into the interview and needs to be used carefully and constructively. Play would be appropriate as a focus for starting discussion, and to help relax a younger child. It should not be a substitute for talking, or for carrying out the functions of the rapport stage: relaxation, continuing assessment, building communication, and setting the context for what is to follow. It is recommended that the rapport stage should not be omitted. However well the interviewer might know the child, this stage offers an important baseline for the interviewers and future viewers by which to assess what comes next. It allows the interviewer to display the child's developmental stage and begin to work out ways of negotiating it. Knowledge of child development is inextricably linked to assessments of reliability in children's testimony. It is therefore helpful if the interviewer uses this opportunity to pre-empt issues which might affect the interpretation of the child's free narrative and response to questions. In relation to the importance of understanding the context of allegations better, and the child's relevance, the following example of a 4 year-old's understanding of kinship relations is given by Saywitz (1990).

> Knowing the name her grandmother is called by doesn't imply she can imagine that her father was once a baby and that he had a mother, just as she does, and that this older woman is that person. This would require the mental operation of reversibility, the ability to change direction of thought. For the same reason, she knows she has a sister, but denies that she is a sister to her sister. Her credibility is compromised by developmentally inappropriate questioning and her subsequent inability to state that her grandmother is her father's mother and that she is her sister's sister.
> p.344

It is impossible to write guidelines for every scenario, but the principle of showing the child's understanding of certain concepts, such as kinship relations, is important to later assessment. In this case the interviewer would have to be very skilled to clarify, without leading, just who is involved in the allegation. However, if some neutral exploration of a topic was carried out at the rapport stage, as suggested earlier, in order to display the child's developmental level, then the kind of confusion that arises in this example can at least be explained in a professional manner. Whilst it may not render sufficient evidence for criminal proceedings because of potential ambiguity about the accused, it may well be useful for civil proceedings to show that something has happened to a child. In addition, this kind of information is crucial for the case-worker who must conduct an initial assessment, and formulate a child protection plan if one is required, whatever the outcome of the substantive interview.

The *MOGP* states that the interviewer must be careful not to over-emphasise his or her authority over the child. There are a number of verbal and non-verbal behaviours that can give the 'wrong' messages. Interviewers must be aware of how their normal speech tone is interpreted by others. Some people speak louder than others, more brusquely, can sound condescending, demanding, or critical without realising it, all of which might provide the child with an assessment of the interviewer's value judgement. Use of physical contact must be avoided; this can be construed as positive or negative reinforcement in the same way as verbal behaviours. Inappropriate body posture can communicate things to a child; for example, lying back on the floor, or being sexually suggestive, albeit unintended. In one interview in the child protection study, a girl of 7 years old had been referred because of alleged sexual abuse by her father. The interviewing male police officer balanced the child with her legs astride his knee, bounced her up and down and said 'right, tell me all about it'. In another, a woman police officer sat throughout with her legs crossed and her short skirt pulled up to show the tops of her stockings.

At some point during the rapport stage, the interview should be explained to the child. How this is done depends once again on the age of the child, how the issue of consent to interview was dealt with, the nature of the allegation, and whether the child has said something specific themselves. The principles guiding this explanation should be that it is non-leading but honest. For example, with an allegation concerning a 7–10 year-old, where the parents are not implicated, and where the child has so far not said anything, something like the following could be appropriate:

We're going to be talking together today so that I can learn as much as possible about you and any problems you may be having. I'm going to think of things that you or your parents might do to help with any problems I learn about. Adapted from Boggs and Eyberg, 1990. p.102

Boggs and Eyberg are writing about general assessment interviews with children. As a consequence, they give a second suggested approach as:

What did your mom or dad tell you about the reasons you were coming here today.

This would not be acceptable for a substantive interview because it breaches the hearsay rule, thus a better way of tackling it would be to ask whether the child knows the reason they are being interviewed. Explaining the interview could link into the introduction. The interviewers should introduce themselves so that the child knows who everyone is, and so that prospective viewers of the tape will know who they are. This, too, must be done carefully so as not to appear pre-judging. For example, it is not alright to say 'I am a social worker, I help children to put their problems right'. This could be said to assume that social workers only deal with problems, thus presuming this child has one, and also that, if she does have a problem, the social worker will put it right, which may not be possible. An alternative could be:

I am a social worker, I try to make sure that the children I see are happy/OK/alright. I talk to children a lot. Sometimes they tell me sad things, sometimes they tell me happy things. My job is to listen to what children tell me, and to help them if they need it, and if I can.

The explanation which could come towards the end of the rapport stage could then reiterate what social workers do and add:

Do you have anything that you might need help with, or that you want to talk about?

The child should be shown the camera which can also be linked into explaining the reasons for the interview. For example, 'we are making a video of this interview so that you will not have to go through the interview again.' This brings up the issue of confidentiality. The child cannot be assured of confidentiality because a number of people might see the video. Children need to be reassured that the video is not like television, in that it will not be broadcast to large numbers of people, and to be told who might see it. The way in which this is done obviously depends on the age and level of understanding of the child. But it should not be assumed that an older child will already know this, nor that a young child does not need to. A possible explanation could be:

> The video will only be seen by a few people who need to see it, people like me who want to work out whether you are alright, and if you are not, we want to find the best way to help.

Finally, the 'ground rules' for the interview need to be established; that is:

> convey to the child the need to speak the truth and the acceptability of saying 'I don't know' or 'I don't understand'. *MOGP*, 1992

Children learn that, if an adult asks them a question, they should answer, and research suggests that children are, like adults, susceptible to social pressure. They therefore need reassurance that this is not a 'right' or 'wrong' type of exercise, and that it is a good thing to say 'I don't know' or 'don't understand' rather than try to answer if they cannot. In addition, they need to know that they can ask for clarification, and ask questions of the interviewer. Explaining the need to speak the truth should be done simply, so that it does not suggest that the interviewer thinks the child might be lying. The form of words in the *MOGP* has been found useful during the pilot stage. That is:

> You can tell me anything you want. I don't want you to feel you need hold anything back. All that matters is that you don't make anything up or leave anything out. Home Office, 1992

This then leads the way into the next stage, the 'free narrative'. For some children, explaining the groundrules and setting the context in the rapport stage, is all that will be required. However, for many it will not. Children can be anxious, and have a mix of feelings at this point (Bentovim et al., 1988). Where should they start, what should they say? It may be they are silent and the interviewer must be comfortable with that, be patient and wait. Once it looks as if the child is feeling uncomfortable with the silence a prompt, such as 'tell me what, if anything, has happened, start at the beginning from where you see it'. The guidance is clear in its directive to the interviewer to resist talking as soon as the child stops speaking, and to be tolerant of what might appear to be irrelevant or repetitious information.

The MOGP recommends that, if nothing of relevance emerges during this phase, consideration should be given to closing the interview. It is crucial that this guidance is not misinterpreted as meaning that the case should be dropped. It has to be acknowledged that the child might not want, or be ready, to say anything, or that nothing has happened. It will be clear from the referral and planning information which is the most likely. Children's feelings and wishes must be respected, and this is a way of establishing trust. Secondly, if nothing has been indicated by the child it is unlikely that the questioning stage will take it further unless direct, and possibly leading, questions are used. This is not advisable since it will prejudice any future evidence. Where suspicion remains because of other information it is better to go at the child's pace; to leave a contact number and continue to encourage contact, and try a second interview at a later date if this is appropriate. As the Cleveland report stated:

> It must be accepted that at the end of the interview the child may have given no information to support the suspicion of sexual abuse and the position will remain unclear. Butler Sloss, 1988

The assessment at this stage should take account of all the available information. If it is thought that there is a strong possibility, on the basis of it, that the child is currently at risk of further significant harm or injury, then it may be necessary to continue the interview with a view to its use in civil proceedings. Even here, however, as the analysis of the Rochdale judgement shows (see Chapter 10) the use of leading questions is unlikely to be acceptable if the *only* information is that obtained by them. The profound impact of that judgement, combined with other recent judgements and inquiries and the principles underpinning the Children Act, 1989, is that social workers and police officers must accept a degree of risk which, hitherto, they may not have done. However, if the case has been investigated sufficiently well and if the evidence can be shown to not be there for the present, there is a greater degree of accountability. This may not save the child, but will save the workers from recrimination, a sad but inevitable indictment of the current context of child protection work.

It is stated in the *MOGP* that the termination of the interview after stage 2 should be exceptional. Most interviews will include a third stage of questioning. The guidance on the questioning stage is clear, and I do not intend to repeat it here. The principles underpinning questioning are, first, a gradual progression beginning with open-ended questions, and only asking one question at a time, and moving towards specific, then closed and, as a last resort, leading questions. The principles are that questioning is acceptable if it is non-leading, and that it provokes as much free narrative as possible (Jones & McQuiston, 1989). This is the point in the interview where the stages are no longer discrete, and the process of moving backwards and forwards begins to operate. If a question starts the child talking, the interviewer should effectively return to stage 2. If the child is beginning to get anxious or show signs of difficulty, it may be necessary to go back to stage 1. This, however, should be considered carefully. The MOGP states that:

> If the child becomes distressed when questioned even in this non-leading way, the interviewer should move away from the subject and consider reverting to an earlier phase of the interview (for example, re-establish through rapport that the child is at ease). Such shifting away from and then back to a difficult topic for the child may need to recur several times in an interview.

However, it may be that it is more appropriate in some cases to be patient and tolerant of the child's difficulty, and to wait to see if the child moves away from the topic. If the child begins to show distress because of the subject matter of their account, rather than the questioning, then it can be important to 'sit with it' and give the message that it is alright to talk and to be upset. It has to be accepted that, in some cases, the interview will not be an easy experience and the child will not be at ease throughout.

Where the child has said something relevant in the free narrative stage, questions can be directed later at further clarification. During stage 2, the lead interviewer (and any accompanying interviewer) should have been mentally noting any points to return to. An important role for the observing interviewer is to assist the lead interviewer. Where an ear-piece is used, the observer can communicate points for clarification to the lead interviewer. These open-ended questions must not contain any new information and take the form of 'could you tell me more about . . . .?', or 'what did you feel/were you thinking when . . . ?'. Specific questions are directed towards getting one answer such as 'when did this happen?'. Closed and leading questions should be used carefully because they are subject to possible legal criticism, and there is a possibility that the child might pick an answer for the wrong reasons (Ross & Ross, 1984). This is particularly the case for 'yes/no' type questions, where the child is asked to choose one of these options for the answer. If it is necessary to use such questions, then an attempt should be made to get the child to clarify the answer with an open question. It is likely that leading questions and their answers could be edited out at a later stage, thus it will require some skill to use the information they prompt. If the child can be guided back into the free narrative/open question stages and the information can be re-obtained, it might survive. As a rule of thumb, leading questions should be avoided where at all possible.

Finally, the interview should be closed. In the child protection study, there were two observations relevant to closure. First, there did not seem to be any agreed 'cut-off' point for the interviewers. The interviews appeared to end when it was felt that there was no more information to be had, rather than on the positive criteria of having sufficient information to investigate/prosecute/proceed. Secondly, some interviews ended very abruptly. It was almost as if, once the interviewers decided it was over, the whole thing stopped, and everyone walked out. Children were sometimes left playing alone in the room. These interviews can be very important events for children, and they might have a mix of feelings to contend with. The *MOGP* states that:

> every effort should be made to ensure that the child is not distressed but is in a positive frame of mind.

The problem is that, for some children, the occasion of 'telling' or giving an account is just the beginning, and, at the end of the interview, they will be acutely aware of it. If the accused is a family member, the repercussions are great. In my research there were instances of the accused being removed from the family home, or leaving voluntarily, and the child was sent home. The following is an account from one of the research interviews:

R = Respondent     I = Interviewer

I: How did your mum know?
R: What about:
I: About your decision, did you tell your mum about [social worker]?
R: No, the police brought her in
I: Oh, I see
R: And they read her the statement. I don't think I'd ever, if the clock was turned back I wouldn't go through it again. I just felt all alone especially in that room [    ].
I: What would have made it easier for you?
R: Well [pause] definitely having someone that was on my side in that [    ] knowing that there was somebody there that knew I was telling the truth, or thought I was telling the truth. That was the worst part and having to go home that night 'cos like I had me mum sat in one chair and me sister [name] didn't know who to believe like, so she was sat there and me sat on the settee and me uncle's down there going 'vindictive little bitch'.

The stepwise approach and the *MOGP* are designed to guide the interviewing of child witnesses in general; they are not about setting the interview in the context of a child protection investigation. They are an ideal approach for a one-off event, particularly perpetrated by a stranger, and are less than ideal for the complex and long-standing repetitive assault cases, because they neither acknowledge the child's trauma and the effect this will have on what they say, nor do they acknowledge the consequences, as in the case above. The aim of the *MOGP* is to improve interviewing for evidence, it is not about improving child protection practice. However, as I noted in the previous chapter, the two are often intertwined.

The stepwise model was devised to be compatible with statement validity analysis, more recently known as 'criteria based statement analysis' (CBSA) which is a means of assessing whether a witness is giving a truthful and reliable account. The rationale for the analysis is that, in general, people are not looking for the right cues in detecting deception. There is a tendency to focus on non-verbal cues such as eye contact and body movements which are associated with nervousness and suspicion, for example, lack of eye contact, shrugs and gestures. It has been argued that these are not reliable indicators of whether someone is telling the truth; in fact, they are the reverse; since they are the most controllable symptoms, they are manipulable to convey truth telling and can be used to cover up deception (Kohnken, 1990). Thus, other criteria have been developed which are thought to be more scientific in their application, which have to do with the content of statements. These criteria fall into five areas: general characteristics, specific contents, peculiarities of content, motivation-related content and offence-specific elements. Once witnesses have been interviewed along the 'stepwise' model, their testimony is available for rating according to such things as its 'logical structure', that is, its consistency, and the unstructured production and quantity of details, that is, its *specificity*. The details can be analysed for such things as: reported conversations, their unusual or unexpected nature, whether they are reported accurately or have been misunderstood, and how they account for subjective mental states of the victim and alleged perpetrator. In Chapter 3, I outlined four structures which were identified from a document analysis in the child protection study. These structures, which were also visible in the treatment of cases which go through the prosecution process, can predict whether a case proceeds or not, whether a child is thought to be lying or not, and whether a referral is substantiated, or not. They were the structures of specificity, motive, corroboration and categorisation. Briefly, if a child's account was very detailed and could be corroborated, if no ulterior motive could be detected, and if an orientation to people's behaviours was such that their behaviour was not expectable or open to explanation except within the context of a categorisation of 'child abuse', then a case could be expected to be substantiated. If children's accounts lacked detail, they could not be corroborated, there was a motive other than genuine concern for a child, and categorisations other than child abuse(r) could be oriented to, then a case could be expected to be not substantiated. These were practical reasoning devices, similar to those observed above to do with the use of non-verbal cues to detect deception. They are also very similar to the criteria used in CBCA (Steller & Boychuck, 1992). The more detailed a child's account, the more validated it becomes. These details are used to corroborate whether the child is giving a truthful account, and some of them have to do with what can be expected of people in a day-to-day sense who are 'telling the truth'. Whilst they are unlikely to be wrong in all cases, there are certain factors that need to be taken into account, particularly for children who have been the victim of prolonged and repeated sexual assault. There is some evidence to suggest, for example, that children minimise their accounts (Summit, 1983). This was reinforced in the child protection study, where some children reported that they told as little as possible. In addition, they were reluctant to give a spontaneous account, a point reinforced by the research reviewed in Chapter 2 concerning the impediments to reporting. If we relate this method of analysis back to the 'stepwise' method of interviewing, it is possible to review the main areas of difficulty in applying the approach to such cases; namely, certain children are unlikely to spontaneously and freely narrate their experiences, and they will require a great deal of support and counselling before they will say anything at all.

For these children, alternative approaches must be considered. The dilemma is to find an approach which is evidentially sound and also sensitive to the particular requirements of the child. The *MOGP* acknowledges that other approaches might be necessary in certain cases, and leaves such decisions to the practitioner. This was done because evaluation of the value of other approaches was awaited. However, any adaptations must bear certain key principles in mind: that time should be spent relaxing and building rapport with the child, that the child should be encouraged to give as much spontaneous information as possible, and that leading questions should be avoided. One potential source of difficulty has to do with the evidential problems concerning the need to do more than one interview. There must now be clear and accountable reasons for doing this; such as where the child has a very short concentration span, or where the case is particularly complex. Two strategies will help to counteract the potential weakening of the evidence if this strategy is considered. First, the Crown Prosecution Service should be consulted if this approach is to be taken, and the reasons fully explained and considered. Secondly, careful attention must be paid to recording time between interviews, accounting for who has had access to the child and ensuring as far as possible that the alleged offence is not discussed between interviews.

Thus it may be possible to adapt certain techniques to the substantive interview. A similar observation could be made about the use of cognitive interview strategies (for a review, see Westcott, 1992; Memon & Bull, 1991). Briefly, the cognitive interview refers to an approach developed from the psychology of memory applied to interviewing eye witnesses (Fisher & Geiselman, 1988). Four techniques are identified to aid recall of information. In the first, the witness is asked to reconstruct the context of the witnessed event; what they were wearing, what the weather was like, what they were thinking about at the time, what they could see, and so forth. The second technique is to ask the witness to report everything s/he can remember about the event. The third technique is to alter the sequencing, so that the witness is asked to remember things as they happened starting from the end of the event and going back to the beginning, and vice versa, or starting from the middle, and so on. Finally, the witness is asked to try and report the event from different perspectives, perhaps from the point of view of others who were present. Certain factors need to be considered when deciding whether to incorporate these strategies into the substantive interview. Firstly, the age and developmental stage of the child will affect how capable they are at utilising these strategies. For example, a very young child may have difficulty in trying to recall information from another's viewpoint and recalling information in different sequences. There is some research which suggests that, for young children, the adult form of the cognitive interview is no better than a standard interview and it is in need of amendment (Memon et al., 1992).

In conclusion, the principles underpinning the model of interviewing proposed in the *MOGP* are important for making a child protection case. However, the 'stepwise' model is not necessarily the best approach in all cases. Preference for it is founded on evidential considerations, particularly on those to do with analyzing the validity of children's testimony. Thus, the principles should be retained, particularly those to do with planning, preparation of the child, types of questioning and closure. Under certain circumstances, it may be more appropriate to consider the incorporation of alternative models or techniques, such as the cognitive interviewing strategies. The choice of approach should be determined by the immediate and prospective needs of the child, as well as by the principles of evidence and the investigating team's individual ability.

# 8 The decision to prosecute

Much of what is contained in the following two chapters is derived from a research study conducted in a Crown Prosecution Service (CPS) branch between January and June, 1991. The aim of the CPS study was to examine the nature of evidence in cases of offences against children where cases were referred and proceeded to prosecution. In particular, I wanted to see how cases were treated by the legal process and what the outcome of those cases was in relation to the types of evidence that cases consisted in. The study involved informal interviews and observations of CPS personnel, court observations, and a file analysis of all the cases involving children over the first six months of the year that passed through the crown court section of the branch.[1] Whilst writing this book, I was approached by a television programme researcher who wanted to know why cases fail in court if the child really has been the victim of significant harm or injury. It is a difficult matter to explain, not least to the children involved, and the following three chapters represent an attempt at a partial answer. The outrage of parents whose children are not returned to them, despite the case against them not being proved, and the risks to children who, by all accounts and purposes, should be returned where the parents are vindicated, all need explanation and public understanding. It is important to retain the rights of the innocent, and it is important to protect the innocent — both victim and accused. A great deal has been done over recent years to accommodate children in the legal process and to promote their right to justice. However, the information I present here shows *how* it is that the legal system remains an inherently difficult one for dealing with cases of offences against children, as well as for dealing with the child him or herself. What became very clear to me throughout both pieces of research was that it is not a straightforward matter that, when something happens to a child, the event is reported and the person believed responsible for the event is prosecuted. There are a multitude of variables which influence the decision-making process, some of which have already been described particularly in terms of the structures which validate children's accounts. Here I want to focus on the legal decision-making process, which begins with making the decision to prosecute, and particularly with formulating an 'abusive' event into a legal statement.

The files in the CPS study contained a lot of detailed information, particularly in the form of 'advice' from barristers, on drafting the indictment appropriately. The indictment represents the offences with which a defendant is finally charged. The routine way in which selecting the appropriate charge was treated as problematic led me to question what it was about child harm and injury that constituted it as a legal problem. Why doesn't it fit neatly, and what are the consequences of it not fitting?

One way of beginning to understand how, and why, things are problematic is to view the legal system as a discourse. Theories concerning discourse and discourse analysis abound in the social sciences, and it is neither useful nor appropriate to explain them here. (For a useful introduction, see Parker, 1992.) The notion, however, that there are systems of statements (not necessarily verbal) which construct objects and contain 'rules' that pertain to their use is helpful in understanding how child protection is constructed in law. The concept is a useful analytic term because it allows us to examine the legal and the child welfare constitution of child abuse as two different sets of statements, objects of analysis and sets of 'rules'. Within discourses, there are voices and silences. It has been argued that, within the child welfare, or protection, discourse, the voices of children are silent (Wise, 1991). Analytically this makes some sense, but, to practitioners within both discourses, it is unlikely to do so. In child protection, great effort is now being made to listen to children and parents, particularly with the advent of the Children Act, 1989, which makes this an accountable part of the work. In the law, serious attention has been paid to making the process easier for children, with the introduction of 'live link', followed more recently by the admissibility of pre-recorded video evidence. It is unlikely to be accepted on a purely practical level, therefore, that children are silent.

However, something happens to the voices of children which are often the starting point for articulating an action of harm or injury, as the observations of evidential interviews have shown. They must be translated, or formulated, within an acceptable framework. Following from the work of Teubner (1988, 1989), King and Piper (1990) suggest that the legal discourse is a closed system which must incorporate the statements and texts from the outside world that are relevant to its purpose. In doing so, a 'hybrid' is formed which reconstructs the 'social' into a legal communication. This can be exemplified by examining the role of 'expert witnesses' who must present their 'science' to courts in a careful and different way. The testimony of experts, as Chapter 10 displays, is open to judgement by legal rules, rather than by the rules of its own discourse. A very similar process is operating in the cases which concern children, and it can be seen in the way that these cases are compiled, written up, talked about and presented in court. Three components to the child protection case; the event of significant and intentional avoidable harm or injury, the alleged perpetrator of the event, and the child — who can stand as sole evidence of the fact(s) — must be constructed so as to be translatable in a legal setting in order to make a case. The legal constructions of each of these components could be drawn out of the research materials from the CPS study. They are not presented here as the definitive construction of the event, the accused and the child, but rather, examples are given of how the constructions emerge in practice. Some observations are made about the consequences of this 'reframing' for the process of prosecution in cases of offences against children, and the outcome in relation to child protection practice and policy, particularly with regard to the process of accepting pleas.

The arbiters of whether a case proceeds to prosecution or not is the Crown Prosecution Service (CPS) which was set up in 1986 to take responsibility for the majority of police prosecutions. One rationale for its instigation was to reduce the number of cases proceeding on weak evidence, and also to act as a counter-balance to the strengthening of police powers under the Police and Criminal Evidence Act, 1984 (Sanders, 1987).[2] All research studies that have followed cases from referral, through investigation to outcome, have shown that many 'drop out' of the system (Giller et al., 1992; Thorpe & Denman, 1992). As indicated earlier, in the child protection study concerning child sexual assault, one reason given for this was a 'lack of evidence' (Wattam, 1991). This category, covering 18% of all investigations, referred to insufficient evidence to warrant further investigative involvement. Hence, there is a filtering process before cases ever reach consideration for prosecution. Some cases continue for the purposes of monitoring, surveillance, counselling and support, but are not submitted for prosecution. The grounds for this are usually where the police decide to caution, particularly in the case of juvenile offenders, or not proceed — also on the basis of a lack of evidence. As Sanders points out:

> The introduction of the Crown Prosecution Service . . . does not directly affect decisions to arrest, charge, summon, caution, or take no further action. So officers aiming at, or seeking to justify, non-prosecution decisions still need only to construct their cases in ways that will satisfy their police supervisors. ibid, p.244

Thus, the police can act as a 'filter' to the decision to prosecute. Those cases that do get referred are generally those where the police side of the investigating team think they have, or can get, the evidence to proceed. All cases that are charged or summonsed are passed to the CPS who become the final arbiters of the decision. The CPS thereby operates as a second filter, sanctioning the final decision to prosecute. It could be expected, then, that, if a case gets this far, it must be a strong one, certainly as far as the investigating team and the CPS personnel are concerned.

A principle which has long been acknowledged within the British legal profession is that:

> At the heart of the issue is the legal fact that it is not the 'truth' that is at issue in court, but the veracity of competing stories. Sanders, 1987

The use of the word 'stories' is based on a social constructionist theory of evidence. The hypothesis rests on there being constructions of what must, in the legal process, be given the appearance of 'facts' and 'truth'. In order to avoid any detours into a metaphysical debate here, it is accepted for present purposes that there are such things that are treated as facts. Where a child has been poisoned, sexually assaulted, hit or even murdered by her parents, this can be construed as a fact.[3] Whilst the argument as to whether these acts constitute 'fact' is not irrelevant, and much can be said about how they might not, the purpose of this chapter is to identify how — on the basis that these events are thought to have happened, and are treated as facts by the parties who investigate them — they become versions of events, rather than retain the factual status that victims, social workers and police officers have already endowed them with. To make this identification is to attempt to bridge the incredulous gap that many fall into in their contact with the legal system.

It is the nature of our adversarial system that one side, the prosecution, and the other, the defence, must prove the facts on which their case rests, and disprove the facts on which the other's case rests. There are three types of facts which are open to proof or disproof: the facts at issue, relevant facts and collateral facts. Facts at issue are:

> those facts which the plaintiff [or the prosecutor] must prove in order to succeed in his claim [prosecution] together with those facts which the defendant [or the accused] must prove in order to succeed in his defence... A relevant fact, sometimes called a 'fact relevant to the issue', . . . is a fact from which the existence or non-existence of a fact in issue may be inferred . . . Collateral facts, sometimes referred to as 'subordinate facts' are of two kinds: (i) facts affecting the credibility of a witness testifying to a fact in issue or a relevant fact; and (ii) facts, sometimes called 'preliminary facts', which must be proved as a condition precedent to the admissibility of certain items of evidence tendered to prove a fact in issue or a relevant fact. Keane, 1989, pp.5–6

One way of deciding which facts are at issue in the first place, or relevant, is from the offence with which the accused has been charged. It cannot simply be said 'this child Y has been sexually assaulted by this man X', for example, and that be a fact. The beginning of a case, and thus the selection of facts open to proof or disproof, comes with the identification of an appropriate charge. In almost half the cases in the research study (49%), the prosecution decided to alter the charges originally designated by the police. Even where they did not, files routinely contained information on the appropriateness of the charge selected. Much of the consideration in arriving at the 'right' charge has to do with anticipating the arguments of the defence.[4] The case example which follows illustrates some of the considerations surrounding settling on the right charge. The case concerned a 15 year-old boy who worked in a garage. He alleged that his employer had befriended him, and, on occasions whilst he was at work, the man had invited him into his home, given him alcoholic drinks and had 'fondled' him and asked him to touch his penis whilst in the shower. The boy himself confessed that he drank alcohol frequently, and this was construed in the file as a 'drink problem'. It was for this reason, the defendant alleged, that the boy lost his job. It was only after losing his job that the allegations were made. Originally, the defendant had been charged by the police with two offences under the Sexual Offences Act, 1956, the other of which related to an 'exposure' to another boy who had admitted to having been in the shower with the defendant after work had finished. The employer had admitted, when interviewed by the police, that he was homosexual.[5]

Counsel admitted to having sympathy for the police officer, who had 'only' added the second charge to give credence to the first one. Thus, it was not that the defendant was thought to have committed two offences and been charged with them, but that having been thought to have committed one, another charge was sought to give strength to the initial charge. The way in which it was constructed, obtained relevance and gave strength to the first charge, was by application of the rules of practical reasoning. Counsel noted that 'in common sense' it was a charge arising from the evidence. Rather than, as the first offence was, a crime committed for which evidence had to be found. Thus, one reason for selecting charges is that they, in themselves, might constitute evidence for each other.

One repercussion of this is that if one charge is used to support another and that charge is not strongly supported by its own evidence, the other might also be weakened. Thus it can happen that whilst a defendant is charged with several offences which on the face of it appears to be a serious matter, the charges are so linked that if one goes they might all be weakened, the case fails and the defendant appears to be vindicated. However, and this must always be a consideration, the way in which charges can (in a practical reasoning sense) operate as evidence for each other, and the way in which relevant charges are therefore *sought for* once a crime is alleged to have been committed, could be construed as a miscarriage of justice, and to put it simply, a way of 'pinning' something on the defendant. Thus counsel, in this case, noted that one problem was whether it was so prejudicial that the defendant would not receive a fair trial, and was the sort of problem which has given rise to the principles and rules of 'similar fact evidence'. Where this is a consideration, one of the ways of revising the evidence is to balance the 'prejudicial effect' against 'probative value'. The exposure and the homosexuality were considered relevant, but 'arguably' even more prejudicial.

Again it is the rules of practical reasoning which are used as the main resource to decide on this. The structures of corroboration, categorisation and motive are present in all the cases in the sample, as they have been in the process leading up to prosecution. In this case categorisation is a salient structure. How else can the categorisation of 'homosexual' be considered, contemplated on, as prejudicial other than through the operation of category incumbent behaviours of homosexuals. We do not need here to speculate about what these might be. The device is in use and its relevance as evidence in a case of child sexual assault can only be obtained through the shared, and known to be shared knowledge, that one category incumbent behaviour is that incumbents (homosexuals) might, could be expected to, want teenage boys to fondle their genitals. This is not to say that this is a right or wrong ascription, we may all have opinions on that topic. It is showing, however, how such rules of practical reasoning are deployed as considerations in the evidence. In this case it was decided that the knowledge would be more prejudicial than probative, and therefore would not be used publicly. However, this decision was taken in anticipation of what the defence might do. If a count had been included in the indictment it was thought that the argument for the defence would have been for a separate trial.

Finally, it was stated that the outcome of this case would depend on the jury's impression of the boy. The information from counsel displayed some of the features which constitute the final charges as they are seen on the indictment. It is not just a case of whether the defendant is thought to have committed a crime and is then charged with that crime. The charge has to fit the alleged offence but, in addition, consideration is given to the way in which the defence might exploit the selection of that particular charge, and how fairly, in this context, the charge fits the crime. Furthermore, consideration is also given to weighing up the relevance of certain 'facts' against their prejudicial value. Whilst it might have been relevant that the defendant had exposed himself to another boy, and had admitted to having a sexual orientation to males, these facts are not strongly relevant to proving that what happened to the complainant did happen. They would, however, be strongly prejudicial, and is itself evidence of the kind of balancing act that goes on in order to ensure a 'fair' trial. The case resulted in a retrial at which no evidence was offered. The CPS clerk who handled the case was of the opinion that it 'would not have run' because it rested on the uncorroborated evidence of a 15 year old, who only complained after getting the sack.

Thus, in terms of indicators for what constitutes a strong case, the above example shows that it must first be one where the act can be adequately translated into an offence, that is, where the charge can fit the 'crime'. The offences under which pre-recorded video evidence is admissible cover a vast range of acts; any act of assault on, injury or a threat of injury to a person, any act which could fit under Section 1 of the Children and Young Persons Act, 1933 (which is essentially any act of cruelty to a child), almost any sexual or violent act perpetrated by an adult on a child, which can be covered by the Sexual Offences Act, 1956, the Indecency with Children Act, 1960, the Sexual Offences Act 1967, Section 54 of the Criminal Law Act, 1977 and the Protection of Children Act, 1978, and finally attempting, conspiring, aiding, abetting, counselling, procuring or inciting any act covered by these offences. The legislation would appear to be able adequately to represent all possible variations of harms and injuries inflicted on children in acts of omission or commission by adults.

There are two features of child abuse, however, that make it difficult to fit into this broad array of legal statements. One has to do with how it is defined, and the other with how it is perpetrated. That child abuse is inherently difficult to define is well known and documented (Blagg et al., 1989; Giovannoni & Becerra, 1979; Finkelhor, 1986; Kelly, 1988). Its definition changes over time (Taylor, 1989) and place (Gelles & Lancaster, 1987). The law does not attempt to define child 'abuse'; rather, it has a list of offences which are drawn on to match up to actions. Some of these actions are quite general — such as cruelty and indecent assault — but what happens is that, once formulated into a charge, it is not the action which forms the basis of legal argument, but whether the action can be properly said to constitute the legal formulation of it.

In the case of a man who waited in the toilets for young boys, and then gave them money for sexual favours, two charges were selected. One concerned 'importuning', the other 'gross indecency'. When the case got to court, the judge and all parties to the case held a discussion about the committal charge, and decided persistency could not be proved. Persistency was a requirement of the importuning charge. The judge stated that an attempt to procure was an act of gross indecency, for which persistency was not a requirement. The clerk dealing with the case reported that a submission was made at which the first count was dropped, and the second count was proceeded with. The defendant was subsequently found guilty on a charge of gross indecency. Thus, it was not the act, *per se*, that was in dispute, but whether the right legal formulation of it had been made. I do not want to suggest that the formulation in this particular case was anything other than the right one. The case reveals the 'rules' in application, and it is the action of applying the rules that can, on occasions, be responsible for difficulties in attempting to deal with child harm and injury through the criminal justice system.

Defining the act is one thing, but there is some indication that a further process is operating: that of orienting to defining a case as 'child abuse'. There were some cases of offences against children, in the sample, where the case was treated in much the same way as an adult offence would be. For example, a case concerning a shooting incident where one of a group of men was charged with an s20 assault. He had fired an air rifle at a 9 year-old boy, who received an injury to his arm. The boy was with a group of peers who were witness to the incident. In this case, no consideration was given to screens or live link for the child witnesses in court. The trauma of court and notions of protecting the child from the court process were missing from the files. The only statement about witnesses were that the orders were 'full for all'. The clerk described the children as confident. In court, they had to describe the area of the incident and they were themselves described as 'responding very well', which was 'proved, really, by getting the conviction'. The fact that the incident might have been an accident was a strong point in considering the case, both for the defence and prosecution. It was the only case involving a child where compensation was awarded, which was also a characteristic of the majority of adult assault cases.

The absence of special considerations in this case points to the way in which a particular approach has been developed within the legal process to orientate towards certain offences against children as problematic for the child victim. The importance of this observation lies, not in criticism about whether all offences concerning children should be orientated to in this way but rather in clarifying what happens to justice for children when special considerations are applied. There is a considerable amount of material in the files which indicates that effort is placed towards protecting certain children, that is, those who could be constructed as the victims of child 'abuse', from the court process. The children in the shooting incident were not orientated to, in the file, as potentially incompetent, unreliable or lying before they got to court. These issues were simply not questioned in the pre-trial process, whereas they were key criteria for deciding whether to proceed in what could be construed as typical 'child abuse' cases (see Chapter 9). Undoubtedly, this had to do with the nature of the offence, but what this tells us is that there is a set of criteria to be considered in child 'abuse' cases, which is not entirely the same set of criteria in all child 'assault' cases. It is important to know that these criteria are operating in order to focus efforts on getting the right evidence, but also to ask whether these are the correct criteria or whether, if a child is considered to be the victim of 'child abuse', they are pre-judged in some way, which they would not be if they had been the victim of another type of assault. Somehow it seems that 'child abuse' brings with it notions of blame, witness competence, reliability, and vulnerability of the child almost automatically, whereas other assault cases consider these issues as they arise. These issues turn out to be extremely relevant variables in terms of the outcome of cases and the decision to prosecute in the first place.

There is general agreement that children have a hard time in court (see Flin et al., in press), and this observation underpinned the considerations of the Pigot working group who outlined a concern:

All of the submissions which we received that addressed the matter indicated that most children are disturbed to a greater or lesser extent by giving evidence in court. The confrontation with the accused, the stress and embarrassment of speaking in public especially about sexual matters, the urgent demands of cross-examination, the overweening[6] nature of court-room formalities and the sense of insecurity and uncertainty induced by delays make this a harmful, oppressive and often traumatic experience. Moreover, because children are less clearly able to understand the reason for the demands which are placed upon them and have fewer developed intellectual and emotional resources than adults to help them cope with these, the effects are generally agreed to be peculiarly injurious and very often long-lasting. Report of the Advisory Group on Video Evidence, para 2.10 p.15, 1989

This reflects a general consensus, observed in the CPS files, that children should not have to go to court unless absolutely necessary. There were many examples of the desire to prevent children from having to give evidence both in the files, and from court observations. In principle, children have the right to justice (Home Office, 1992); however, in practice, it appears that their right to justice is filtered through well-intentioned attempts to prevent them suffering further trauma and distress. This desire to protect children has a profound influence on the result of a case, particularly through the process of obtaining and accepting pleas.

The majority of cases in the CPS sample resulted in guilty pleas, although these were not always pleas to the original charges. Protecting children from court was frequently given as the rationale for accepting pleas, as the following file extracts illustrate:

Clearly the young boys should not have to give evidence. It will be necessary to ensure a sufficient number of pleas are forthcoming from the defendant even though this case can properly be described as a 'tip of the iceberg' situation. (To obtain such pleas it may be necessary to substitute count of indecency with children for indecent assault.)

and:

It may, of course, be that [defendant] will tender pleas of guilty to the incidents in June, and I should have thought in those circumstances we ought to save this little girl the trauma of giving evidence unless those instructing me have other views . . .

Early on in the study, I was informed that 'plea bargaining' was not the right term to describe the frantic activity which seems to precede the appearance of some defendants in court, and that legal practitioners were involved in 'meaningful discussion'. Plea bargaining is a sensitive legal topic, and one which is largely hidden from researchers and the public domain (Baldwin & McConville, 1977). Pleaing is an acceptable, and built-in, part of the legal process. Defendants can be charged and they can accept the charge, or reject it outright; that is, they can plead guilty or not guilty. In the CPS study, this covered just over half the cases, with 26% pleading guilty and 26% pleading not guilty from the onset of the case. Then there is the option for the defence to state, quite early on, which charges will be selected for a guilty plea, and the prosecution decides whether to proceed on that basis. 28% of the sample pleaded guilty to selected charges[7] and it is to this group I now want to turn.

Much concern has been expressed about the time that it takes for cases to come to court, and measures are being taken to speed up the process. Some of the problems have been put down to organisational factors, such as availability of video link and court listing practices. Whilst both of these are important, there is also delay because of the decision-making process surrounding pleaing, and the uncertainty about whether, and how, the defendant will plead. The following case concerning the administration of toxic substances to a very young child by her parents, illustrates this. The clerk had noted that whilst the idea of an attempted murder charge had been mooted, the prosecution could not make up their minds until they knew what the nature of the admissions was. Thus, delay was a result of the process of reviewing the evidence. It was also recorded that the clerk had been informed 'off the record' that the defendant had admitted to giving the substances to her child, but did not know why she had done it. The defendant had been prepared to plead to administration, and attended court ready to do so, but her own Counsel had persuaded against it.

It is this kind of 'off the record' knowledge which sustains negotiations about pleas, but about which anyone outside the legal process — and on occasions those within the courtroom — have no knowledge. The noted information gives some indication of the relationship between pleaing and deciding the charges, that is, it has to do with which charges are likely to obtain a guilty plea, and which charges should be included in the event that the defendant pleads not guilty to some of them.

In relation to delay, the advice given by counsel on the case stated that he had decided to draft the indictment since there had been a number of applications for extension of time and the defence were anxious to have sight of the indictment. The extensions were largely as a result of indecision on the part of the defendants in terms of whether they would plead guilty or not. Because of the indecision over the plea the case was delayed, with the prospect of future delays because it would be necessary to have a further conference and serve additional evidence upon the defence. The indictment was drafted to take possible options into account. Four counts were included. The first two related to one defendant alone and were intended to be alternatives. So that if the defendant were to admit the administration of only one of the drugs it might not have been necessary to insist on a plea which covered the administration of both.

The third count related to both defendants and was intended to cover the administration of toxic substances by one or other of them. However, it was noted that if the defendant entered a guilty plea to either of the first two counts a guilty plea to the third count should not be expected. The fourth charge was a wider count covering neglect of the child by both parents. It was considered to be a minor count compared with the other counts in the Indictment. The option was left that if the defendant wished to plead guilty to the offence occurring at some other time this was something which the prosecution would have to consider. Furthermore, counsel felt that if any guilty pleas were offered, the acceptance or rejection of those pleas would have to be considered in the light of new developments.

These observations not only show how delay can be caused, but also display how consideration of the defendants plea influences the drafting of the indictment, and thus the final charges to which the defendant will plead. In this way it can be seen how attendance to pleaing becomes a variable in the final result. In the majority of cases (64%) the result matched the plea offered by the defendant, and only 8% of these were 'not guilty'. Cases where not guilty pleas were accepted tended to be those where the CPS decided not to go ahead because of a critical weakness in the evidence, generally because a crucial witness, such as a parent, indicated that they would change their account if called. Only 9% of the pleas were obtained at the last moment, and were characteristic of the kind of last minute 'plea bargaining' referred to earlier. Thus, much hinges on the day to day work of clerks and solicitors who must compile evidence and negotiate on the basis of it, all of which happens outside the courtroom.

A further issue in relation to charging in cases of offences against children has to do with the occurrence of child abuse over lengths of time. Very often it is not a one-off event, particularly if it is serious enough for prosecution to be a consideration. Over half of the cases in the research sample (57%) concerned actions alleged to have been committed over a continuous period. This ranged from less than 7 days (7%) to more than three years (15%). Approximately two-thirds of these case were sexual offences, and the remaining third contained cases of physical assault, neglect and poisoning. In these cases charges again had to be selected to represent the 'crime', rather than operate as a description of the actions themselves. A method of making 'specimen' charges is used to get round the problem which is acknowledged between legal professionals. An example was a case concerning a sexual relationship between a girl, now aged 16 years, and her stepfather. The way in which counsel write about drafting the indictment shows a shared knowledge of the difficulty, by stating that counts were selected to demonstrate the continuing nature of the assaults by the defendant upon the complainant over a period of approximately four years and spanning the ages of 12 to 16. These were regarded as specimen counts and it was suggested that the defence should be informed that the prosecution intended to put their case at trial on that basis.

One problem with specimen counts, as with seeking other relevant charges, is that sufficient corroboration might not be available for them all. In other words, they too can be proposed to lend support, to act as practical (rather than legally acceptable) evidence, to allow the court to get a clearer picture. The nature of offences against children often means that evidence must be constructed by 'reading between the lines'. The formulation of children's cases within the legal discourse creates problems. The methods by which cases are generally tested do not apply easily to violent or sexual assaults perpetrated in private, in secrecy, in relationships where many complex components are in play. Thus, the law has a problem. How can it use its own rules to formulate a case for its own purposes. One solution is that specimen counts appear to be selected to give the 'flavour' of the case.

It can be seen that the relationship between a harmful event, or set of events, the selection of the right charge, and the final result, is a complex and consequential one for children. The legal discourse cannot respond to child 'abuse', although it orientates to cases as child 'abuse' cases. Child 'abuse' in the criminal domain must be formulated in terms of a crime. Many factors influence the selection of the right charge, which have much to do with notions of 'fairness', representation and acceptability, based on calculations as to the predicted response of the alleged offender and the defence. The event itself remains outside the legal discourse, as an experience of the victim, and elements of that experience are only articulated as they become relevant to making a case within the legal discourse. The legal discourse, in a sense, knows what it is looking for, and constructs the case in terms of its own language, so that it can be judged in its own language, which brings with it at least two sets of consequences for children. The first is that the choice of charge(s), and how this is made, has implications for sentencing, treatment of offenders and future risk to the child. Pleaing to a lesser charge produces a lower sentence, and reduces the perceived importance of therapeutic intervention for the offender, both for the offender him or herself, and their families. Secondly, when it is legal terms that become the point of issue, rather than what happened to any particular child, the process is not, and cannot be 'child centred'. It may be that some would argue that it should not be. However, it is important to note how it is not because of the relationship between the civil and the criminal system. If a child has been significantly harmed and/or injured by a caretaker, and is thought to be at risk of further significant harm or injury, and that caretaker is found not guilty of the act, it may be difficult to justify the making of an order under the Children Act, 1989. Yet, the caretaker may have been exonerated on the basis of a dispute about the legal formulation of the act, none of which needs be made known to the civil court, or even to the social worker involved with the child. Such an event is quite a strong possibility in cases of sexual assault, where the non abusing parent is torn between the child and his or her partner. They may well use such a finding to convince themselves that their partner did not commit an act, and accept them back into the home. This not only exposes the child to further risk but also leaves the child with the problem of leaving home, either under an order or voluntarily.

In conclusion, the decision to prosecute rests firmly on the available evidential facts and whether they can support an act being adequately translated into a 'crime'. Two fundamental features of child harm and injury, to do with how it is defined and how it is carried out, influence the availability of such facts by making them unlikely. There are indications that certain cases are oriented to as 'child abuse' cases, in an attempt to exploit the evidence to its full effect. However, this has some consequence for the process for children, and the outcome of cases. One clear factor influencing outcome is the orientation towards the vulnerability of children and a desire to protect them from the court. The facility for negotiating over pleas and charges is operated, in part, on the basis of preventing children from having to encounter the court. This process has the effect of reducing the severity of charges (and thus sentencing), of increasing delay, of giving mixed messages to children and their families, of influencing civil proceedings and, arguably, of denying children their full right to justice.

# Notes

1.  The CPS do not distinguish between offences against adults and offences against children in their recording systems. All files relating to offences which could have been committed against either were examined (259), and 62 cases were identified as concerning children.
2.  Thus, in the case of offences against children, where it is known that evidence is often lacking or weak, it might be anticipated that the impetus is not to prosecute. This was not the case in the area I studied. Only four cases were reported as not proceeded with during the data collection period. There are inevitable local variations, and much depends on the personality and interests of the Chief Crown Prosecutor (CCP) in the region. In this particular area, the CCP was very sympathetic to such cases, and personally attended to the majority of them in some way.
3.  These acts can similarly be viewed as social constructions, in and of themselves, without reference to the legal system. For a brief account of this position see Taylor, 1989.
4.  In some cases, this is stated directly, in others, it stands as a rationale for any debate about the charges. Also relevant and articulated are notions of 'fairness' and 'fair trial', which reveal a consideration for both sides of the argument. Sanders (1987) noted that the CPS was intended to have an inquisitorial role as well as a prosecution one, but that this, in practice is very difficult to achieve. The articulated notions of 'fairness' may well represent attempts at independent assessment of the facts.
5.  As with all the case studies in this book some of the circumstances have been altered to maintain confidentiality. The substance of the case remains the same.
6.  I suspect that this should read 'overwhelming'.
7.  At the time of writing the pleas in the remainder of cases were not known (20%) because they had not been entered on the files.

# 9 Relevant evidence for practical purposes

There are at least two very practical reasons for examining the nature of evidence in cases of offences against children. First, to comprehend the way in which evidence is constructed more formally is to gain insight into what it is that might be focused on during the investigation. Legal evidence, as it was interpreted by practitioners in the child protection study, appeared to be quite narrowly focused on physical signs and symptoms, or a confession from the accused. When cases failed to proceed because of lack of evidence, these were the features lacking. Having observed cases in court, it became clear that, whilst this kind of evidence was important, even where it was present, much depended on the credibility of witnesses and how this was verbally constructed within the court setting. With the introduction of pre-recorded video evidence, the act of interpreting what children say has become extremely important in determining the 'strength' of a case. Thus, to ask the question of how children's testimony is used to construct a case, even prior to its availability on video, is to provide useful information for the investigating team conducting the substantive interview. It also gives critical scrutiny to the construction of validity and credibility by the legal discourse of, and about, children and their accounts. Secondly, the *MOGP* brings with it a requirement to involve the CPS at a very early stage of the child protection investigation. An understanding of the nature of evidence in criminal proceedings will enable better links to develop with the CPS when they are compiling a case and to know where use of the service will be appropriate.

In order for cases to proceed in both civil and criminal proceedings there must be evidence. Under the Children Act 1989, all evidence must be disclosed beforehand to give everyone a chance to read or see it. This brings the format of pre-court preparation in civil proceedings closer to that of criminal proceedings, in that cases are similarly compiled pre-trial. In fact, much of the evidence — except that of hearsay, and in some cases, experts — will be relevant to both. Thus, although the burden of proof in civil proceedings is less, in practice the standards required are likely to be the same; particularly in relation to pre-recorded video statements. It would be too simple to think that evidence is merely a statement of facts. Evidence is a construction, of what is considered to be relevant, in ways that are legally acceptable, and crucially, must show information in ways that are common and shared within our culture. Evidence is not merely a representation of an event, or set of events, it is a formulation of events in ways that any 'reasonable' person will understand. It would not be possible, for example, to represent a statement as an abstract painting which could only be understood as one person's representation of the facts. There are customs, practices and rules to do with what will stand as evidence, by which the detection, compilation and presentation of a case is guided.

There are legal definitions about evidence and what is considered relevant. To understand what is relevant in a strictly legal sense is a matter of applying the legal 'rules'. What I want to talk about in this chapter is different, though not entirely. Observations of the legal process in cases of offences against children, and analysis of the files concerning them, reveal certain features about the nature of the evidence, as it is handled in a routine, day-to-day, way. It is not a coincidence that an analysis of these materials comes up with some of the same terms as the legal discourse itself uses, since the legal discourse was my resource. However, I am not going to talk about what should, or could, stand as strong evidence according to some kind of textbook formulation. What follows is less to do with the 'rules', and more to do with rules observed in use. Lawyers need to know the 'rules', of evidence, of court; in short, of the whole legal process. The investigating team in a child protection case does too. It might, however, be better equipped if it knew how the rules are applied in practice. In the previous chapter, I referred to 'relevant facts'. These facts must attain a status of relevance, and they do so by the application of what could be termed the day-to-day rules of human conduct. These 'rules' derive from what is known, and shared, as known in our culture: how we define 'promiscuity' for example, or a 'good parent'. Such 'rules', which are not the same as the rules of evidence but are formulated in the context of them, could be found in my research material. These were the 'rules' by which the 'rules of evidence' were applied.

The strength of a case rests on its evidence. This can be the testimony of the child and other witnesses, including the defendant, forensic, medical or 'expert' evidence, and 'real' evidence, such as objects. They are not strong in themselves. Their strength derives from the relationship between the alleged offence, the person or object which is the source, and their content. Strength depends on how well the evidence proves the facts. The question is, what proves what? Does the statement that a child did not cry out in pain prove that she was not in pain, for example, or that because a child did not report a sexual assault immediately after it had happened, only after he was sacked, it did not happen? There is something missing that we would need to know about; the circumstances and context under which these statements are made. In, and of, themselves these events are meaningless. However, if put together with certain circumstances (as the case example in the previous chapter shows) these events can serve to weaken proof that an offence has been committed. In the wrong context, they might completely undermine a case.

Underpinning the evidence is the fact that the complainant is a child. Thus the usual rules about admissibility of evidence concerning a complaint apply, but, in addition, the 'reliability' of the child as complainant becomes an issue. The reliability of any complainant requires testing out in all cases. However, the criteria used to make judgements about reliability are different between adults and children. There is an extensive amount of research literature on the reliability of children, most of which seeks to show how reliable children are in relation to adults (see, for example, Spencer & Flin, 1990). The research activity directed at this topic has, arguably, been as a consequence of the perceived status of children in the legal system: that they have not been presumed reliable, or as competent as adults. The debate about this issue continues, although some agreement has been reached that the key factors appear to be the ages of the children, their susceptibility to social pressure, and the quality of the information they can give, rather than the quantity. None of the experimental research can adequately duplicate the conditions of the real world, in terms of context (the investigative process, the courtroom) combined with the meaning of the experience (sexual and/or physical assault or neglect). I do not here want to enter into an analysis of what the literature can tell us about the reliability of children. For a broad review, readers are directed to Spencer and Flin (1990). Very little attention has hitherto been paid, however, to the way in which the reliability of children is used as a topic and resource in the construction of evidence concerning them. A more relevant question would be, why is it that children are considered unreliable in the first place? Is it that we just don't know how reliable they are, and all that is needed is good research to decide the matter one way or the other? Or is it that criteria for reliability in the legal discourse serve another purpose. After all, it is not just children who are potentially unreliable, adults could, and are, considered so as well.

Judging reliability is a practical problem. How do we know, in a practical, every-day sense, that information given to us comes from a reliable source? One way in which this is done is through the activity of categorisation, and through category incumbent behaviours. For an account of an event, for example, we might look for the category 'people who were there'. We would also need to know something about this particular person's viewpoint; is he going to give a biased version of events? Thus it would be important to know other identity descriptions such as age, gender, ethnicity or occupation; descriptions which could give information about a possible way of interpreting and recounting the event. This is not to say that any of these descriptions necessarily bias statements one way or another but merely to suggest that, in practice, they can operate as criteria for assessing the judgements of others in relation to our own. There are other identity descriptions, such as degree of interrelationship — a different account might be expected from a friend, for example, rather than from a reporter working for the tabloid press, or alternatively, the quality press — all of which might influence the interpretation of reliability attributed to the account. When we come to receive the account, in a newspaper, for example, part of our interpretation of it will depend on how reliable we think it is. Reliability will be achieved, in part, by this kind of categorisation of information source. Thus, an assessment of source reliability is a resource for interpretation. There was material in CPS files to support these 'rules' in operation, in cases concerning adults and children. For adults, particularly in relation to the sexual offences, the method of applying the 'rules' was the same, but the criteria were different. Categorisations had to do with persons of 'good character' who were not, for example, 'promiscuous', or culpable through identity descriptions in some other way (such as the use of homosexuality in the previous chapter). The reliability of children is less easy to test by the same categories that are available for adults. There is a ubiquitous quality to the category 'child' which does not stand in the same way for adults. Children cannot, for example, achieve categorisation in relation to occupation. In fact, they are categorised almost wholly by their age particularly in relation to maturity and relationships. The problem in cases of offences against children is that very often these are the only devices open to achieving reliability of the evidence and that, very often, the only evidence is the child's testimony. Put simply, the question might run like this — 'Is this what could be expected from a child of this age in this kind of relationship with this person, given the things that have been said?' What is expected is used to test out the allegation, and the allegation is juxtaposed against what is expected.

In this way reliability becomes a topic in the legal process. How reliable someone is becomes a subject for consideration, talking about, giving evidence of. Its relevance as a topic stems from the need for it as a resource to interpret the evidence. So the child's reliability is not only a resource for interpreting the evidence, it becomes part of the evidence itself. It is known that the reliability of children is at issue, but not precisely how the issue pans out in practice. In one case, for example, concerning two 12 year old girls, their reliability was called into question by drawing attention to the inconsistency of their accounts. This inconsistency was both inherent within the accounts and also between them, a fact which was taken as a possible unwillingness of the girls to tell the entire truth that they permitted continuing indecencies for money. This way of interpreting inconsistency acknowledged that the offences may still have occurred but there were reasons for not telling the full story. Yet the acknowledgment of inconsistency meant that the children were not considered good witnesses, and without other evidence the case would fail. Thus, again, it can be seen that the nature of offences against children mitigates against their adequate formulation in the legal discourse precisely because of that nature. That the events can be perceived as blameworthy, shrouded in secrecy and matters that are difficult to be truthful about, also makes accounts of them appear unreliable.

The reliability criteria in the girls' evidence was 'consistency' both within and between accounts. Its use as a resource — to assess whether the girls are telling the truth — and a topic, as evidence of a potential truth that they were content to permit indecencies for money, could be seen in action. The use of reliability is immensely consequential for children. It means that what is focused on, in the first instance, are the criteria by which their reliability as witnesses is achieved. Because of the adversarial nature of our legal system, and because, very often, the only evidence is the testimony given by the child, it is the reliability of children which is called into question. The facts cannot be considered without first deciding whether they are reliable or not.

In the files, the testing out of reliability was a routine matter formulated as a request for a witness assessment. This was generally done by the police, although there was one case in the sample where prosecution counsel decided that a child really was 'telling the truth' after having a cup of tea with her. Typically, the assessment was communicated in memo form by the police to the prosecution. I am unable to quote directly[1] but the following is an example of an 'unsuitable witness' assessment, compiled from typical material in the files:

> 'She seemed quite immature for her age, and her attention span was limited. Despite the fact that she had made an additional statement to me and is adamant that no further incidents have occurred, I am of the opinion that there are still matters she has not told us.
>
> I feel that Sandra would be an unsuitable witness at court.'

Alternatively, children would be described as good witnesses. One memo referred to an 8 year-old girl who would be 'a little star' in court. Whilst much of the research literature examines the reliability of children, as if they had abilities or characteristics of a kind, the examples above show that much has to do with the impression given by the child. It is not about children in general, being reliable or not, or even about a particular child being reliable. The legal process demands that they exhibit reliability criteria. What is being considered is impression formation — how the child gives the impression of being reliable for the purposes at hand.

Inconsistency is one criterion for unreliability, yet little attention is paid, within the legal process as to how inconsistencies might come about, or even how it might be a product of unreliability. Children have to wait for some time to come to court, several months on occasions, they must give their account early on, they might well have given it several times before coming to court, and each telling could alter in some small detail. The context of the offence itself could cause inconsistency; a child might be fearful, not know how much she can safely say, and so forth. Whatever the case there is, on the one hand an acknowledgement that children must be 'good' witnesses for a case to proceed — and one criterion for a good witness is that s/he can appear reliable — and, on the other, an acknowledgement that there is a truth to the matter which can be judged on the same criteria. The criteria such as consistency, specificity, motive are not — as a routine matter in the files at least — called into question. This is not to say they are never questioned, or that they are not available to questioning. But the criteria are overwhelmingly present as factors on which to decide about children and evidence. These are the criteria by which reliability is judged, and if there is to be help for children at all, it is to expose these practical reasoning components of impression formation for the devices they are. This, of course, is what lawyers do on occasions to make their case, although, because they use such everyday devices — criteria that any 'reasonable person' can accept — it does not appear that way, it merely appears 'reasonable', such as, for example, when a child is accused of lying because she is upset at the discipline she received (motive for complaint).

The perceived reliability has an influence on the outcome of a case. If a child is considered an unreliable witness prior to court, the case may not proceed, and, if a child can be shown to be unreliable in court, the case may fail. The intrinsic reliability of a child is less central than the way in which other relevant facts to the case combine to give a sense of reliability, or not. In a case concerning children with learning difficulties, for example, an expert was called upon to comment on their reliability as witnesses. The report put doubt on their interpretation of facts, and the advice contained a reference to these comments. However, the police noted that they felt much of what the children alleged did, in fact, take place. Counsel's reply was that although this might well have been the case, the views of the expert on the children's reliability should be respected. Thus in the opinion of the police, and possibly counsel, these children had been assaulted, but they could not use the children's testimony concerning the assault because an expert had concluded that the evidence of children with this particular learning difficulty could not *always* be considered reliable. The children's testimony was problematic, not because it was untruthful or wrong, but because these were children in an 'unreliable' category and it would be anticipated that the defence would exploit this categorisation.

Thus, and in the above case it was articulated, it is not what is likely to have happened, or how accurate the child's report is perceived to be by the investigating team, but how reliable the child can be shown to be that is at issue. To return to the idea of day-to-day 'rules' in use, there are observable rules by which unreliable connotations of the child can be achieved. In sexual offences these often had to do with the age of the child; looking at the age they were, behaving in intimate relationships according to their age, and so forth. In a case where a 21 year-old had allegedly had sexual intercourse with a 12 year-old girl, these 'rules' about age, and age-appropriate behaviour, were framed so as to inform the legal issues to do with consent; a feature which cropped up in many cases. The child had known the man for a few days and they were at the house of a mutual friend. The offence came to light as a result of a police interview because the victim was missing from home. The key witnesses claimed the child appeared older than she was, and also that she appeared older to the accused. Thus witnesses were using certain rules to do with the assessment of age. The accused claimed to have been drunk and said that the victim had told him she was 16 and that she joined him and started kissing. The girl was interviewed a second time to establish her 'suitability as a witness'. It was noted that she had a mature physical appearance but mentally she was quite immature. During the interview she became upset and refused to answer further questions. She informed the police officer of details concerning the offence and it was felt that she was not being entirely truthful. The conclusion was that she could not be relied upon to give evidence consistent with her statements, and that she should not be called as a witness.

Thus other factors, particular to the case, are weighed in terms of their influence on reliability. Any final statement, 'expert' or otherwise, on the reliability of children cannot cancel out these factors fundamental to the decision-making process. Many of them can be grouped into the category of 'motive to lie', which (as a general rule) if it can be shown, will be shown. Once again, the every-day rules can be seen in the construction of the legal case. One case, for example, noted that the defendant would contest the case, claiming that the relationship between father and daughter had been a difficult one and that the girl was trying to get back at her father. A view supported by the CPS clerk who commented that this was the line taken in court by the defence.

This example begins to highlight a fundamental problem in making judgements about whether or not something has happened to a child using the legal system. There is an inherent conflict to do with what is expectable. For example, that children love their parents but children are not expected to love their parents if they are significantly harmed by them. The example above can make sense in terms of the 'rules' of day-to-day family life and discipline. It depends for its interpretation on what is expectable. Thus, it is expectable that children will be disciplined by their fathers, and that they may not like it. However, it is also expectable that children will not like being abused by their father, and may try to 'get back'. It is a problem of versions, and which version is selected depends very much on what else there is to go with it — hence the search for identity descriptions and relevant activities, such as watching pornographic films. The more of these that can be found, to do the work of supporting a version, the better.

One such feature which strengthens the evidence — or version of the evidence — has to do with the recency of the complaint. The *MOGP*, following the Pigot recommendations, endorsed the need to conduct a substantive interview as soon as possible after a complaint has been made. In my file study, it seemed that, where a complaint lacked recency, it weakened the evidence, and the chance of proceeding. Recency of complaint was discussed wherever it was an issue, that is, wherever there was a time lapse between the alleged event and the reporting of it. In a typical case example concerning an alleged assault by a stepfather on his 13 year-old daughter, the question of prosecution was considered 'at length'. It was noted that there was no corroboration and whilst that of itself did not prevent proceedings, the gap between the incidents and the complaint was identified as 'the crucial test'. It was pointed out that a 'golden opportunity' arose for the child to tell her mother which she did not take up. It was in consideration of such matters that the case did not proceed.

The emphasis on recency derives from the point that, in cases of rape or sexual offences, a complaint made shortly afterwards is admissible to show consistency of conduct with the complainant's evidence. This is 'when it is made at the first opportunity after the offence which reasonably offers itself' (Keane, 1989). If it is not made at the earliest opportunity, the issue of recency gets tied to the issue of motive: 'why is the complaint being made now'? Communications on file articulated this in many ways. It was stated that it was hard to believe that a child could be assaulted over a period of time and not tell anyone, particularly if there was an apparant opportunity to do so, such as when the person believed responsible left the home. A factor reinforced by the case in the final chapter of this book.

Whilst research on reporting shows that child sexual abuse is a difficult thing to talk about, (Russell, 1986; Finkelhor, 1986) that in such cases children may not tell until the abuse has stopped and, in addition, they are given the right opportunity, none of it is taken into account here. The recourse is to more traditional lines of moral reasoning — if the child did not tell, there must have been a reason, and one possible reason is that he has been 'making up the story'. Research in a legal setting is generally left to the 'experts', thus, what is known by the investigating team, in terms of their own professional expertise, cannot be taken for granted as known by lawyers. It is important that practitioners make full use of the research evidence on reporting when communicating with lawyers and interviewing children.

In conclusion, this chapter has indicated three crucial variables in the strength of evidence in cases of offences against children; reliability, recency of, and motive for complaint. In terms of practical guidance, there are two possible recommendations that follow from these observations. The first is that practitioners seek ways to compensate for these features, if they appear potentially problematic, in the substantive interview. There is a need to direct the child, in a non-leading way, so that they have the opportunity to justify such matters as inconsistency, how it was that they first told of their experience at a certain time rather than another, how it comes about that a motive for complaint (such as an argument) can act as a precipitating factor rather than evidence of a false account, and so forth. All these features, to do with consent, recency and motive, must be counteracted in the gathering of evidence if children are to be taken seriously. The difficulty for social workers and police officers is to do this in a way which does not undermine or appear doubting to the child. Thus, for example, asking a child why they did not tell anyone can seem to be blaming. The *MOGP* directs practitioners to probe this topic if possible. One way would be to ask 'how' it came about that they were able to tell. It will take skill and patience to enable a child to give this information, but the common sense reasoning that appears to be applied to children as witnesses in a legal setting must be anticipated and counteracted, if children are to be adequately afforded justice.

## Notes

1.  Many documents, such as memoranda between police and CPS personnel, are regarded as 'privile ged'. The Crown Prosecution Service considered that some of the research materials fell into this category, and therefore could not be cited directly.

# 10 Expert evidence and the construction of child abuse

Experts can be called to give evidence on matters which, in the court's opinion, require expertise. In criminal proceedings, in cases of offences against children, experts tend to be clinical psychologists, psychiatrists, physicians and forensic scientists. Experts are usually restricted to making comment only on the abnormal, such as where the accused or the complainant suffers from a mental illness or disability (Ormerod, 1992). They are not routinely called to give evidence on child abuse, whereas, in civil proceedings, they are often called to do so, as are doctors and forensic scientists where appropriate.

Most people accept in the course of their day-to-day lives that there are such things as 'facts'. Within the legal discourse, there is an acceptance that science can help to define the facts, and also that these facts are available for scrutiny as to their relevance and value in relation to the case at hand. Critics of the adversarial system argue that pitting experts against each other creates an unnecessary conflict, whereas advocates of it suggest that any other system (for example, an inquisitorial system) could encourage the ascendency of one particular form of expert knowledge over another, and bias the result. Technically, experts are valued because they are able to give independent 'objective' advice to the court. Therefore, the side that calls them should not matter. However, in any legal dispute, under any legal system there will be an attempt to represent different points of view. The material in this chapter shows the way experts are used to validate a preferred version of the 'facts'. In cases of offences against children, almost all the facts can be argued, and ultimately, someone — the judge, and in criminal proceedings, the jury — must decide on which version of the facts to accept. An analysis of how decisions are reached within the court is crucial to an understanding of outcomes, and the material in this chapter shows the way in which experts are used in the decision-making process to validate a preferred version of the 'facts'.

A recent case of alleged ritual abuse in Rochdale is used as the basis for analysis here. The judgement in that case was presented at the end of a process which involves weighing up evidence with what is known about child abuse and the investigation of it as it applies to the particular problem at hand. Thus, these judgements incorporate some of the recent history of child protection investigations, particularly the Cleveland inquiry, and they were given because, in the view of the judge, they gave rise to areas of genuine public concern and had implications for future proceedings. Their consequence has been to reinforce the principle underpinning the Children Act, that children are better off in their own families, and to shift social work practice into balancing the probability of risk of further harm and injury against the emotional trauma of familial separation. The judgement in the Rochdale case is important for two further reasons: it acts as a judgement about how to constitute a form of child abuse, and also as a judgement on what counts as a good expert.

The cases concerned alleged satanic or ritual abuse. The interest value of ritual abuse here is not the concern of whether or not it exists, rather it lies in the opportunity to examine practical reasoning about how a form of child abuse is defined by a court. That is, how a case is made to substantiate that a way of behaving and a set of events is child abuse, which, in this case, happens to be ritual abuse. This is not to diminish the importance of the recognition of 'ritual' abuse, but there are important lessons to be learned about the informal rules that guide the construction of evidence about child abuse in general.

The judgement in open court was given by the honourable Mr Justice Douglas Brown in March, 1991. It begins with an overview of the development of the case, which began in November 1989 when teachers reported their concern about a 6 year-old boy. 'His behaviour had been strange and withdrawn for some weeks and he had talked to his teacher about ghosts and a ghost family that were part of his life. There were clear signs that he was very disturbed.' Social workers were not allocated to the case until February. A month later the boy and his sister were interviewed on two consecutive days, after which a Place Of Safety Order was taken. The Police were then involved in a joint investigation based 'largely, if not exclusively' on what the children said. The focus, therefore, was almost entirely on children's accounts and how they might be corroborated. As a result, four months later, 12 more children from four families became wards of court. A further child was warded during the same month and a sixth family became involved three months later when three more children were warded.

Three children in one family were dewarded in December when the hearing began in respect of the remaining 17 children, 14 of whom were still on interim care orders. Of these, 10 had 'no or very little access to their parents'. The hearing lasted 47 days, and evidence was given from the local authority, parents, psychologists and psychiatrists. The judge stated that:

> The reason underlying this unusual and protracted hearing stems from the belief of local authority social workers, supported to an extent by clinical psychologists, that a number of the children had been subjected to or were at risk of organised satanic or ritual abuse by adults either involving the parents or with their co-operation or complicity. I have also had to consider whether the children had been subjected to or were at risk of emotional neglect and physical neglect . . . a complex and difficult case.

The decision on the cases concerning 20 children resulted in 16 of the children remaining wards, 12 of whom were returned home under various conditions, four remaining in care, and four children being returned home and dewarded completely.

This result reinforces the principle that children are better off in their own families. The judgement is peppered with comment that supports that principle and makes it clear that the trauma of removing children from home should only be done on the strongest evidence. The curtailed interview of N, who was sobbing, distraught and 'greatly distressed at being removed from home', was described as 'one of the most abiding and disturbing parts of the evidence'. Using the recommendations of the Cleveland inquiry, the judge reinforced that the removal of children was an 'onerous responsibility' and should only be carried out where there is cause to believe there is a high risk of further immediate abuse. Children cannot be removed on the basis of suspicion alone and the possibility of abuse, it was stated, was not sufficient to prevent the return home of a child.

The assessment of 'insufficient evidence' in the cases of the children returned home was based on an analysis of information, all of which was presented to the court either to support or disprove the case for them having been subject to abuse. A summary of the history of the matter in relation to ritual abuse was given in the judgement.

The starting point for ritual abuse came from family 1 of whom it was noted that both parents may not have been typical but their problems were familiar. They had a poor home background and were regarded as educationally subnormal. This way of 'framing' the family became significant later when one criterion for ritual abuse was the involvement, cited in the American literature (Finkelhor, 1988), of predominantly middle class 'intelligent' people. In 1985, the parents claimed that their house was haunted by a ghost and a poltergeist. It was blessed by a priest and the manifestations stopped. This information is subsequently correlated with the children's talk of ghosts and the suggestion is made that the talk could have derived from, and been related to, this event. This example of the retro-prospective feature of practical reasoning identifies a key feature of evidence; that making sense of what comes later in the light of what has gone before, and vice versa, is a corroborating device.

The child's (B) teacher, who was viewed positively by the judge, gave evidence. An assessment of the teacher preceded an account of her comments, in which it was stated that she was 'not very experienced' but 'intelligent and shrewd' with 'an old head on young shoulders'. We are then told that the teacher described B as 'disturbed', 'unhappy', 'withdrawn', with 'no self-esteem', often tired and cold to touch, he had sudden outbursts of temper and was attention seeking. All of these characteristics could be indicators of parental maltreatment, though not, in themselves, indicators of ritual abuse. The judge then goes on to describe how the social services became involved. Before commenting on what the children had said, the point is made that the social workers had read articles on ritual abuse, one of which contained the passage:

> Even if what the children are saying is untrue, it is clear they believe it to be true so something dreadful must have happened to them.

This stance was said to have informed the social worker's interviewing. It is wholly unacceptable in a legal framework to be seen to prejudge an issue — the facts must speak for themselves. By using this quote, the judge begins to discredit both the social workers and the evidence they obtained in one instant. In prefacing the teacher's account with a positive character assessment, her statement is credited and cannot be so easily dismissed. Thus, there is a case to examine, first, but the next piece of information immediately begins to undermine the foundations on which it rests.

Thus the 'believing stance' becomes a crucial issue for future investigations, as well as this case. Evidence, in its legal sense, should be an adequate document of the matter under consideration.

The distinction between 'social' and 'legal' evidence is made by Dingwall, Eekelaar and Murray (1983). Social evidence is what people might require in an everyday sense, to establish whether something has happened, and it does not hold the same 'probative value' as 'legal' evidence. It would not be possible, or desirable, to have to prove all matters beyond all reasonable doubt in everyday life. This point is made in Chapter 5 where, in interviewing children, one unordinary feature is identified, that of not suspending the 'rule of doubt'. 'Social' evidence is interpreted in the light of what is already known about a person's moral character, or a given set of circumstances. This cannot be the case for legal evidence, for example, in relation to identity:

> The evidence must formulate the identity of the accused; it must not be the case that the evidence itself becomes understandable only on the basis of prior knowledge of the accused's guilty identity. Rules of admissibility of evidence exist to ensure that the sequence of formulation, at least as it takes place inside the court, proceeds from documents to identity. Frank, 1981.p.181 cited in Dingwall et al., 1983 p.151

Evidence which may have started its course as 'social' evidence, as much evidence in cases of offences against children must do, takes on a 'legal' status when presented in court, even though it might not have been obtained under the same 'rules'. There can be no prior formulation through which the information is judged. Unfortunately this might lead to a misunderstanding of the 'believing stance' which is not about an unquestioned belief in what the child says, but directs practitioners not to enter the encounter with the child in a state of disbelief.

There is a clear sense in which certain actors in the Rochdale case are construed as credible and reliable, and others are not. The activity of constructing a credible source and then interweaving this with a decision on the evidence runs throughout the judgement. The evidence rested almost entirely on what the children said in interview with the social workers. It was stated that two factors had to be established in relation to that evidence: that it had to be obtained in a reliable form, and that it must have been correctly and accurately analysed. Much of the judgement centres on showing how the children's accounts were not so obtained, for example:

> I have considered the evidence of Mrs Scott-Fordham but I infinitely prefer the opinion of Mrs Valerie Mellor, a consultant clinical psychologist instructed on behalf of the family 1 children, that the interview work was done with little regard to the Cleveland recommendations and breached many

of the requirements which she would regard as essential. The breaches were not minor, trivial or infrequent, but substantial breaches which rendered the information received from the children valueless and unreliable.

That opinion is shared by Professor Elizabeth Newson, Professor of Developmental Psychology at Nottingham University, whose report, commissioned by family 4, contained a devastating and detailed analysis of the shortcomings of the social worker's investigatory technique.

It is clear that certain experts are given authority and credibility and others are not, and that this authority is used to further discredit the already discredited. First, I will show some of the grounds for the experts being 'credited' or 'discredited'. Professor Newson and Mrs Mellor were mentioned in the context of certain statements which could arguably act as criteria to support their status as good 'experts'. These were: basing statements on clinical and research evidence and their 'vastly greater experience', which included professional involvement 'in some 16 to 18 cases with some 70 to 80 children' of which approximately half were found by the court to be proved, this experience confirmed the literature, 'they gave evidence of having had a meticulous examination of the material available and have reported on the result of their work in detail'. Mrs Scott-Fordham, called by the local authority, was discredited by the following criteria: not reading the full Cleveland report, altering previous statements under cross-examination, she was not a child psychologist, not having the same amount of experience in 'understanding a child's mind' and the 'effect upon it of the kind of questioning to be seen in the transcripts', having no experience of ritual or satanic abuse but 'basing an understanding on writings', she was not supported by the literature she relied on, she had read only the family 1 transcripts and was thus considered unprepared. Miss Fisher, also relied on by the local authority, had: 'limited first-hand experience of ritual abuse' with adults, 'she made frequent reference to what she called the literature to support her theories, but she had not brought any of the literature with her and was only able to give vague citations', she did not have the 'detachment which the court expects . . .' anything that did not fit she explained away. If the evidence supported her theory, she would use it and, if it didn't, she would discredit it'. This final comment is interesting since there is evidence to suggest that this is precisely what the judge himself was doing. There are a number of comments in the script which refer to probability, and the normal bounds of human behaviour. It could be argued that the judge was operating, in part, on his own theory based on what is expectable, 'normal', and thus believable, within our culture. All the evidence that he was able to accept acted to reinforce that position, and all the evidence that was rejected did not do so. For example:

> The other clearly unprompted statement by B, much relied on by the local authority, is in relation to the cemetery. Mrs Mellor said that he would have called it a cemetery if he had been there with his parents and not a church garden. That is speculative and I am not persuaded of it, but nevertheless I find it very difficult to accept that he was discussing real experiences. Although no search of the cemetery was made, there were no reports to the police or the authorities of graves being disturbed, animal remains being found or strange activities taking place, all of which would have been expected if graves had been dug up and animals had been killed and eaten.

> The likeliest explanation of what B said is that this is further fantasy . . .

Quite unusually, in the context of the rest of the judgement, the judge suggests that a 'credited' witness is being speculative. He, nevertheless, uses her speculative comments to precede his own opinion, that the activities the child alleged to have happened were difficult to accept: that only in the face of 'real' evidence could they be believable. In the absence of such evidence, the child's comments are reconstructed as fantasy, remaining within the 'expectable': children can be expected to fantasise.

There were a number of facets to this case, of which the distinction between fantasy and reality was one. Others were: how the information was obtained, whether drugs were administered, whether ritual abuse can occur without sexual abuse, and the culpability and intention of the parents. Each of these issues was discussed and a verdict reached on a probable explanation of what the children had said in the context of them. This technique of forming probable explanations for particular parts of the evidence had an interpretive echo for the evidence as a whole. Thus, if it could be shown that the interviewing of the children was unreliable in part, all of the information obtained in interview — which comprised the main part of the evidence — was discredited. If it could be shown that a child may have been fantasising in one part, this cast doubt on his whole account. If it could be shown that sexual abuse was an intrinsic component of ritual abuse, and the children had no physical symptoms of sexual abuse — despite one child actually having them — then the children were considered not to have been the victims of ritual abuse.

I will take one example to display how each of these features is

played out in the decision-making process; that is, the use of one
expert to discredit another, the preferred version of events which
seeks to accommodate the 'normal' and 'expectable', and the way in
which one part of the evidence has an interpretive echo for the rest.
The part of the judgement selected concerns the issue of whether
sexual abuse is an intrinsic part of ritual abuse.

> Mrs Mellor's clinical experience confirms the American
> literature. In every case of satanic or ritual abuse, sexual
> abuse has been a component. In Mrs Mellor's view, which
> I share, it is in the highest degree improbable that adults
> would go to the trouble of dressing up and performing rites
> with children, some of them of a horrific nature, without sexual
> activity of some kind being involved . . .

Thus the grounds are laid on the basis of probability — what can
be expected, and not expected on the basis of what is known in
common about people in our culture, in this case that there must
be a reason for certain types of behaviour, and that reason has
to do with sexual gratification. The credibility of the experts who
support this view is then outlined, in a way which continues to give
it strength:

> . . . those who have had to deal with ritual or satanic abuse, Dr
> Holt, Mrs Mellor and Dr Heller, are of the view that satanic
> or ritual abuse is always accompanied by sexual abuse. The
> strongest opinion is expressed by Mrs Mellor who has the
> greatest experience . . .

The experts are defined as having a warrant to comment and their
comment is given. Thus:

> In these circumstances I have no hesitation in rejecting the
> evidence of Mrs Scott-Fordham. She had no clinical experience
> of a relevant kind and little experience of child sexual abuse.
> She was a surprising choice, in my view, by the local authority,
> as an expert witness in this field. She is not supported by the
> literature she herself relies on. She had no realistic answer to
> Mrs Mellor's opinion that the children not only had no signs
> of sexualised behaviour but showed no fear and they did not
> use any of the words or terms of satanic abuse. They did not
> mention church ornaments or an altar, apart from what I regard
> as an unreliable drawing of what is said to be a chalice, they
> did not talk of demons or wizards or witches, or boss man, a
> term which Mrs Mellor had heard from children to describe the
> organiser of the abuse.

I want to stress here that I am not in pursuit of a right or
wrong interpretation of the facts, what I want to show is how

the business of interpretation gets done, so that any future work
on interpretation in a legal setting can be anticipated, and publicly
understood. The use of experts as a device to credit or discredit
others is clearly articulated above. There is a further dimension to
this; the use of experts as validators of a preferred version of events.
To take the final statement concerning the level of fear exhibited
and use of words or terms associated with ritual abuse, Pamela
Hudson (1991) gives a summary of reported acts in relation to
ritual abuse cases in America. They include: being locked in a cage
or 'jail', told that parents, pets or younger siblings would be killed
if anyone is told of the abuse, being drugged, being hung from a
pole or hook, perpetrators wearing robes and/or masks, observing
animals killed, being taken to churches, other people's homes and
graveyards for the ritual abuse. There are different forms of ritual
abuse, and not all children report the same events, however, these
and some others such as: live burial in caskets, coffins, boxes, water
torture, threats with guns or knives, drug injections, filming and
still photography, were reported by several children in Hudson's
study. The children in Rochdale talked of being put in cages, being
chained to a wall, being given special drinks and sweets that made
them fly, digging in a cemetery, burying people and ghosts, killing
sheep and eating them, killing babies, ghosts, monsters and adults
who wore silver clothes. It may well have been that this information
was obtained in an unreliable form, but there can be no doubt
that they used the words and terms which were relevant to an
assessment of ritual abuse, although these were not the words and
terms selected in the above extract by the judge. The judge himself
points this out later in the judgement, and continues to dismiss each
component of the allegation by use of the 'experts'. For example, in
relation to killing babies:

> The potentially alarming statement of killing babies and seeing
> babies killed has to be seen against a background of Professor
> Newson's and Dr Holt's clinical experience. In their experience,
> in Professor Newson's case going back 30 years, children talking
> of killing babies is commonplace. Dr Holt said the talk of
> slaughter of babies is the rule rather than the exception.
> Professor Newson said this was frequently encountered with
> children who had for certain not been abused in any way.

By taking the topic of 'killing babies' on its own, and applying
the credited expert's opinion on that topic alone, it is brought
within the realms of the normal. One is mindful of Freud and his
interpretation of the accounts of his patients relating to childhood
sexual assault. Within his own time and culture this too was
thought to be wholly implausible, and the pressure of opinion

was great enough to force Freud to rethink his hypothesis, to bring it within the acceptable framework of fantasy. This method of breaking down the evidence into isolated events, out of their context, and dismissing each in turn was characteristic of the judgement. No comment was made about the numbers of children, in the experience of the 'credited' experts, who talked about killing babies, for example, in the context of ghosts, being put in cages, given magic toffees, and so forth. It may be that this is also commonplace, but the question was not accounted for in the judgement. In addition, there are at least five references in the judgement to the children being frightened when talking about the alleged events, yet in the statement above they are described as showing 'no fear'.

First it must be remembered that, in general, very little is known about ritual abuse. Secondly, what is known, in a professional and particularly legal arena, is known because there has been sufficient evidence to warrant intervention. The sexual assault of a child would constitute such a warrant. Thus it is not surprising that the experts have only encountered cases where sexual assault is a feature. But rather than acknowledge it as a possible requirement of this form of abuse to reach a status sufficient to come to court, it is interpreted as a criterion for defining the abuse itself. In contrast, there has been a dearth of 'alternative' literature, mainly in photocopied pamphlet form, given out where the topic is discussed, for example, at social work conferences (for example, the BASPCAN Conference at Leicester, 1991) which seeks to show that, whilst ritual activities, even 'satanism', take place, they do not include such components as sexual and physical assault on children, or child murder. Because so little is known, or believed, about ritual abuse, it is not possible to give status to either side. Yet, in the absence of a definitive view on the nature of ritual abuse, this judge has had to reach a decision as to whether the children in Rochdale were victims of it. To examine how this was done, as an instance of legal reasoning, shows, once again, how evidence is reflexively formulated. That is, it is 'made sense of' in terms of the way it is produced, and it is produced in terms of the way it is, and is to be, 'made sense of'. Evidence in this and many other cases of child abuse, is not a 'hard and fast' 'there or not' thing. When the only evidence is a child's account, the matter is open to opinion.

Some further observations about what might affect the strength of a future case can be observed from the judgement. The fact that there was no 'accused', and an absence of complaint about sexual abuse meant that the case almost had to be constructed from scratch, based on what the children said. There were certain assumptions which would need pre-empting; for example, that there are abnormal conditions in childhood which are not necessarily linked to child abuse, and that, if they are, those links must be evident, or that children will show an aversion to activities which could be associated with the abuse perpetrated on them, that parents are not likely to be co-operative unless highly intelligent, and that some children talk nonsense, are suggestible or unreliable.

Finally, in relation to the interviewing, certain points were made, most of which are now accounted for in the *Memorandum for Good Practice*. It was stated that all the interviews should have been taped, and notes taken, that leading questions should not be used, that interviews were started when the child began to 'disclose', thus denying the opportunity to see what preceded the video, and that the social workers had not checked the equipment which they clearly should have done. Criticisms of the videos themselves included the indifferent technical quality, figures were visually distant, and facial expressions were not observable. The sound was muffled and the interview technique was thrown into high relief because interviewers could be heard but the child couldn't. There was only one camera position and one child had her back to the camera for long periods of time. In the pilot evaluation (Wattam, 1992) a number of technical 'hitches' occurred, even where interviewers were trying to follow the *MOGP* with an eye to technical quality. These included: problems with the earpiece repeatedly falling out, the child hearing feedback through the interviewer's earpiece, visibility of the equipment to the child, one child was able to see the light reflected off the TV monitor, and another was acutely aware of the camera, all of which caused distraction. There were also difficulties caused by the positioning of the child and interviewer; the child was often not facing the camera (in one interview, the child was at 90° to the camera throughout) all participants being quite distant (the co-interviewer was only observable by her legs in two interviews). Finally, in one interview, the time declared by the interviewer at closure did not match that on the tape timer (by approximately 10 minutes), and in one interview, either the insert box or the in-built date/time mechanism covered the child's face. The need for training in using the technology was clearly and strongly expressed. The importance of technical quality as an evidential variable cannot be underestimated. The technical annex in the *Memorandum* gives advice on camera position, equipment and expectations about visual and sound quality, all of which are important to the interpretation of the tape and its admissibility in evidence.

In conclusion, as in the previous chapter, the key for investigators is to anticipate and compensate for the reasoning about children's testimony in court wherever possible. Given that the testimony to be presented in court is known beforehand, and increasingly so with video, it should be scrutinised for the retro-prospective way of interpreting evidence as a corroborative device, and compensation made where possible. That is, the accounts of children should be examined for topics and themes that might relate retro- and prospectively, just as a family history which included reference to ghosts was used to corroborate the fact that a child might have been confused in the Rochdale case. If it is known that these historic features do not corroborate current events, some attempt must be made to display that they do not before such inferences are drawn by others who would, in terms of practical reasoning, have good cause to do so.

Previous chapters have shown how evidential facts are, in fact, versions of events. This chapter has depicted, through legal statements of, and about, experts, how experts are used to validate these versions of events. Expertise is a claim, in that it must be exercisable, and it is an achievement. Like a knowledge claim, a claim to expertise must rest on a demonstrable exercise of the relevant things and skills the expertise is claimed to involve. The Rochdale judgement includes statements about what the relevant skills are: what makes a 'good' or 'bad' expert, such as things to do with thoroughness and experience. However, there is an indication that such skills are defined in the context of the preferred version of events, and the valued attributes of an expert are used to back up that version. One way in which this is done is by breaking down the evidence into discrete parts and by applying the expertise to each part — such as in the case of children 'killing babies' — without examining the evidence as a whole, in its own context.

# 11 Making a case in court

In this final chapter, I want to present a transcript, which is more or less complete, of a case which I observed in court. There was nothing very unusual about this case, it was a routine, run-of-the-mill case for the CPS clerk, except that it was a case about child 'abuse'. This case had been through all the stages outlined so far in this book. That is, it had been referred to a social service agency, it had been categorised as a case warranting investigation, the child had been jointly interviewed by a police officer and social worker, and her case had been put forward for prosecution. The person believed responsible, her stepfather, had been charged and had denied the offence of indecent assault with which he was charged, so the case had come to trial.

## The case

B1   = prosecution counsel
B2   = defence counsel
CPSC = Crown Prosecution Service Clerk
X    = the child complainant

We returned and were sitting in court for 2.15. Another case came on first, the defendant in our case was called at 2.30. The jury are sworn in and told to give 'a true verdict according to the evidence'. The indictment is read by the clerk, 5 counts.

B1: 'These are specimen charges, let me tell you a bit about the circumstances. Generally (X) is 12 and lives at [address] she is [the defendant's] stepdaughter. [I refer to the] timing of [X's] behaviour change, mother put this down to adolescence [date] things came to a head, X made allegations. Mother tried to talk and it was then that a very serious allegation was made of sexual abuse that went back till 5 or 6. Initially this was touching but went on to more serious acts as the years went on. Mother, quite properly reported this to the police. By X's account, I won't go into detail, she says it started by touching private parts, not that serious but this is how it started. She recalls, aged 7, touching and she resorted to wearing knickers in bed, that didn't work. She recalls getting into bed in a dressing gown, that didn't work either. From [date] the incidents stopped for no apparent reason, she hadn't said anything. Unfortunately they started again, when she was about to start junior school. It was even more serious this time. I won't go into detail but there was at least one occasion when the defendant attempted sexual intercourse. The police were alerted and he was sent for trial to this court. Why here? Because of the video link. It was a condition of bail that he stayed away, went to a hostel, a further condition was that he stay away from [home town]. I mention this because it was important, because, not long after, X and her mother went to the solicitors and wrote a letter saying it was a pack of lies. Either it was a pack of lies or she had been put under enormous pressure. It was up to the police to find out and their inquiries really were quite fruitful. The family had actually been up to see him in the [Btown] area and immediately he put pressure on her, told her she might get into trouble, she would be put into a home, that her mother [        ] but it didn't stay just like that, for thereafter the defendant clearly broke his bail conditions and, for a certain time, took up residence in the family home. The jury must decide either this is a girl who has made it up or this is the truth of the matter. The charges are merely specimens and you must consider the charges separately, of course.

The judge then announced that we would move to another court where the video link equipment was installed. I ask CPSC about the child, and am told she arrived this morning and a WPC has been looking after her. We move to another court (2.55). Barristers chatting (only people who are, everyone else silent) '. . . we'll finish the girl today'.

Judge turns on the video link equipment, we can see the child is giggling and looks surprised, sitting back in a chair.

Judge: 'Hello can you hear me talk, I'm going to ask you some questions [        ] er lies d'you know what lies are? . . . good, I'm going to push another button now and you'll see another man.

B1: [name] that is your name? and you lived at [address]. Take it slowly and tell me in your own words what [the defendant] did.

C: He tried to kiss me and that.

B1: Anything else?

C: Tried to take his trousers off and get in on top of me.

B1: Did he do this when you were 5?

C: Yes, he did this when I was 5.

B1: Do you remember where it all took place?

C: The bedroom or living room.

B1: Where was your mother usually when this happened?

C: If it was the morning, in bed, if night she was usually out.

B1: Now this is when you told us you were about 5, when you were 6, was it still a lot or only sometimes?

C: Sometimes quite a lot.

B1: D'you remember when you were 7 and can you tell us what happened?

C: He got on top of me and tried to get my knickers off [pause]

B1: Once or twice, or more than that?

C: More than that.

B1: Now X, did you ever go to bed in anything else?

[gap here in notes]

I want to go on to when you were 9, had you still got your cabin bed?

C: Think so, not sure.

B1: What happened?

C: I was watching telly and my dad got onto my bed and pulled my pyjama bottoms down.

Judge: What was that — I'm going to ask you to say that again, can you shout up a bit?

C: Yeah, I was watching telly and my dad got onto my bed and pulled my pyjama bottoms down and put his privates on top of me.

Judge: Just a moment, Judge turns to barrister, what was that, pulled my pyjama bottoms? (B nods, 'yes').

Judge: What was that, privates in to me?

B1: Privates on top of me.

C: on top of me.

B1: What happened then X?

C- I told him to get off . . . and then went downstairs.

B1: When you were 9. Always on your cabin bed, anywhere else?

C: Sometimes on a couch downstairs.

B1: Where would your mum be and your brothers be?

C: Neighbours, out.
B1: Would you always be alone in the house?
C: Not always mum might be in bed or something.
B1: Did you ever tell your mum?
C: No.
B1: Why not?
C: Scared she might shout at me.
B1: Do you remember a time when your mother was in hospital
for 2–3 weeks. D'you remember what happened then?
C: [Def] kept coming in my room and saying can I have a look
at your privates.
B1: What could you see then?
C: His privates.
B1: And what did he do?
C: He got on top of me.
B1: And can you tell us what he did when he got on top of
you?
C: He kept moving up and down.
B1: Now I'm talking about when your mother was in hospital,
did this happen once or more than once?
C: More than once.
B1: More than once. After your mother came out of hospital I
think it stopped for a while, is that right?
C: Yes.
[There followed a question on the next time something
happened in the context of schools, leaving old school, dates,
how old the child was at the time]
B1: Did anything else happen again round about then?
C: Yes.
B1: What happened?
C: [He] came into my room and sometimes had his dressing
gown on. He pushed me down and then he got on top of me.
B1: Just pause for a moment, and then?
C: And then he hurt me and covered my mouth so no one could
hear me and then he went downstairs.
B1: Just stopping there for a moment, just wait a minute
[pause] can you tell me how he hurt you? I know this is
difficult for you.
[child says something]
Can you speak up?
C: He hurt me in my privates.
B1: Sorry, say that again.
Judge: what did she say, in her privates?
[          ]
C: I started crying and went downstairs for a glass of water.

B1: Did anything else happen that time, was this just one thing?

C: Not sure.

B1: You were still at your new school and er during [dates] did anything else happen?

C: Don't know.

B1: Did things stop then?

C: For a while and then they started again.

B1: We're just trying to get the dates, let's go on to after that Xmas.

C: He asked if I wanted to wash his privates.

Judge: He asked?

B1: If I wanted to wash his privates. Doing the best we can, I appreciate it's not easy for you to remember anything, this was in the second term at your new school. D'you remember the summer term. Start of the second year at your new school?

C: Yeah, he came in and said, can I rub your privates?

B1: And was this morning or night [          ]
What was the next thing you remember happening?

C: He kept trying to look at my breast and then I said no and he pulled my top off and began feeling them.

Judge: He kept trying to look at my breast?

B1: And he pulled my top off and began feeling them. Did you tell anyone else about this at school, or your mother?

C: No.

B1: And did this happen once or more than once?

C: Quite a few times.

B1: Now did this upset you, going to school?

C: Yeah

B1: Did you get any money from [the defendant]?

C: About 70 to 80p

B1: Did you get the money the same time or a different time?

C: Same time sometimes.

B1: Did anything else happen that you haven't told us so far?

C: No.

B1: D'you remember a row with your mother about going to the post office. Did you tell your mother?

[reply]

Do you remember that after you told the police officer [the defendant] went to live somewhere else in [town]?

C: Yes.

B1: That's what I want to ask next.

[child explains what the defendant had said to her]

'Why have you told them, it's no good, the judge will just say you're just telling lies.'

B1: [what did your mother say?]
C: She told me to say that I was just making it up to get me Dad into trouble.
B1: Did you want to go?
C: No
B1: Why did you tell the solicitor that?
C: 'Cos me mum was ill, she was making herself sick and she was always crying. I just hoped that me mum would be alright.
B1: And did you go to [town] again?
C: Yeah
B1: And did you stay?
C: Yeah
B1: Was that in a little hotel?
C: Yeah
B1: And was anything else said to you again?
C: No. He was mostly with me mum.
B1: Now X, did you see your dad in [home town] at all?
C: It was after Christmas [       ]
B1: And did he stay at the house for a long time or what?
[       ]
Were you back at school this time, or not?
[       ]
When you saw him, was anything said about what you'd said to the police?
C: No not really.
B1: Can you help us X, when you say not really, just what he said in the [supermarket]?
C: Your mum's gonna get took away for seeing me.
B1: Did you believe him?
C: Sometimes.
B1: What happened then? Eventually he left did he?
[       ]
Someone else is going to ask you some questions.

This extract represents an almost complete account of the child's examination in chief. It is the part that the child will no longer have to give in court, but will be on pre-recorded video. The 'rules' underpinning the question and answer format are clearly different from those advocated in the *MOGP*. There is no attempt at establishing rapport, and no free narrative stage, with questioning beginning at the start. The questioning style tends to be closed, and more than one question is often asked at a time. Many of the questions have the sense of acknowledging that both participants know what they are referring to, for example:

B1: . . . let's go on to after Christmas.

C: He asked if I wanted to wash his privates.

and could therefore be described as leading. The child is interrupted whilst giving her answers, by the judge, and there are attempts to get certain points emphasised by requesting they are repeated. Almost all the rules that are established as good practice in the *MOGP* are ignored. This observation indicates one of two possibilities in terms of the implementation of the MOGP. The first is to do with how much more licence barristers have in interviewing children, and how little licence practitioners will have in the future. This may have the repercussion of inhibiting the availability of evidence, which it has previously been possible to get at, since children cannot be interviewed in the same way. Alternatively, it may mean that the investigating team, whilst attempting to follow the guidance wherever possible, can feel safer relaxing into less stringent 'rules' because, traditionally, the courts have accepted such an approach.[1]

The examination in chief is followed by the cross-examination. Despite the recommendations of the Pigot working group, this will still take place in court on the day of the trial.

[Defence barrister starts]

B2: When you first met [the defendant] you liked him didn't you and until last year [the defendant] took mum's side, told you you were naughty and horrible towards mum. D'you know what it means if someone makes discipline. D'you understand?

C: No.

B2: Follow the rules?

C: No.

B2: Like at school. He wouldn't let you have your own way, shout at mum, swear at mum, go out late.

C: No.

B2: And you got very angry at [defendant] taking your mum's side.

C: Yeah.

B2: You wanted him to go.

C: Yeah.

B2: You knew that you'd have to say something terrible to get [the defendant] to leave.

C: Yeah.

B2: And it was only when [          ]. These are lies these accusations.

C: What does accusations mean?

B2: See, you told us that you wanted him out of the house.

C: Yes, no [child is showing some distress]

B2: You've accused [the defendant] of some terrible things haven't you?
C: [shouts] IT'S TRUE [gets up and walks out of room away from camera crying].

Judge adjourns [3.50] and orders the jury to be back at 4.00 pm.
   On their return, the judge speaks to the child through the monitor, who is now back but still looking upset.

Judge: Are you prepared to go on?
C: [Yes]
B2: Before the break, was that true?
C: No, you got me confused.
[B2 asks question, unable to hear from my position]
C: Because you was confusing me. I didn't know what you was on about.
B2: Did you hate him?
C: Only cos he was doing things to me.
B2: Did you get on well with your mum?
[          ]
B2: Why did you not say a word to your mum?
C: I was scared she'd shout at me.
B2: Why were you scared, when all you were doing was suffer because of [the defendant]?
C: [Because I didn't tell anyone]
B2: Didn't tell anyone?
C: No.
B2: At your school there's a big notice.
C: Don't know, never seen it.
B2: But you knew you could tell a teacher.
C: Yeah.
B2: The first time you made a complaint was in a fit of temper.
C: Yeah.
B2: Why were you in a fury with your mother and father?
C: Because she asked me to go to the post office.
B2: You didn't want to go.
C: No.
B2: It wasn't anything to do with [the defendant]
C: No.
B2: Were you trying to upset your mum when you said these lies?
C: They're not lies.
B2: Were you trying to upset her because you knew she would be upset?
[child crying]

[pause] when you went to the solicitors you said you'd told a pack of lies, is that right?
C: Yeah.
B2: You actually said to the solicitor [ . . . ] that [ . . . ]
C: Yeah.
B2: Did you say that because she was sitting beside you?
C: [inaudible]
B2: How long was the pressure on you?
C: Since after Xmas.
B2: Speak up a little bit, slower, when did mum first put pressure on you?
C: After Xmas.
[        ]
B2: You've had a social worker to help you.
C: Yes.
B2: Did you ever complain to the social worker?
C: Sometimes.
B2: Did you ever tell the police?
C: No.
B2: Did you ask your social worker to [        ]. This is a pack of lies.
[child is crying]
B2: Why didn't you scream?
C: He put his hand over my mouth.
B2: Why didn't you tell your mum?
C: I don't know.
B2: Certainly you knew it was wrong.
C: Yeah.
B2: Why didn't you tell your mum?
C: Don't know.
B2: There were long periods of time when nothing happened. In the summer of 1989 nothing happened did it?
C: No.
B2: Can you say exactly when it stopped, in 1989?
C: Don't know, can't remember.
B2: D'you remember when you went back to school? How long since you went back to school?
C: Four weeks.
B2: If I suggested that it was a lot longer?
C: No, a few weeks.
B2: How long before it started up?
C: [        ]
B2: Before that when it started again when had it finished, would it be a long time?
C: Yeah.

B2: Would it be perhaps as long as six months?

C: Don't know.

B2: [What about town] why did you go if you didn't want to see him?

[gap in notes]

Judge: Is this a good summarising of what you said that you went to [town] because there was nowhere else for you to go?

C: Yes.

B2: The reason you'd gone to [town] is that you wanted to see [the defendant] is that right?

C: No.

B2: You have been giving your mum a terrible time lately. Swearing, shouting, staying out late.

C: I don't swear.

B2: Just so the judge knows what your answers are, have you been swearing at your mum?

C: No.

B2: Have you been staying out late?

C: Yes.

B2: Have you got into trouble with your mum for staying out late?

C: Yes.

B2: Has your mum smacked you?

C: Yes.

B2: Have you said to her that you'll have her put away? You see what I have to suggest X is that it's all lies.

C: It's not.

Judge: this seems to be a good point to break, case adjourned till tomorrow.

There is nothing in the cross-examination about the alleged assaults. The focus is on the child's character, and the language is designed both to confuse the child and also to get a certain message across: this child is unreliable, inconsistent, badly behaved. The barrister opens by suggesting the child is 'naughty' and 'horrible', that she does not understand 'discipline', she shouts and swears, and goes out late. There is an attempt to bring up the notion of 'taking sides', and that the child wanted the defendant to go, but this is situated in the context of argument rather than sexual assault. She is attributed with a self-knowledge which is extremely negative, she knew she would have to say something 'terrible', and this is constructed as 'lies' 'hate', a 'fit of temper', 'fury' and trying to 'upset her mother'. This is followed by the observation that she did not tell anyone when she, apparently, had the opportunity: to a teacher, her mother, the social worker, or the police, even to

herself, she did not 'scream'. However, having suggested clearly
that the child's statement consists of lies, the barrister then asks
exactly when 'it' stopped and talks around 'it' stopping. This
double message is confusing, the child is confused and her replies
are vague. Eventually, the judge must intervene and the barrister
then reiterates the 'terrible' time the child is giving her mother,
repeating the words 'swearing', 'shouting', and 'staying out late'.
The case is adjourned with the suggestion once again that the child
is lying. These are all tactics, and known as such. The barrister
was only stopped once, and there is a tacit acknowledgement that
this is acceptable behaviour: it is the job of the defence to expose
the weakness in the prosecution case. The jury are left with the
notion that this might be a confused, inconsistent and unreliable
child, with some ulterior motive for making the allegation. Here
we can begin to see the structures for making a case in their full
legal formulation. Specificity is lacking, the child gives one-word
answers on most occasions, there is no corroboration and the
child is depicted and orientated to under the category of 'badly
behaved child', which, even if she was, has nothing to do with
the alleged assault, but which does the work of mitigating against
the categorisation of 'victim'. This is instantiated by the comment:

> B2: Why were you scared, when all you were doing was suffer
> because of [the defendant]?

the implication being that if this child was a genuine victim, a
genuine sufferer, she should not be afraid. This line of defence
is reinforced the following day after other witnesses, the mother
and a police officer, had been called. The jury was given a break
while counsel and the judge discussed the evidence. The defence
suggested that it was a case of 'no case to answer' and gave a
reference (Hollinghorne, Criminal Law Review 87/88, Sheffield
Crown Court on a murder, p.767 November]. The defence stated
that there was no evidence on count 2, and no allegation from the
child for that time. He points out that this is a case that stands or
falls on the child's evidence and asks whether there is consistency.
The complaints were not recent, there is no corroboration, and, he
maintains, there are material inconsistencies. These come by way
of evidence of two retractions and admissions that she had lied.
There is a problem because the mother's testimony changed at the
last minute, and she decided to support her husband. Thus there
is a suggestion that there is 'no case to answer' because the mother
is put forward by the Crown. The evidence of the two witnesses
should not contradict, rather, together they should establish the
facts of the case. B2 suggests to the judge that the jury have to
look at the mother's evidence and see two contradictory accounts,

and also an admission that the allegation is a lie. He states that this is plainly a situation where the girl has the clearest possible motive to lie: she said that she hated him. The case is framed so that the jury are faced with the uncorroborated evidence of a child who hates the defendant, a girl who has retracted on two occasions, the first before she had seen the defendant and before the mother has given evidence that she has admitted that she has lied.

The judge reads the case of 'no case to answer' referred to by the defence. The prosecution attempt to counteract this move by suggesting there is corroboration.

> B1: On the first thing I say . . . factually, I'm not sure that the evidence goes as far as she told her mother that she wants to withdraw. I think your honour is better dealing with the letter . . . there is the corroboration of pressure, what about the corroboration.
> B2: Not corroboration at all — it may be a man trying to assert his innocence.

Corroboration, here, as on so many other occasions, consists in a concept, in this case 'pressure', the meaning of which is determined in the first place by its usage within everyday life. Once again, the structure of categorisation is a resource for decision-making. How else can the judge, and subsequently the jury, decide on what is reasonable, expectable, behaviour for an innocent man? Understanding what is being referred to here, how the notion of 'pressure' could amount to corroboration in the first place, is dependent on shared-in-common knowledge of the culture. This knowledge is exploited by both sides, it is the resource, on the one hand, to indicate guilt and, on the other, innocence.

The judge notes that the case was not opened on the basis that pressure was corroboration and that it needs 'mulling'. He retires and returns to say that he has decided not to accept 'no case to answer'; it is a matter for the jury to decide whether there was pressure or not. The jury are called back in and addressed.

> B1: Members of the jury, you've now heard all the evidence. We got to a stage where is this a case of having fabricated ( . . . ) or, alternatively, do we have a case where substantial pressure has been brought to bear. First of all you have seen X on this new practice of video link — almost as if she was on TV as it were . . . invite you to be very critical . . . try and put yourself as it were, right in the centre of the picture here. She's been criticized that she didn't make complaints. But look at it from a child's point of view. It may well be that that's just the sort of behaviour that you would expect. You know that

the girl made a complaint to a police officer . . . Ask yourself
this, why should she go to the solicitor . . . a case of divided
loyalties . . . an impossible situation to be in . . . why is it
that this girl retracted her complaint? Just think of the thought
process, why's she giving evidence?

B2: . . . Even we as lawyers don't understand it at times.
What the law says is . . . it is dangerous to convict on the
unsupported, that means uncorroborated, evidence of a child
[emphasises this several times, then] there is no evidence
that supports X's evidence . . . be aware of all the dangers
that are attendant on her evidence. What possible motive
that girl could have for telling wicked lies. In many cases
there is no obvious motive, sometimes it is better not to
look for a motive but in this case you have the perfect
motive. The defendant is in the always difficult position of
step-father, he has to assume the role of disciplinarian . . . is
there anything in that evidence that . . . the circumstances
in which the complaint was made, not one final significant
attempt by her step-father, it was her mother saying she
would be put away. Over the last 5 years possibly more,
possibly less, and she has known for probably about two
years that what he has been doing was wrong. Members of
the jury, why, why, why was there never a complaint to
anyone, mother . . . friend . . . teacher . . . aunt . . . do
you think there would not have been a single solitary piece
of evidence . . . if it had happened as frequently, of screams,
protest, marks, torn clothing . . . You can't get as good a
picture as we get when they're [on video link] . . . got a picture
of a completely relaxed girl . . . [pressure . . . consistency . . .]
It is no task of [the defendant] to prove his innocence to you,
it is the crown's task to prove his guilt . . . in simple words
members of the jury, you can only convict if you're sure of his
guilt . . . evidence that's going to confer in some material part
not only that the crimes have been committed but that it was
the defendant who committed those crimes, must come from
an independent source. So in this case X can't confirm herself.
Members of the jury I tell you now there is no such evidence
in this case. The evidence relied on by the prosecution or the
evidence of the mother herself.

Judge [        ] turn to the evidence [mine is not complete]. You
add the evidence that you think has that relevance. Don't worry
too much about the dates, the only two stable dates are change
of school and date of complaint. The video link obviously
lessens the stress, lessens the impact, direct impact of the

witness on the jury, so bear that in mind when evaluating her evidence . . . absence of recent complaint . . . note no medical evidence and remember on one occasion she said it hurt . . .

Ultimately, the defence rested on the possibility that the child was lying and the prosecution rested on whether the child had been put under pressure to retract. The jury are asked to draw on their knowledge of the culture, to consider the behaviour they would expect, of a child victim of sexual assault and of a step-father exerting discipline. The importance of 'pressure' as corroboration becomes clearer when the defence emphasises that it is dangerous to convict on uncorroborated evidence. This must be, and always will be so. However, it was part of the submission of the Pigot Working Group that the duty for the judge to warn the jury of convicting on uncorroborated evidence be dropped. They concluded that there were sufficient safeguards within the judicial process without the need to emphasise the warning. As yet, the duty to warn remains intact but it clearly mitigates against reaching a guilty verdict in such cases. As Garfinkel (1967*a*,*b*) points out in his study of juror's decision-making, one of the rules making up the official line that the juror follows is that:

> Between what is legal and what is fair, the good juror does what is legal. p.106

The warning articulates a legal 'rule' which juror's would therefore have a tendency to follow, despite their possible belief in a child's account.

There was an acknowledgement by all the legal personnel involved in this case that it could have gone either way, that is, that the verdict could have been guilty or not guilty from the start. This possibility is present even in the context of knowledge which suggests to any given party that, in fact, there is a 'true' verdict in the case. The defence barrister had, on other occasions, acted for the prosecution and therefore had a certain kind of relationship, one which permitted the case to be talked about outside of the court. This kind of talk generally has to do with what evidence you have, and what kind of a chance of conviction you have, on the basis of the evidence. He had indicated that the defendant had probably 'done it', but it was mutually acknowledged that his job on this occasion was to defend the accused. The defence is not a denial, rather it is an exploitation of the weaknesses in the prosecution's evidence, the child's account. The two kinds of 'realities', inside and outside the courtroom, allow strategy to be discussed, particularly in breaks. In one break I overheard the two barristers saying, for example:

> Well hold on, I don't follow this at all, if it's a plea it'll go through court, if it's not a plea . . . well I'll tell you what I'll do, I'll speak to the senior probation officer . . .

This talk could not be conducted when the court is sitting, it is an outside negotiation which acknowledges that there are different possible outcomes, which need to be thought about, accounted for, anticipated. It further exemplifies how justice is not a hard and fast thing to do with representing the 'facts' and reaching a decision about them. The facts, as we can see from the above, are constructed within the court for the purposes at hand. They are versions of events, of people, and of truth. This has quite profound consequences for children, because it depends greatly on the ways that children are categorised and oriented to within our culture: as victims, as well behaved, badly behaved and so forth. It turns out to have less to do with what has actually happened, if that can ever be known, and much more to do with how children can be presented within the legal system. This is further exemplified by the references to video link: the way in which it might give an artificial picture of relaxation and lessen the impact of the child's testimony. Whilst there is some dispute as to whether this is an effect of video link (Davies & Noon, 1991), what is of interest here is the way in which video link was drawn upon as a resource, a factor to consider in assessing the evidence, that is, the child's testimony. The prosecution state:

> First of all you have seen X on this new practice of video link — almost as if she was on TV as it were . . .

What relevance can this observation have to the evidence? This becomes clear when the judge states:

> The video link obviously lessens the stress, lessens the impact, direct impact of the witness on the jury, so bear that in mind when evaluating her evidence . . .

The relevance is obtained through categorisations of children as victims, who are not expected to be relaxed, who are expected to be stressed, who are expected under non-video link circumstances to have an impact on the jury. In other words, these are the kind of criteria upon which children are acknowledged and known to be judged, and the comments above show that it is known to be known. This is problematic because, quite clearly, not all children are the same, they do not experience sexual assault, or any other adult inflicted harm or injury, in the same way, nor do they respond to questioning similarly. Thus, in terms of making a case whilst it already happens that some account is taken of categorisation as a structure underpinning decision-making, it may also be necessary to highlight any particular child's difference, to state quite clearly how it might happen that they are not as they are expected to be.

The same is, of course, applicable to adults. But adults have more of a choice, about whether to make a complaint, about how to respond to questioning which they are better equipped to interpret and understand. Adults have a better chance of knowing the rules, and, as the above clearly displays, a child's ignorance of them can be a resource for exploitation by the defence. In this case, the jury reached a verdict of 'not guilty'. Some weeks later I was informed that the defendant had moved back into the family home, and had freely admitted his guilt. The child remained in local authority care. Even if she had been allowed to give her evidence in chief on pre-recorded video, it is likely that the rest of the case, the cross-examination, the testimony of other witnesses, the silence of the defendant, the issues of 'pressure' and corroboration, would have remained. It must therefore be clear that, despite the piecemeal implementation of Judge Pigot's recommendations, children may still not be afforded justice. It is this observation which underpins my concluding remarks in the following chapter.

## Notes

1.  The CPS have indicated that it may be inappropriate to draw conclusions on the basis of this one case, and that another example of court proceedings may have shown a more rigorous adherence to rules of evidence and painted a different picture. Whilst this may, or may not be so, it does not take into account that these barristers, the judge, and all other legal personnel involved had been involved in many other cases of this kind and did not find it relevant to comment that the overall proceedings were anything unusual. On the contrary, this case was treated in a very routine way. Indeed, 'exceptional' or different features were a matter to be commented on, for example, by the judge in his account to the jury of video link. So the fact that this is one case is irrelevant to the comments I make.

# Conclusion

In the light of material presented in this book, one cannot fail to ask the question of whether the law is an appropriate device for responding to child abuse. Many, including the Lord Chancellor, view the introduction of the Children Act, 1989, as a step towards family courts, 'with welfare and justice going hand-in-hand as equal partners ready to solve any problems and resolve any conflict involving children's interests' (King, 1991). This could present an improvement on the present system. However, as King argues, following Teubner (1988, 1989), family courts would constitute a hybrid institution with the legal discourse continuing to dominate and interfere with a child welfare discourse. King concludes that:

> The overriding lesson of Teubner's ideas for child psychiatrists, child psychologists and social workers is not to place their faith in the creation of some romanticized family court. Rather, they should seek to develop their own mechanisms for dispute resolution and conflict management outside the confines of the legal system, much as the out-of-court conciliation movement has done. Only thus could they ensure that their world view and their procedures for reality construction would be preserved. p.319

King reaches this conclusion by showing how the legal discourse, in attempting to accommodate child welfare discourse, reconstructs child welfare science as legal communication and thus gives it a quite different meaning. This is evidenced in part by the dilemmas faced by 'expert witnesses', who must couch their own professional talk for a legal audience, particularly with a view to cross-examination. In Chapter 9 it was shown how the child's account similarly takes on the status of a legal communication, which makes it subject to different criteria for its interpretation, and which often renders it inadequate as a legal device. The section on interviewing children displays how the known requirement for the child's account to stand as a legal communication structures the approach to the child and the type of information sought. The consequences of this were discussed, one of which is to make the process very difficult for the child. King cites Furniss who writes of his own experience as an expert, and the problem presented by cases which fail for 'legal reasons'. Furniss explains how such outcomes 'provoke further abuse' and contribute to a system of 'abuse-promoting child protection'.

King's analysis is useful in terms of helping to make sense of how it is that the law is so difficult to influence, and how it must shape whatever it deals with under its own discursive 'rules'. However, the material contained in this book clearly indicates that legal reasoning is situated within the context of practical reasoning, even if they are not entirely the same thing.

It has been shown how legal professionals draw on their knowledge of every-day life, on the culture and matters known to be known 'in common', in order to do their work. There is also some indication that the legal discourse has been open to change in relation to children, particularly with regard to the Children Act, 1989, and that it is, therefore, more open than King suggests (James, 1992). Thus, the answer may not be to avoid the legal system altogether. Rather it should be used to the benefit of the victim. There is no point in going to court if you are clearly not going to have the potential of effecting some planned and desired change (Morrison, 1991). If prosecution, or the seeking of a child protection order, is considered by the victim and those who work with him/her to be beneficial, then it may be appropriate to go to court. There will also be many cases where court is not the best course of action, and a large number of children and families might need diversionary intervention (Masson, 1992). The problem for the practitioner arises in deciding which course to follow.

The investigation of child abuse has become increasingly a joint endeavour, between the police and social services. Each has their own interest, their own role, and their own organisational requirements. Observations from an evaluation of the pilot of the *MOGP* suggest that the joint working relationship will have some consequence for the decision-making process. It may, in practice, be the case that decisions about how to handle children's cases are taken by default, rather than on the basis of criteria designed to consider the child's best interests. The case examples given in Chapter 6 show how the criteria for conducting a substantive interview on video begin to operate. In this concluding chapter, I report on some of the observations from the pilot of the *MOGP* which have relevance to decisions about when, and when not, to video. In doing so, I will make reference to the key themes of the book, to do with the structures underpinning decision-making and the ways in which children's evidence is constructed and interpreted.

Arrangements for joint working vary across the country. One point of interest for future research would be to see how these arrangements affect the implementation of the *MOGP*. There were clear differences in the two pilot areas. In Area 1, after a referral is received, a strategy meeting is arranged as soon as practicable. It is recommended within 12 hours, and in any case within 24 hours unless exceptional circumstances warrant delay. The meetings need not be face to face and are sometimes conducted over the telephone (often after office hours). They include a nominated worker, a police officer and social services team manager. Occasionally, a senior police officer will participate. The strategy meetings are designed for workers to decide the next step.

The process, in prototype, runs as follows:

(*a*) Meeting held.
(*b*) Officers (SSD and/or police) contact parent and, if further information is needed to establish that an offence has been committed, the child is seen in the presence of the parent.
(*c*) If a strong enough allegation is made, then the strategy meeting makes a decision on the type of interview required: joint, video or statement, and which worker will lead.

In practice, all the strategy meetings attended during the research period ($N = 8$) resulted in an initial interview with the child prior to the main evidential interview. This highlights the issue about when a referral actually becomes a legally constructed complaint. Because of the growing emphasis on joint investigation there has been an assumption that the two are synonymous. However, referrals are often ambiguous and the two are clearly not the same thing. The Pigot Working Group recommended that an interview should be conducted as soon as possible after the *complaint* had been made. This might operate as one criterion for deciding when to video the substantive interview. That is, to ascertain the feelings and wishes of the child, depending on age and ability, and to establish whether or not the child him or herself, or the parent where appropriate, wishes to make a complaint. This will not be applicable to all cases, and needs to be handled carefully, bearing in mind the 'rules' of evidence in any encounter with the child beforehand and the particular circumstances of the case, particularly the severity of the offence.

In Area 2, arrangements for joint working were clearly in operation, but seemed to be less formal in their organisation. Much appeared to depend on the good working relationship between a managerial social worker and the local police child protection team. Thus, in this area, the decision to video was based in one agency who then get in touch with the other. The effects of different joint working arrangements on the substantive interview are strongest at the pre-interview stage, and can be summarised as follows:

(i)  *'Filtering'* Where one agency decides to contact the other, much depends on a subjective assessment of appropriate referral. Therefore, some referrals may be filtered out at this stage (Moran-Ellis et al., 1991; Wattam, 1992; Giller et al., 1992).

(ii) *Planning the interview* In some areas it may be that joint planning can appear to be somewhat irrelevant, and has not been previous practice, since the police assume that they will organise and lead the interview. In some cases, initial planning is conducted at the case conference, and strategy concerning the interview is left until shortly before (10 minutes was mentioned) the interview time. Possible effects in areas of the country where such informal arrangements prevail would be:

(a)  inadequate information gathering,

(b)  no choice in the light of information gathered about who would be the best person to interview,

(c)  the possibility of one agency actively prejudicing the work of the other — either the criminal investigation or responding to the needs of the child and his or her family.

To counteract these problems, a clear joint working policy needs to be in operation which allows the initial referral assessment to be undertaken jointly.

Resourcing represented a third criterion for the decision to record the substantive interview. This had to do with the availability of an interviewing suite, access to the right equipment, and knowledge of personnel in terms of operating the equipment. Both pilot areas had at least one operating video suite, with the prospect of more becoming available. There is clear guidance in the *MOGP* about the kind of technical equipment that should be used to attain the standards afforded by video link. Many areas will be reviewing their equipment in the light of the guidance. The principle behind the guidance was to keep equipment as simple as possible, but conforming to court standards. Whilst the *MOGP* does allow for interviews to be conducted and recorded in the child's own home, or in some other convenient place, the realities of legal scrutiny will dictate that these standards be met. The availability of only one suite in Area 1 had consequences for the decision to video interviews, because the area covered was geographically extensive. Almost all interviews conducted by one district, and some from another, had been considered for video, but, for areas distant from the facilities, this was not so. In Area 2, the sole use of the suite for child protection purposes was thought sufficient. However, this did mean that child witnesses to other crimes had no video resource, thus impeding the implementation of the relevant section of the Criminal Justice Act.

The perceived status of the *MOGP* was an underlying theme throughout the observation, and a fourth criterion relevant to making a video of the substantive interview had to do with decisions made about departures from the guidance. There was some confusion about who would decide to depart, and at what level. Linked into this was a concern about the task and role of each respective agency. The police primarily want to investigate, and departures from the *MOGP* might come where their investigatory role is compromised. An example was given where a child had described all the actions leading up to potential buggery, but had not mentioned penetration. As a last and final resort, the police officer concerned felt that the requirements of the investigation meant that he should ask the child a (leading) question about this. The difference in charging would have been highly consequential for sentence. A relevant comment given in interview was that the police felt 'torn' by the conflicting interests of the social services and of the CPS. This example highlights a potential pressure, which needs to be considered in the context of joint working, that is, the potential conflict of roles. Each agent needs to be clear, both about their own role and the requirements of the other, so that the decision to interview is not based on each agency trying to meet their own ends separately. In the pilot, at least, the social services expressed some concern that their child protection practice might be compromised by over-emphasising evidential requirements. Thus the impetus to depart from the *MOGP* may come as a result of an assessment about the child's best interests. However, there was a fear that the *MOGP* would be used to exclude tapes because the defence will interpret the guidelines too rigidly and will criticise any deviation from the 'recommended good practice'. Thus, the impetus was to adhere to it, possibly at the expense of the child. Linked to this was the concern that the defence will not want the videos shown in court and will find arguments to prevent this, leading to a danger of 'trials within trials'. This highlights a key role for line management, who are likely to be the final arbiters of difficult decisions. If the tendency is to video, this needs to be counteracted by the child's interests.

A fifth criterion in making the decision to video was that of consent. If the child didn't want to be on video, there was some confusion about whether the child's consent had to be sought. In one case, the interview was held up because the child was adamant she did not want her mother to know about it, and the investigating team felt they could not interview without the mother's consent. The Children Act, 1989 has brought the issue of consent into sharp relief. Whilst the *MOGP* acknowledges that formal written consent to video is not required, it also suggests that the child's consent, or parent's where appropriate, should be sought. In the absence of consent, a strong case would have to be made for removal of the child, and an application for an assessment order will probably be more appropriate. However, this will only be granted if there is reasonable cause to suspect that the child is, or is likely, to suffer significant harm, that an assessment is required to establish whether or not this is the case, and that it is unlikely that such an assessment could be made without an order. The child may refuse to submit if he or she is considered capable of sufficient understanding. Hence, whilst formal consent to be video recorded is not required under the *MOGP*, the child could withdraw it under certain conditions.

In addition, the issue of consent to 'substantive' interviews also highlights the issue of compellability. If a child has the right not to submit to an assessment order, is s/he compellable? Technically, a court could subpoena a child to give evidence, but it would still be up to the child to decide how much s/he was prepared to say. On most occasions, without the child's testimony, there is unlikely to be any case to proceed with in the first place, unless there is very strong evidence from another source; physical, forensic, or eye witness, and these are rare. In the case of a child who does not consent to the substantive interview, it was stated at the *MOGP* drafting stage that it should be put to them that, if they did not do the interview, they may have to go to court to give their evidence in chief. In practice, similarly, it is unlikely that a case would proceed where a child did not want to give evidence in court. So, whilst technically the child does remain compellable, in reality, this is unlikely to be enforced, and the need for the child's co-operation remains important.

The decision to video was also made on the basis of a preference for statements, the presenting information, and the training of the interviewers. In practice, it was felt that statements were easier to obtain than video evidence. When taking a statement, not all of the questions might be written down. Mistakes were not so obvious. Thus, police officers had ways of getting the information they required whilst retaining evidential credibility. Given that the original aim of the admissibility of pre-recorded video evidence was to minimise trauma to the child by preventing the need to appear in court, and the fact that this aim has not been achieved, the option of continuing to take statements may still be the preferred route.

In terms of presenting information, this is best given by example.

# Case 1

AB had alleged touching, stroking and squeezing his legs over his clothes by a 75 year-old man, a relative of his friend C. Both children were present at the time of the offence and had gone to the man's house to get some money off him in return for him touching them. The strategy meeting had decided on a joint interview and video, subject to mother's approval. When the investigating team went round to see AB at school, he retracted the allegation, saying he had told lies. The nominated worker was thus reluctant to video the interview because if, at a later date, it came to light this offence, or any further offence, had, in fact, occurred then the first video would have to be produced thus showing that AB might be prone to lying.

**Deciding factor**

(a) Concern about use by the defence, and general interpretation by the court,
(b) parental consent.

# Case 2

The case of a 14 year-old autistic child displaying extreme sexual behaviour and knowledge. The child was considered to be a non-communicator, and thus video was not judged to be a viable option.

**Deciding factor**

Competency. However, visual evidence of this child's behaviour may have been useful though this was not considered — the emphasis is still on the written statement, i.e. a verbal record. This was endorsed by an officer in one of the interviews concerning the recent number of cases involving babies and very young children who said he 'couldn't conceive of doing it with a 3 year-old' (meaning the substantive interview). The research literature offers some support for the value of interviewing very young children (Jones & Krugman, 1986).

## Case 3

DE (12 years) had been displaying explicit sexual behaviour towards his 5 year-old sister. He had been seen by mother undressed with his sister, who had her clothes off, simulating intercourse. The mother had reported this to a health visitor, who had passed it on to the education social worker (ESW) who regularly visited the family. The ESW saw DE and his mother and asked him about his behaviour, and enquiries were made at school where teachers felt it was unlikely he had learned the behaviour there. On the second visit, the ESW discovered the whole family had been shown a video which contained explicit sexual information by a friend of the family. In this case, the decision was made to see the family friend, and for a social worker to see the boy about his behaviour and the source of his sexual knowledge. The police wanted more evidence before they became involved. The meeting decided to re-convene if more information came to light. A video interview was not considered an option at this stage.

### Deciding factor

Type of information not considered sufficient. In the case mentioned earlier (Chapter 6) concerning the suicidal teenage boy, who alleged sexual assault by his uncle, this was clearly seen as serious enough to warrant a video. Under the *MOGP*, both could be candidates for a substantive interview. It may be that, in fact, Case 3 was more appropriate — the evidential needs could be met and the child is not reported as unduly distressed at this stage. Whereas in the case in Chapter 6, the child clearly needed therapeutic support for a life-threatening condition — the evidential needs should have taken a secondary position.[1]

All of these cases point to the need for the development of assessment skills about when to consider the substantive interview and the need for well-trained staff. The availability of trained staff may also turn out, in practice, to be a criterion on which decisions to video are based, as the following example from the pilot evaluation highlights.

> Police: We need to proceed quickly with this . . . either by statement or video . . . but [district A] is the only suite available . . . I'm committed for two days, and the suite needs to be booked . . . I am a trained user . . . all time consuming elements.

Team leader: Is it agreed to have a joint interview, I don't know about videoing, that's something for you two to decide. Do you both have to be trained?

A further discussion followed about the necessity for both officers to be video trained or whether it was alright to proceed if only one was trained. The police officer telephoned for clarification on this, and it was confirmed that only one needed to be trained, although the trained person would have to be leading interviewer and the non-video trained worker would have to be 'comfortable' about going ahead with videoing. The nominated social worker was not willing to use the video for interviewing the victim.

This issue is likely to improve as training becomes more comprehensive, but highlights the need for preparation before the *MOGP* is fully implemented. Thus, in practice, the decision to interview appears to be founded on the following criteria: where there is a complaint, the organisation of joint working arrangements, technical and human resources, line management decisions about when to divert in the child's interests, consent, a preference for statements, the presenting information and training.

In addition to observations concerning the decision to interview in the first place, there were some data on potential problem areas to do with the interview itself. The first of these was the practice of 'admonishing', and an indication that it might be problematic. For example, one officer who asked a 10 year-old child, 'Tell me what your understanding is of truth', to which the child replied 'What do you mean, truth?'. The officer then went into great detail about telling lies, how it feels if you tell lies, if someone tells lies about you and resulted in the officer saying 'you might be confusing telling lies and telling tales'. This should be a very simple part of the rapport stage of the interview where children need to be given the opportunity to show that they understand they must speak the truth. It is important to do this early on because, if it arises later, children feel that what they have said may be doubted, in the context of an approach which is already pre-disposed to engender such a feeling.

Secondly, it was felt by almost all the officers spoken to in the pilot that the *MOGP* was too rigid with regard to the actual interview phases, and that, if the interviewer did not adhere to it exactly, the defence would use this to discredit the tape. For example, in one interview observed, the child 'disclosed' immediately. There was some confusion about whether the rapport stage would need to be returned to. In connection with this was the feeling that the *MOGP* did not recognise individual differences between children, and the way in which they needed to be interviewed. A related issue was that the word 'stepwise' has been taken out of the guidance but the structure and model is still salient. Stepwise tends to focus on an event which it is assumed the child will be able to freely recall. Whilst in some cases it might hold, in others it may be necessary to take an alternative approach. One model which does this is SAGE (Roberts, 1992) which has a 'modular' framework. This approach is probably more likely to obtain better information from certain children because, rather than directing focus on the abusive 'event', it focuses on what might be relevant to the child and factors which might inhibit recall. For example, in a custody and access dispute, a child might be more traumatised and affected by the danger of being seen to take sides, or discredit a parent, than sexual assault that may have been perpetrated in a 'loving' context. The modular approach would concentrate on the relevant issues so that, in this case, it would dedicate a module (which may be whole or part of an interview) on the parental separation. The *MOGP* acknowledges other approaches in terms of suggesting that the methods it outlines 'are not recommended as the only, or necessarily the best, for all cases'. Thus there is some discretion required about when it may be appropriate to follow it, and when not.[2]

Thirdly, the use of questions was a difficult area. Interviewers appeared to be conscious to the point of inhibition in some cases, of the dangers of using leading questions. This seems to have been generalised into concern about using anything but 'open' questions, or even using questions at all. For example, the comment made in interview that it was impossible to use 'all open questions . . . [you've] got to bring children back to what they're there for'. However, it was occasionally felt necessary to use them for investigative purposes at the very end of the interview. A further indication of this problem was again to do with the competing interests of justice and the child. One police officer commented that he thought the police remit was different from that of the interviewing remit of social services. He felt that evidence gathering, 'rather than being entirely child orientated', would, in itself, alter the type of questions that were asked. This confusion between what are perceived to be competing demands serves to mask an important misconception, that being child-centred means losing evidence. Whereas, in fact, talking to children about the things that are important to them can actually render more evidence in the long run.

Fourthly, in general, it was assumed that the police should lead the interview. One observation was that social workers did not feel sufficiently trained to do it and preferred to allow the police to take the lead. The recommendation in the *MOGP*, that only one person should lead the interview, seemed to be narrowly interpreted to indicate that only one person should speak throughout. Where training was available, this was thought to be a potential source of friction between agencies, that is, if only one person could do the interview, who should it be? This points to a deeper concern underlying the shifts noted in the earlier chapters of the book, that of an increasing legal influence, and policing of child protection. In the context of a purchaser provider, climate and resource constraints, social workers are required more than ever to substantiate their role.

Concern was expressed about the lack of training given, and what was meant by 'training' under the *MOGP*. Observations were also made by the researchers about interviewing practices they recorded. Many of these could be resolved by good training. For example:

- Not using the child's terminology, and substituting adult terms, e.g. penis for 'willy'.
- Use of questioning which emphasises the child's culpability. For example, after a child stated why he hadn't told anyone (he felt guilty, wasn't sure if it was wrong, liked the perpetrator, and so on) he was asked 'Did you tell him to stop', 'So you could have said stop'.
- Trying to identify times and dates but not helping the child with guides, for example, 'was it a weekday or weekend?' 'Was it day or night?'.
- Use of negative comments. For example, when a child stated dislike of football, and talk about his own hobby (collecting epitaphs) the interviewer responded with 'That's a bit strange isn't it?'
- Allowing the interview to 'drag on' and lack focus, particularly when children are distracted by toys.
- The use of leading questions. There was some indication that interviewers did not realise they were leading when, in fact, they were.

These observations reinforce the points made concerning the practice of interviewing children prior to the *MOGP* in Chapter 5. Whilst many practitioners, particularly the police, are conversant with interviewing children under evidential constraints, they are still not following the guidance which is also designed to make the process as child-centred as possible, where it is assessed as the right route to take for a child, even when they are trying to follow it. However, we should not lose sight of the fact that much of the material in this book reveals how the whole process, from assessment through to prosecution will remain, despite the *MOGP*, a very difficult one for children. The *MOGP* gives good advice, founded on experimental and clinical research, about interviewing child witnesses, particularly those who are not traumatised by the event. Many child protection cases will not fall into this category, and account must also be taken of the need to deal with the child's trauma. Theoretically, it should now be possible, in consultation with the CPS, to offer the child therapeutic intervention after the substantive interview. This is a considerable move forward from the days when children had to wait for their court appearance before receiving help. It does not, however, address the idea of a therapeutic route to 'disclosure'. Disclosure can quite clearly be viewed as a process, where children can slowly give more information over time (Wattam, 1991). There is evidence that they may need therapeutic or counselling help to do this (Bannister, 1992). Since Cleveland, the term 'disclosure' has been discredited, and the *MOGP* clearly advises that the substantive interview should not be known as the 'disclosure' interview, for all the reasons to do with prejudging the evidence and taking a 'believing stance' that I outline in Chapter 10. Up until Cleveland the term had been defined only in so far as it was a dynamic in cases of child sexual assault, one that could be anticipated (Sgroi, 1982; Summit, 1983). Absence of the concept denies many years of clinical practice, and does not afford the child the opportunity to tell others of their predicament.

A great deal of concern was expressed about access to, and storage of, tapes. Generally these were: a fear of copies getting into the 'wrong' hands, the resource issue to do with cost of copies, the prospect of taking the tape to the defence, and security. In one area it was felt that, in the light of current concern about the misuse of statements, interview videos should be stored by the police, that there should be only one copy in addition to the master copy, and that private viewing arrangements should be made for interested parties. As one police officer commented 'video porn is eminently more marketable than pieces of paper, and that's what will happen'. Clearly, great care must be taken to ensure that the videos are not open to misuse, and the resource implications attendant on copying, access and storage must be seriously considered by each agency. The *MOGP* now recommends that viewing should be preferred to copying, but this will require a change in working practices which could be difficult to accommodate.

This book has attempted to highlight some of the key issues in making a child protection case, in practice. The final judgement, about what sort of a case should be made, must rest with social workers, police officers and their line managers, whom, it is hoped will listen to children in their deliberations. Overall, the admissibility of pre-recorded video evidence is likely to have a considerable impact on the decision-making process. However, it must be remembered that the introduction of pre-recorded video evidence, whilst representing a step forward, is still problematic. This is because it is a piecemeal reform of an already difficult legal process. Full implementation of the recommendations of the Pigot Working Group (Home Office, 1989) would go some way to making further improvements, particularly the introduction of pre-trial hearings, the use of an interpreter in difficult cases, and dropping the requirement to warn the jury that it is dangerous to convict on uncorroborated evidence. Deeper questions, concerning the criminalisation of child protection, the development of alternative solutions, and the impact of the adversarial system on resolving private, traumatic, and often intrafamilial, problems remain unresolved. Whilst this is so, making a case in child protection may still present practitioners and children with the dilemma of a 'no win' situation. Justice for children has a long road to travel.

## Notes

1.  In a personal communication from the CPS it was stated that the child's behaviour in this case would not give rise to a specific suspicion of criminal conduct. It was, therefore, understandable that a video would not be made at that stage. This is a pertinent observation which encapsulates the difficulties practitioners must face — namely, if the video should be made as soon as possible after a case has been reported, does a referral of suspected harm or injury constitute a report? Whilst, under other circumstances it would not, in cases of offences against children if it is found that they have been interviewed prior to the substantive interview, for whatever reason, it may be exploited by the defence.

2.  There is a possibility that the SAGE approach and the *MOGP* can be combined. Interviewers using *MOGP* can incorporate its principles, but training must encourage investigators to shift their focus from a crime event to matters relevant to the child (which may amount to the same thing in some cases, though not in all).

# Bibliography

Altemeier, W.A., O'Conner, S., Vietze, P., Sandler, H. & Sherrod, K. (1984). Prediction of child abuse: a prospective study of feasibility. *Child Abuse and Neglect*, 8, 393–400.

Aries, P. (1973). *Centuries of Childhood*. Penguin, Harmondsworth.

Baldwin, J. & McConville, M. (1977). *Negotiating Justice*. Martin Robinson.

Bass, E. & Thornton, L. (eds) (1983). *I Never Told Anyone: Writings by Women Survivors of Child Sexual Abuse*. Harper & Row, New York.

Barford, R. & Wattam, C. (1991). Children's participation in decision making. *Practice*, 5 (2) 93–102.

Bentovim, A., Elton, A., Hildebrand, J., Tranter, M. & Vizard, E. (1988). *Child Sexual Abuse within the Family: Assessment and Treatment*. Wright, London.

Berlinner, L. (1983). Child Sexual Abuse Investigation. A Curriculum for Training Law Enforcement Officers in Washington State, Criminal Justice Training Commission Victims of Sexual Assault Programmes, Department of Social & Health Services, State of Washington.

Besharov, D. (1986). Unfounded allegations — a new child abuse problem. *The Public Interest*, Spring, 18–33.

Biestek, F. (1957). *The Casework Relationship*. Unwin University Books, London.

Bittner, E. (1965). The concept of organization. In Turner, R., (ed.) 1974. *Ethnomethodology*. Penguin Books.

Blagg, H., Hughes, J.A. & Wattam, C. (1989). *Child Sexual Abuse: Listening, Hearing and Validating the Experiences of Children*. Longmans.

Boggs, S.R. & Eyberg, S. (1990). Interview techniques and establishing rapport. In La Greca, A.M. (ed.) *Through the Eyes of the Child*. Allyn and Bacon, Boston.

Bray, M. (1989). *Susie and the Wise Hedgehog go to Court*. Hawksmere, London.

Brearley, P. (1982). *Risk and Social Work*. Routledge.

Bull, R. (1991). Commentary: the issue of relevance. In Doris, J. (ed.). *The Suggestibility of Children's Recollections*. The American Psychological Association, Washington, DC, pp.134–137.

Butler-Sloss, E. (1988). *Report of the Inquiry into Child Abuse in Cleveland*. HMSO, London.

Burgess, A.W., Groth, A.N., Holmstrom, L.L. & Sgroi, S.M. (1978). *Sexual Assault of Children and Adolescents*. Lexington Books, Toronto.

Browne, K., Davies, C. & Stratton, P.(eds) (1988). *Early Prediction and Prevention of Child Abuse*. Wiley.

Children's Society (1991). *Working with Sexually Abused Children: A Resource Pack for Professionals*. Children's Society, London.

Cohen, R. & Harnick, M.A. (1980). The susceptibility of child witnesses to suggestion. *Law and Human Behaviour*, **41**, 201–10.

Conroy, S., Fielding, N. & Tunstall, J. (1989). *The Surrey Constabulary/Surrey Social Services Joint Investigative Initiative in Cases of Child Sexual Abuse*, Interim Report. Department of Sociology, Surrey University.

Conte, J.R., Wolf, S.R. & Smith, T. (1989). What sexual offenders tell us about prevention strategies. *Child Abuse and Neglect*, **13**, (2).

Creighton, S. & Noyes, P. (1989). *Child Abuse Trends in England and Wales 1983–1987*. NSPCC, London.

Davies, G. (1986). Context effects in episodic memory: a review. *Cahiers de Psychologie Cognitive*, **6**, 157–74.

Davies, G. & Flin, R. (1988). The accuracy and suggestibility of child witnesses. In Shapland, J. and Drinkwater, J., (eds.). *Issues in Criminological and Legal Psychology*, No. 13, The British Psychological Society for the Division of Criminological and Legal Psychology.

Davies, G. & Noon, E. (1991) *An Evaluation of the Live Link for Child Witnesses*. Home Office.

De Francis, V. (1969). *Protecting the Child Victim of Sex Crimes Committed by Adults*. American Humane Association, Denver Co.

DHSS (1982). *Child Abuse, A Study of Inquiry Reports, 1973–1981*, HMSO, London.

DHSS (1988). *Working Together: A Guide to Inter-Agency Co-operation for the Protection of Children from Abuse*. HMSO, London.

DOH (1991a). *Child Abuse: A Study of Inquiry Reports 1980–1989*. HMSO, London.

DOH (1991b). *Working Together Under the Children Act 1989*. HMSO, London.

DOH (1992). Children and young persons on child protection registers year ending 31 March 1991, England. *Provisional Feedback*. Department of Health, London.

Dingwall, R., Eekelaar, J. & Murray, T. (1983). *The Protection of Children: State Intervention and Family Life*. Basil Blackwell, Oxford.

Driver, E. & Droisen, A. (eds) (1989). *Child Sexual Abuse: Feminist Perspectives*. Macmillan.

Elliot, M. (1985). *Preventing Child Sexual Assault: A Practical Guide to Talking With Children*. Bedford Square Press/NCVO, London.

Everson & Boat (1989). False allegations of sexual abuse by children and adolescents. *American Academy of Child and Adolescent Psychiatry*, **28**, (2), 230–5.

Finkelhor, D. (1979). *Sexually Victimised Children*. The Free Press, New York.

Finkelhor, D. (1986). *A Sourcebook on Child Sexual Abuse*. Sage, USA.

Finkelhor, D. (1984). *Child Sexual Abuse: New Theory and Research*. The Free Press, New York.

Finkelhor, D., Meyer Williams, L. & Burns, N. (1988). *Nursery Crimes: Sexual Abuse in Day Care*. Sage.

Fisher, R.P. & Geiselman, R.E. (1988). *Evaluation and Field Implementation of the Cognitive Interview*. Final Report to the National Institute of Justice.

Flin R. & Bull, R. (1990). Child witnesses in Scottish criminal proceedings. In Spencer, J., Nicholson, G., Flin, R. and Bull R. (eds). *Children's Evidence in Legal Proceedings: An International Perspective*. University of Cambridge, Faculty of Law.

Frankel, J., Parental Participation in Case Conferences (1990). Unpublished research report (available from NSPCC Hedley Library).

Garfinkel, H. (1967). *Studies in Ethnomethodology*. Prentice Hall, New Jersey.

Garfinkel, H. (1967b). Good organizational reasons for bad clinical records. In *Ethnomethodology*, Turner, R. (ed). Penguin Books.

Gelles, R. & Cornell, C. (1985). *Intimate Violence in Families*. Sage.

Gelles, R.J. & Lancaster, J.B. (1987). *Child Abuse and Neglect: Biosocial Dimensions*. Aldine de Gruyter, New York.

Giller, H., Gormley, C. & Williams, P. (1992). *The Effectiveness of Child Protection Procedures*. Social Information Systems Ltd.

Giovannoni, J.M. & Becerra, R.M. (1979). *Defining Child Abuse*. Collier Macmillan, London.

Goodman, G.F., Jones, D.P.H., Pyle, E.A., Prado-Estrada, L., Part, L.K., England, P., Mason, R. & Rudy, L. (1988). The emotional effects of criminal court testimony on child sexual assault victims: a preliminary report. In Shapland, J., and Drinkwater, J. (eds.). *Issues in Criminological and Legal Psychology*. No. 13, The British Psychological Society for the Division of Criminological and Legal Psychology.

Goodwin, J., Sahd, D. & Rada, R.T. (1982). False accounts and false denials of incest: clinical myths and clinical realities. In Goodwin J. (ed.) *Sexual Abuse: Incest Victims and Their Families*. pp.47–56, John Wright, London.

Greenland, C. (1987). *Preventing CAN Deaths: An International Study of Deaths Due to Child Abuse and Neglect*. Tavistock, London.

Hallet, C. & Stevenson, O. (1980). *Child Abuse: Aspects of Interprofessional Co-operation*. Allen and Unwin.

Herman, J. (1981). *Father–Daughter Incest*. Harvard University Press, Cambridge MA.

Higginson, S. (1990). Under the influence. *Social Work Today*, **22**, (14), 20–1.

Hobbs, C. & Wynne, J. (1989). Sexual abuse of English boys and girls: the importance of anal examination. *Child Abuse and Neglect*, **13**, (2), 195–210.

Home Office (1989). *Report of The Advisory Group on Video Evidence*. London.

Hudson, P.S. (1991). *Ritual Child Abuse: Discovery, Diagnosis and Treatment*. R&E publishers, Saratoga CA.

Hughes, J.A. & Wattam, C. (1989). Some aspects of confidentiality talk and the disclosure of child sexual abuse. Working Paper 3, Sociology Department, Lancaster University.

James, A.L. (1992). An open or shut case? Law as an autopoietic system'. *Journal of Law and Society*, **19** (2), Summer.

James, J., Womack, W. & Strauss, P. (1978). Physicial reporting of sexual abuse of children. *Journal of the American Medical Association*, **240**, 1145–46.

Jayussi, L. (1984). *Categorisation and the Moral Order*. Routledge Kegan Paul.

Jones, D. & Krugman, R. (1986). Can a three-year-old child bear witness to her sexual assault and attempted murder. *Child Abuse & Neglect*, **10**, 253–58.

Jones, D. & McGraw, J.M., 1987. Reliable and fictitious accounts of sexual abuse of children. *Journal of Interpersonal Violence*, **2**, 27–45.

Jones, D. & McQuiston, M. (1989). *Interviewing the Sexually Abused Child*. The Royal College of Psychiatrists, Gaskell.

Jones, D. & Seig, A. (1988). Child sexual abuse allegations in custody or visitation disputes. In Nicholson, B., (ed.) *Sexual Abuse Allegations in Custody and Visitation Disputes*. American Bar Association, Washington DC.

Keane, A. (1989). *The Modern Law of Evidence*. 2nd edn, London: Butterworths.

Kelly, L. (1988). *Surviving Sexual Violence*. Polity Press, Cambridge.

Kelly, L. & Regan, L. (1990). Flawed protection. *Social Work Today*, **21** (32).

Kelly, L. (1989). Bitter ironies. *Trouble and Strife*, **16**, 14–21.

Kilkerr, A. (1989). A police response — devising a code of practice. In Blagg. H., Hughes, J.A. and Wattam, C. (eds) *Child Sexual Abuse: Listening, Hearing and Validating the Experiences of Children*. Longmans.

King, M.A. & Yuille, J.C. (1987). Suggestibility and the child witness. In Ceci, S.S., Toglia, M.P. and Ross, D.F. (eds). *Children's Eyewitness Memory*. Springer-Verlag, New York.

King, M. (1991). Child welfare within law: the emergence of a hybrid discourse.' *Journal of Law and Society*. **18** (3).

King, M. & Piper, C. (1990). *How the Law Thinks About Children*. Gower, Aldershot.

Kohnken, G. (1990). The evaluation of statement credibility; social judgement and expert diagnostic approaches. In Spencer, J.R., Nicholson, G., Flin, R. and Bull, R., (eds.). *Children's Evidence in Legal Proceedings, An International Perspective*. University of Cambridge.

Korbin, J. (ed.) 1981. *Child Abuse and Neglect: Cross-cultural Perspectives*. University of California Press, Berkeley, CA.

La Fontaine, J. (1988). *Child Sexual Abuse*. An ESRC Research Briefing. ESRC.

Lealman, G.T., Haigh, D., Phillips, J.M., Sloan, J. & Ord-Smith, C. (1983). Prediction and prevention of child abuse — an empty hope. *The Lancet*, **8339**, 1423–4.

London Borough of Brent (1985). A Child in Trust: Report of the Panel of Inquiry Investigating the Circumstances Surrounding the Death of Jasmine Beckford.

Madge, N. (1983). Identifying families at risk. In Madge, N. (ed.). *Families at Risk*. Heinemann.

Masson, J. (1992). Managing risk under the Children Act, 1989: diversion in child care? *Child Abuse Review*, **7**, 1–20.

Memon, A., Cronin, O., Eaves, R. and Bull, R. (1992). Cognitive interview and child witnesses. Paper given at the DCLP 2nd Annual Conference, 25–27th March.

Metropolitan Police and Bexley Social Services (1987). *Child Sexual Abuse Joint Investigation Programme, Final Report*. HMSO, London.

Midgely, M. (1991). Rights-talk will not sort out child-abuse: comment on Archard on parental rights. *Journal of Applied Philosophy*, **8** (1) 103–14.

Morrison, T. (1991). Paper presented at BASPCAN Conference, Leicester, September.

Moran-Ellis, J., Conroy, S., Fielding, N. & Tunstill, J. (1991). *Investigation of Child Sexual Abuse: An Executive Summary*. Department of Sociology, University of Surrey.

Nash, C.L. & West, D.J. (1986). Sexual molestation of young girls: a retrospective survey. In West, D.J., (ed.). *Sexual Victimisation*. Gower, Aldershot.

National Centre for Child Abuse & Neglect (NCCAN) (1981). *Study of Findings: National Study of Incidence & Severity of Child Abuse and Neglect*. DHEW, Washington DC.

Nelson, S. (1987). *Incest: Fact and Myth*. Stramullion, Edinburgh.

Nobile, P. (1978). *Incest: The Last Taboo*. Penthouse, January, p.117.

NSPCC (1990). *Child Protection Adviser's Resource Pack*. Paley, J. (ed.), NSPCC/DOH

Packman, J. (1989). Decisions in child care. In Kahan, B. (ed.). *Child Care Research, Policy and Practice*. Hodder & Stoughton.

Parton, N. (1989). Child abuse. In Kahan, B. (ed.). *Child Care Research, Policy and Practice*. Hodder & Stoughton.

Parton, N. (1991). *Governing the Family: Child Care, Child Protection and the State*. Macmillan.

Peters, J.J. (1976). Children who were the victims of sexual assault and the psychology of offenders. *American Journal of Psychotherapy*, **30**, 398–412.

Pfohl, S.J. (1976). The 'discovery' of child abuse, *Social Problems*, **24**, 310–23.

Plotnikoff (1992). Information Pack for Child Witnesses. Currently being prepared in conjunction with the Home Office.

Roberts, H. (1992). Gathering evidence from children: a systematic approach. Paper presented at the Second Annual Conference of the British Psychological

Society, Division of Criminological and Legal Psychology, Harrogate, 25–27 March.

Raskin, D.C. & Esplin, P.W. (1991). Assessment of children's statements of sexual abuse. In Doris, J. (ed.). *The Suggestibility of Children's Recollections*. The American Psychological Association, Washington, DC. pp.153–164.

Russell, D.E.H. (1986). *The Secret Trauma: Incest in the Lives of Girls and Women*. Basic Books, New York.

Ross, D.M. & Ross, S.A. (1984). The importance of type of question, psychological climate and subject set in interviewing children about pain. *Pain*, **19**, 71–9.

Royal College of Physicians (1991). *Physical Signs of Sexual Abuse in Children: A Report of the Royal College of Physicians*. Royal College of Physicians, London.

Sacks, H. (1966). The search for help: no-one to turn to. Unpublished PhD Dissertation, Department of Sociology, University of California, Berkeley.

Sacks, H. (1971). SS132, Fall 1971, Lecture 3, October 31.

Sacks, H. (1972). *On the analysability of stories by children*. In Turner, R. (ed.), 1974. *Ethnomethodology*. Penguin Books. pp.216–232.

Sacks, H. (1984). Notes on methodology. In Atkinson, J.M., and Heritage, J. (eds.) *Structures of Social Action*. Cambridge University Press. pp.21–27.

Sanders, A. (1987). Constructing the Case for the Prosecution. *Journal of Law and Society*, **14** (2), 229–53.

Saywitz, K. (1990). The child witness: experimental and clinical considerations. In La Greca, A.M. (ed). *Through the Eyes of the Child*, Allyn & Bacon, Boston. p.344.

Sgroi, S.M. (1982). *Handbook of Clinical Intervention in Child Sexual Abuse*. Lexington Books, Toronto.

Spencer, J. (1990). Children's evidence in legal proceedings in England. In Spencer, J.R., Nicholson, G., Flin, R., & Bull, R. (eds.). *Children's Evidence in Legal Proceedings, An International Perspective*. University of Cambridge.

Spencer, J.R. & Flin, R. (1990). *The Evidence of Children: The Law and the Psychology*. Blackstone, London.

Stone, M. (1990). *Child Protection Work: A Professional Guide*. Venture Press

Straus, M.A., Gelles, R.J. & Steinmetz, S.K. (1980). *Behind Closed Doors: Violence in the American Family*. Anchor/Doubleday.

Sudnow, D. (1967). *Passing On: The Social Organization of Dying*. Prentice Hall, Englewood Cliffs, New Jersey.

Summit, R. (1983). The child sexual abuse accomodation syndrome. *Child Abuse and Neglect*, **7**, 177–93.

Taylor, S. (1989). How prevalent is it? In Stainton Rogers, W., Hevey, D. and Ash, E. (eds). *Child Abuse and Neglect: Facing the Challenge*. The Open University.

Teubner, G. (1988). *Autopoietic Law: A New Approach to Law and Society*. Walter de Gruyter, Berlin.

Teubner, G. (1989). How the law thinks: towards a constructivist epistemology of law. *Law and Society Review*, **23**, 728–57.

Thorpe, D. (1991). Patterns of child protection intervention and service delivery: report of a pilot project. *Research Report No. 4*. Crime Research Unit, University of Western Australia.

Thorpe, D. & Denman G. (1992). A Local Child Protection System. Unpublished research report.

Underwager, R. & Wakefield, H. (1990). *The Real World of Child Interrogations*. Charles C. Thomas, Illinois.

Undeutsch, U. (1990). Conference Paper presented at the Testimony of the Child Conference, Leeds University.

Vizard, E. (1991). Interviewing children suspected of being sexually abused: a review of theory and practice. In Hollin, C.R. and Howells, K. (eds). *Clinical Approaches to Sex Offenders and Their Victims.* Wiley, Chichester.

Wakefield, H. & Underwager, R. (1988). *Accusations of Child Sexual Abuse.* Charles C. Thomas, Illinois.

Waldby, C. (1985). Breaking the silence: a report based upon the findings of the war against incest phone-in survey. Honeysett, Sidney.

Waldby, C., Clancy, A., Emetchi, J. & Summerfield, C., for Dympna House (1989). Theoretical perspectives on father–daughter incest. In Driver, E. and Droison, A. (eds.). *Child Sexual Abuse: Feminist Perspectives.* p.101.

Wattam, C. (1989). Teachers' experiences with children who have, or who may have been, sexually abused. *Occasional Paper*, No. 5, NSPCC, London.

Wattam, C. (1991). Disclosure: the child's perspective. A research study. NSPCC evaluation (unpublished, available from NSPCC Hedley Library).

Wattam, C. (1992). Pigot Code of Practice Steering Group. Pilot of 4th Draft: NSPCC evaluation (unpublished, available from NSPCC Hedley Library).

Weir, K. (1991). Fabrications and false allegations in sexual abuse cases. *Scan,* **11,** 67.

Westcott, H. & Davies, G. (1990). Underwager and Wakefield: child abuse evidence abused. *Interesting,* August.

Westcott, H. (1991). personal communication.

Westcott, H. (1992). The cognitive interview. *British Journal of Social Work.* In press.

Williams, R. et al. (1985). Medical confidentiality and multidisciplinary work: child sexual abuse and mental handicap registers, *British Medical Journal,* **293,** 1315–8.

Wise, S. (1991). *Child Abuse: The NSPCC Version. Feminist Praxis.*

Wynne, B. (1989). Establishing the rules of laws. In Smith R. and Wynne, B. (eds). *Expert Evidence.* Routledge, London.

Wyre, R. & Swift, A. (1990). *Women, Men and Rape.* Hodder & Stoughton.

Yuille, J. (1989). *Credibility Assessment.* Kluwer Academic Publishers.

# Index